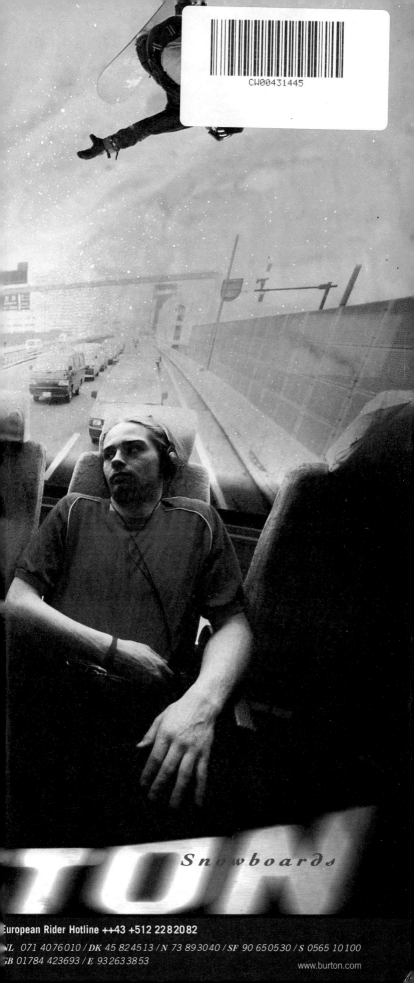

Snowboards

CONTRIBUTORS

Alban Thom
Allison Coates
Dot Tsikou
Eddie Spearing
Euan Baxter
Matthew Beck
Ian Sansom
Nick Dales
Simon Smith
Steve Bailey
Stig Sturgon
Sara Hall
Thomas Reider
Viv Jenkins
Christoph Schare
(German ski writer and publisher of
Ski Wetweit and numerous guide books)
All the Tourist offices listed
and their representatives for
their contributions.

Acknowledgements to
All those numpty chaps at SUK

Jeremy Sladen ——— Snowboard Asylum

Heino ——— Burton Austria
Nick Bolton ——— Rocky Mountain
Snowboard Tours

Tony Brown one of the UK's original snowboarders who
founded the UK's first ever snowboard shop, first jumped
on a snowboard back in 1986 with the Innsbruck posse
from the club known then as the Burton Snowboard
Division. This book was devised by Tony whilst working in,
of all places, the Sahara Desert in 1993.

Tony would like to offer special acknowledgements to;
Maggie Gilfian and her twin sons Gordon and Graham for
meals on wheels, dog handling and being cool neighbours.
Cathy and Neil Baxter for dog sitting.
Pink Floyds Delicate Sounder of Thunder album for travel
music (the only cassette for 5000 miles of Euro driving with
the radio packed up). The Italian policeman who refrained
from shooting me in Milan. Fords crap Fiesta which was home
for 2 months. All those that may have helped along the way in
producing this book which has taken 2 1/2 years, especially
those who funded me, allowing me to eat and buy beer.
Lastly Max Plotzeneder, Thomas Marsh, Andy Ortner and
Junior for the early days.

PS, to any one from Ashburton High School in Croydon,
where I was in O&N between 1992 & 1997.

Kaya Dog.

Very special shouts to;
Bruce my son.
Sisters & Family Ossian.
Lyndsey "D"

USG is dedicated to Kaya the Dog as well as all free
thinking people around the globe.

Front cover picture
Rider: Burton Team Rider Johan Olofsson
Photographer: Vianney Tisseau
Location: Zermatt Switzerland

4

Universal Snowboard Guide

Snowboarding around the globe in winter & summer, above and below the equator

Universal Snowboard Guide
Published by
ICE PUBLISHING
45 Corrour Rd,
Dalfaber, Aviemore
Inverness-shire
PH22 1SS
Tel (01479) 810362
Fax (01479) 801362

Associate Publishers
Air Publications
1a Franchise St
Kidderminster, Worcs.
Tel (01562) 827744
Fax (01562) 755705

Compiled by Tony Brown

Design and Layout:
Simon Mayoh,
Tony Brown
Repro: Quad Colour
Printing: Cradley Print Ltd

Destribution:Macmillans Ltd
Tel (01256 29242

CONTRIBUTORS, CONTENTS

KEY TO SYMBOLS

 Around the Mountain

 On the Mountain

 To the Mountain

 Beginner Runs

Intermediate Runs

 Advanced Runs

 Terrain rider styles

 Half pipe & Funparks

 Lifts and lift passes

 Snowboard Instruction

 Snowboard Hire

 Snowboard Repair/Service

 Snowboard Shops

 Heli-boarding

 Paragliding / Hangliding

 Rock Climbing/Wall

 Bungee jumping

 Snowmobile Hire/Rides

 Skateboarding

 Night time hangouts/Boozing

 Eating joints

Rider: Jonny Barr : Photo Ken Achenbach, Verbier.

 Accommodation

 Tourist information.

 Flying

 Bus travel

 Train travel

 Car Hire from airports

 General driving tips.

Could this be the start of a series of journals put out by wide eyed business men with dollar signs in their eyes, telling us to do this, do that, ride this board, wear that jacket.

Actually no, Universal Snowboard Guide (USG) is none of that. What USG is, is a simple to use no nonsense guide book compiled and written by snowboarders from around the world. It doesn't do in-depth analysing of your snowboard technique or style of snowboard pant, and it does not dictate where you should or should not go in order to snowboard. What I have endeavoured to do is set out a guide of what is available as it was found, with the information given for your guidance, aimed at assisting you. You are an individual who will snowboard on the mountain of your choice, wearing what you like and riding the board you want.

Getting in on the act of snowboarding, it being a growth industry, has become the thing, but what a lot of dudes have missed out on is the sports direction.

However, the roots of the sport and what snowboarding first stood for in the eyes of many an old school riders is the freedom, the lack of preconceptions and the lack of restrictions that other mountain sports impose coupled with the pleasure of riding a mountain as an individual. Snowboarding was never meant to be a technical over hyped pastime for the gold credit card elite. It is a sport that appeals to those with a street eye and attitude, and those who want the simplest fun.

There is a trend in certain sections of the winter sports industry to bring snowboarding into line with its main rival "Skiing" when it comes to rules relating to standards of instruction, mountain behaviour and so on. Granted some rules are necessary, but what has not been understood by those trying to get snowboarding to toe the line is that the sport doesn't want to be ruled or restricted, and snowboarding should be kept simple in all aspects. Snowboarding is a sport in its own right and not a variation of skiing or windsurfing which some still think its linked too. Snowboarding's roots are Surfing and Skateboarding which are free spirit sports without the need to compete all the time.

Snowboarding is growing big and fast though it suffers - like so many new sports - from serious growing pains. Only a few years ago the Federation International du Ski (FIS), skiing's world governing body, had brushed it all aside as a fad with no future, but now, having been proved so spectacularly wrong, they are trying to split the sport and take over from the established and much-respected world snowboard administrators, the International Snowboard Federation (ISF). The FIS has been staging race programmes to rival the ISF, taking no account of the loyalty shared by the world's top snowboarders or the snowboard industry. Pro riders are boycotting FIS races, and it certainly hasn't helped the FIS cause calling snowboarders 'ski boarders', either.

The reason for the sudden FIS involvement is the inclusion of snowboarding as a future Olympic sport with thousands of wannabe medalists turning their back on skiing. But lets not be short sighted and forget the profit snowboard companies are raking in at the expense of many ski companies, and of course ski resorts now promoting snowboarding. The conflict is set to run, but in the end it must be the snowboarders under the ISF who win the day. Not out of touch geriatrics.

Snowboarding, like Surfing and Skateboarding, all have a simple laid back appeal which Universal

Rider; Mat Beck, US rider at Okemo USA

Snowboard Guide sets out to convey. The idea of the USG was initially conceived in the Libyan Sahara Desert (somehow) at a time when I was working for an American company under the watchful eye of Colonel Gadaffi (all hush hush). After subsequently owning a snowboard shop, and school for a number of years I carried on the idea of a need for a snowboard guide. I was constantly being asked "Where is the best place to snowboard". I have snowboarded in Europe and America, and I knew that if a snowboarder didn't get pen to paper and produce a simple to use snowboard book, then a greedy ski publisher type would come out with a boring, over written, nappy changing and totally unimaginative ski style guide. Snowboarding is no big deal so going away to do it shouldn't been seen as so either. A guide book that helps, without the fuss and propaganda is what you need, and USG is that book.

Snowboarding is universal and no two resorts are the same, so USG is not an A to Z of what's tops and what's not, that's for you to decide. The type of information that can help prior to going away are costings, and a rough idea about the resort and the slopes.

USG gives details on to 301 resorts in 58 countries, listing basic mountain facts with travel guides to the resorts. We give prices of lift passes, accommodation, hire and instruction as well as beer and food prices. I have also given an indication of any skateboarding available and what ISF events are going on in resorts, plus a little info on snowboard hang outs.

What I haven't done, is rattle on with the same old boring dribble that is all to common in ski journals. Who the hell is interested in whether a mountain resort has panoramic views, (it's a mountain lets get real here) or if the chalets all have cosy traditional styles. Please spare us ski chaps with your ABC on skiing. They all sound the same.

I've often been asked where is a hot place to go, I simply reply that it depends on the tastes and expectations of the individual. What is hot to one can be sad to another.

Over the next five years mountain resorts all over the world will be vying for most-favoured status and changing accordingly, upgrading their facilities and services for the new mountain breed of snowboarders, so expect to read a whole host of new facts in this journal next year.

The information that has been included in this issue is a guide and unfortunately information may differ from what you find, i.e. USG may indicate a halfpipe or funpark at this or that resort, however when you get there they may be gone. We have no control over the weather and some resorts only build pipes when certain amounts of snow have fallen. Where we list prices this is based on information supplied by resorts and shops. Prices obviously can vary, so before you go anywhere pick up the phone and communicate with people. You will find out a lot, especially if you call a resorts snowboard shop. You'll be able to find out the best deals at the last minute, or how good the powder is or whether the funpark is open. Call the resort Tourist office too as they will help, after all they want your money so it's in their interest to be helpful. So Call.

Tony Brown: Core snowboard dude

Photo: D. Welsh, Waterville Valley USA

Can I go Snowboarding ?

Check out	Remedy
Parents Guardian or Landlord	If they say no go anyway after all you will have to leave the nest one day.
Wife or Girlfriend	If she says no leave her, you're bound to find a snowboard chick while you're away.
Husband or Boyfriend	If he says no chuck him, he's certain to be a skier or worst a windsurfer.
Cat Dog $ - £ -DM	Feed it to the Dog. Give it to your parents. Low on funds, scam a lift pass and borrow a board.

— Travel options

Photo: Stig

Accommodation

Hotels
Guest houses
Chalets
B&B's
Bunk houses
Youth Hostels

Insurances

You're sick of school, University is doing your nut in and the boss at work needs a thumping. Time to go snowboarding and leave reality behind. Life is too short to worry about the norms, and anyway a snowboard trip no matter what time of the year, will put you back in the right frame of mind to tackle anything when you return.

Taking a snowboard trip is easy. If you have half a brain you can get to any resort with the minimum of fuss, (unless you're the sort that wants the lot done for you, sad gits). Like any holiday or trip away from home and perhaps the loved ones, you will need to be sure of a few things and will have to do the ground work. Check out the 'Can I go Snowboarding' chart.

There's no point dictating why you should visit this or that country, each has something to offer. It may be that you're partial to garlic and euro carving in hard boots which means France is the place, on the other hand you may prefer over priced lifts, bleak weather and a little freeriding in softs making Scotland the choice.

Whichever country you choose you'll have to make a few plans before setting off. Note! whatever info we give you in USG, you should

Equipment hire
Instruction
Lift passes

Money
Passport
Visas

Resort facilities

tips

always check on up to date information prior to leaving by calling resort tourist offices and snowboard shops.

Nowadays 95% of the worlds ski resorts happily allow snowboarding, and many go out of their way to attract it. A lot of resorts are now providing 'snowboard only' areas served by snowboard lifts - Avoriaz in France, Hintertux in Austria or Winter Park in the US are just a few. In a number of resorts you now find gondolas and cable cars with snowboard racks, and rules covering snowboarders using T-bars and drag lifts are becoming more clearly-defined and standardised. For instance, it's no longer a rule all over France that you must have your back foot in the binding, or in Italy that you are obliged to use a small ski on your free foot.

When considering a snowboard holiday it's an idea to bear in mind whether or not there are good beginner areas reachable by foot, or user-friendly chairlifts. It would be a nightmare for any enthusiast to reach the bottom of a slope to discover that the only way back is via a drag lift which travels at the speed of sound taking you through a pine forest while completing a 90° turn.

As a beginner or even an intermediate, you will need flat open piste with well connecting lifts dispensing with the problematic scooting all over the shop. Chair lifts and gondola's will help beginners get up the mountain without the T-Bar tackle, however other important points should be pointed out. For instance cable cars are OK but usually crammed with hordes of skiers with dayglo suits and bad breath. Gondola's on the other hand are far more civilised and usually only take up to about six persons, which makes partying on the way up a lot easier. What's more if you happen to be in a gondola with just you and your loved one you will be able to have a quick hump with out being disturbed.

Many of you will need to find out what levels of instruction are available. Check if there are any specialist schools in the resort and what age groups they cater for. All countries are now offering some form of snowboard instruction. You can have a series of beginner lessons or learn to freestyle; you can also get slalom and race training. Beginners should plan to have a couple of hours tuition in the morning over the first three days of a trip, after that you'll be able to gauge your progression. It may be that you can get by after a few days tuition, without spending more beer money.

Snowboard beginners generally progress more quickly than skiers and can therefore tackle the harder runs much earlier than the novice skier, so check out the piste map, and plan to take on the next grade up.

Should you be planning a snowboard trip with a loved one then remember an important rule "Don't act as their instructor" as it will soon end in tears, plus you'll soon become bored and will miss out on some riding. Send the beginner to the local snowboard school and be done with it.

Certain snowboarding styles suit particular terrains, e.g. a freestyler will want natural jumps, gullies with high walls and so on, as well as funparks and halfpipes; a eurocarver in hard boots will prefer wide-open flat piste, while the expert freerider will look for a combination of all those elements.

If you're low on funds don't pick out the big resorts to go to, some of the small resorts are far more friendly. A point to note is that a resort boasting hundreds of Kilometres of marked piste is all well and good, but you will never get to see it all in a dozen trips.

If you can only get away during certain periods due to school or work commitments, try and schedule a trip that doesn't clash with local and school holidays, these periods are stupidly busy with ski clones and happy families, plus you pay more for lifts and accommodation. Avoid Christmas, New Year and Easter, January is OK, as indeed is April.

Summer is a great time to go snowboarding. You can find resorts with heaps of good snow, no lift queues, you get the chance to ride in Tee shirts, and more importantly the two plank wonders usually stay at home. Prices for accommodation and lift pass are usually cheaper in the summer periods. Summer is also the time when many of the pro's run camps where you can learn and laugh. There are a number of specialist snowboard tour operators running camps to most of the summer destinations. Summer snowboarding takes place on glaciers, but don't fret, you won't find your self shooting down a slab of ice, Glacier resorts are snow covered in the same way as low lying resorts. Depending on the weather you'll find powder runs, extremes, bowls, as well as halfpipes and funparks.

Travelling for some people is a bind. Riders who live on a mountain have it easy. For them it's out of bed, ollie over the balcony, and into a lift line all in the space of a few yards and minutes. However the rest of us have to pack the kit and travel. If you are going away with the parents don't worry too much, chances are they are still in 70's and 80's mode, and will want to ski in bright coloured tight fitting matching suits, ditch them as soon as you arrive at the resort, you will soon meet up with local riders who will show you the best areas.

Travelling as an individual is no drama. As soon as you arrive at a resort check out the main snowboard shop to get the low down on places to kip, and where the locals ride, you'll also find out info on places to work if you're job hunting. Resorts are always looking for casual workers, take a night job or work weekends leaving midweek for boarding.

As few and far between as they are, snowboard tour operators give the best service because they understand what a snowboarder wants. However beware of ski companies in drag, acting as snowboard tour operators, at least for the next couple of years anyway.

Flying around the globe with a snowboard shouldn't prove to be a problem, however make sure that you check with the airline, or travel operator, about baggage charges, some airlines have been known to charge snowboarders extra with a snowboard. If you are told that you have to pay more, ask why, and point out that a snowboard is generally much shorter, and lighter than a pair of skis with bindings. If you have a good size board bag, you can pack your board and boots along with all your clothing, so doing away with the need for a suit case, saving even more space and weight.

Once at you're destination you'll need to know details about onward travel from airports so check out train and bus links. If you're going with a package tour operator transfer arrangements will usually be included in your programme but be sure you don't have to pay extra when you arrive at the airport. Note: hitching a lift from an

tips

airport is not as easy as you may think, so avoid this method of onward travel.

When you're hanging out in airports on the way home, don't buy snowboard mags in the news stands if you can help it, they cost you a lot more than they would have done in a resort and one other thing, don't drink all your duty free booze at the airport.

No need to rattle on about Trains and Buses, only an idiot wouldn't know how to use either. Trains and Buses are generally the cheapest form of long distance travel if you are on a tight budget, however you will have to add considerable time to your trip, and may need to make a number of connections, check in advance how long you will be travelling and your change-overs so that you don't miss out on snow time. In certain places trains run directly into resorts, but for most you will need to take a train to the nearest main town and then transfer by bus.

If you are going to the continent via a ferry crossing a tip when driving is not to drink on the ship during a short crossing unless you can get some one else who has not been driving to drive off, because you will be over the limit, feel like shit and end up falling asleep at the wheel. However do fill the boot with as much duty free a possible to drink when you arrive. Walk on, walk off passengers check out onward travel services at ports i.e.: if you can get a bus or train. You can (if you didn't realise) travel between the UK and France by train through the channel tunnel which can be handy and quick.

Driving from your home to a resort gives you the independence to travel at your own pace. Always check out the particular countries driving laws and whether or not you can take a car into a certain resort (some resorts ban cars). Plan your route and take a map, their are varying ways to get to most resorts however, to save money avoid toll roads and remember to strap down your snowboard on the roof rack (a lot of nerds forget too). If you're going in an old clapped out camper van have the sense to be properly covered with valid foreign driving insurance. Common sense dictates you shouldn't camp out in a van during the winter because of the cold, and snow can fall quick and deep, you could end up being buried. Vehicles should be equiped with snow chains and some emergency survival things, such as·a blanket, a torch, a candle, a can or two of Red Bull, maybe some tinned nosh, definitely a crate of beer, and perhaps a wooly hat.

Accommodation in resorts varies from country to country. Hotels, guest houses, bed and breakfast's, chalets and apartments, are always covered in the ski guides, but they forget to mention Bunk houses, Youth hostels or even camp sites, which will usually offer the cheapest places to stay and let you have the best laugh. It's pointless paying big bucks for a head rest considering the amount of time you're in the place, after all you'll most likely to be snowboarding all day, and partying all night. Some resorts boast special snowboarders accommodation which are worth checking on. If you're planning a summer snowboard trip you'll be able to camp officially at some resorts, while at others you will have to take a chance. Wherever you stay always remember that the more people you squeeze in to sleep on floors etc. the cheaper it costs, but don't get caught. Useful things with any accommodation is a drying room and a secure board store, a bar, all night entry, and no night watchman so you can get into the kitchen for a night feed.

Insurance; this should speak for itself. Don't be an egg head and go away without it, because you could well live to regret it, what's more there are a number of countries where you are not allowed on the slopes without personal insurance cover, America is very strict on this. As well as personal injury insurance make sure you have adequate cover for your belongings i.e. your board and camera etc. And if you are on a package deal make sure you are covered for cancellation and other mishaps. Tour operators have a number of insurance schemes available but make sure you check the small print and be sure that the word SNOWBOARDING is mentioned in any policy. You will find that some countries offer a special insurance policy which can be included for the valid period of the pass. In France this policy is called Carte Neige, check out the details at the resorts for confirmation and to see what cover exists.

If you have your own snowboard equipment, then obviously take it with you, but have the sense to have the board pre waxed and serviced before you leave. For those who will be renting the tips are, either rent at your local shop because if subsequently you want to purchase the board the hire charge can be knocked off the price; alternatively, don't rent at your local shop, wait till you get to a resort and visit a snowboard shop. The advantage of this is that you only pay for the days you use the equipment, plus you can change boards to suit your needs. The other advantage is that you don't have to lug equipment through customs, and on and off transport. The downside is you might not get exactly what you want. In some resorts you will be able to rent snowboard clothing, however it is highly unlikely that you will find anywhere to rent snowboard gloves so don't leave home without a pair.

Lift Passes; like it or not, you are going to have to pay for them (unless you can scam one). There are places that operate special passes that cover snowboard only areas, which is where the pipes and fun parks will be, passes covering these areas may be cheaper, check to see which resorts have snowboarder concessions. Passes can usually be bought as $1/2$ day, full day or in multiple days. Resorts often have passes that can be used in other resorts, the pass will usually cover linked resorts and local buses. Be sure to take a few passport size photos wherever you go, because you may well need them for multiple and long stay tickets.

A very useful card to have is the 'Snowboarders Pass' which can be used for discounts at thousands of places around the globe. The credit card style pass will get you discount on travel, insurance, accommodation and lift

tips

passes as well as discounts in restaurants and shops. It can be purchased for around £25.00 and lasts a year and is well worth the cost.

Snowboarding is not the only thing to check out at resort, places to eat, drink, hang out and chill, are also important. Quite a few resorts have a skate scene with ramps, rails and street especially during the summer, but most have very little for skateboarders. To save on money live off burgers and pizzas, as well as supermarket food, don't bother with fancy restaurants, save your dosh for other things such as pool and partying. In most resorts you will find loads of places to buy snowboards, however there is usually only one or two truly independent, snowboard only shops, that don't have a link with another ski shop. The full on snowboard shop is the place to buy a board but remember two points about buying snowboards at resorts. One, you will not get any after sales service, which will be a pain if you find a problem when you get home. The other point is prices can often be higher in resorts than at home unless you are buying in the US or Canada, where prices are half of what you pay at home.

For some strange reason snowboarders have, in some areas anyway, acquired the image of low life dudes who wreak havoc where they descend, be it on the slope or in the bars, but it's hardly a truly representative one. You will find resorts with bars and cafes which thrive on a snowboard culture with music likely to be more thrash and indie rather than Euro pop, played in many après-ski bars. However just as fashion on the slope changes so does the main hangouts.

As far as snowboard life-style goes in the evenings REMEMBER that snowboarders DO NOT DO APRES SKI, snowboarders do not wear silly bright coloured lip stick or face paint, and dance around in silly groups at tea time bar sessions.

Skater: Russ Ward

16

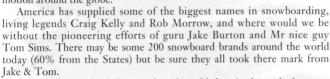

AMERICA

The world's third largest country, with the third largest population, having gained its independence from Great Britain in 1776. Yep the land of the hopeful, the free, the guns, the hamburgers, and Frank Sinatra. For this is the country where it all began, America is snowboarding. Great riders, the best snowboard manufacturer's, full on snowboard clothing and half decent music (with an exception for Country). Back in the sixties when surfers were experimenting by dragging their surf boards out of the sea, and up to the snow capped mountains of California, little did they know what they were setting into motion around the globe.

US pro Rob Morrow : Chilling.

America has supplied some of the biggest names in snowboarding, living legends Craig Kelly and Rob Morrow, and where would we be without the pioneering efforts of guru Jake Burton and Mr nice guy Tom Sims. There may be some 200 snowboard brands around the world today (60% from the States) but be sure they all took there mark from Jake & Tom.

America having lead the snowboard world, hasn't always had resorts open to snowboarding. For instance in 1989 only 70% of resorts allowed snowboarders in, and even today although a good 95% do allow snowboarding, some still ban or restrict snowboarders. Still, don't fret because these are the crap areas anyway. There are even reports that some resorts are snowboard only, skiers are the ones banned. There are over 700 resorts in the US, split between the East, Mid and West coasts.

Americans go in for big time snowmaking, which helps to insure snow almost everywhere, though America does have a good 'real' snow record with areas that get stupid amounts of deep powder. Most US resorts try and open at 'Thanksgiving' (November) and generally go through to April, with a few more northern areas managing to operate lifts in May and June.

Rider- Temple Cummins- Photo Chris Carmel. Crystal Mtn

Resort Page finder

AMERICA

AMERICA

American resorts are varied and tend to be smaller than many European areas. You don't find 600km linked resorts with hundreds of lifts. What you do get is compact and well set out on mid range mountains. Full on well groomed runs are cut between thick wooded forest which allows for a lot of tree lined snowboarding with logs for freestyle grommets readily available. One of the things that stand out about US resorts is how few drag lifts there are. 99% of lifts are chairs which often move with great speed. Chairs solve the problem of having to skate between lifts and help novices get around with out having to tackle T-bars or Pomma's. The few drags (surface lift in US terms) that you do find are generally around beginner areas but don't fret they are beginner friendly. Some resorts state that you need to wear safety leash's but rules aren't always enforced and there is no big drama about riding drags with your back foot clipped in too.

Lift queues are usually short and while you're waiting people will talk to you. The Americans don't have the European (especially British) skiers snobbery attitude. American runs, which will suit all styles of riding, does tend to favour freeriding and freestylers in softs, although carvers in hards will find plenty of places to cut big arcs. One thing America is certainly a pioneer of, is Half Pipe and Fun Parks, you'll find them everywhere, with many resort having more than one pipe and numerous parks, some with DJ's and sound systems as well as floodlights for night riding which is quite common in the US.

On the Eastern side, where resorts are spread out over Maine, Vermont and New Hampshire, you will find nearly all the snowboarding is in tree lined cut out runs, Sugar Loaf is an exception to this with its high up open snow-fields. The east coast often gets some pretty harsh and cold conditions and is known for it's irregular snow, that's why you find a very high use of snowmaking facilities Mount Snow being a prime example. Probably the most famous east coat snowboard resort is Stratton in Vermont where Burton began is boarding success.

The Midwest areas covering the Rockies offer some of the best snowboarding in the US. Places like Vail and Aspen in Colorado (dollar hungry and star studded), or Snowbird in Utah noted for it's powder and big bowls while Breckenridge is a snowboard legend.

The West coast is the area for sun, deep snow and late riding. Big old Mammoth Mountain up there in northern California is a main choice, while around Lake Tahoe you find loads of snowboard friendly areas. Head on up to Washington State for another US classic, Mt. Baker. Small it may be but history it has.

Through out the US many resorts are close to each other and some do connect on the mountain while others can be reached by car or bus. You will be able to use lift passes in other areas where indicated.

America is almost totally Freeride and Freestyle oriented, with soft boots the norm. Hard boot carvers are few and far between, however it is catching on in some areas. The States accounts for 40% of the worlds snowboard market and it is estimated that there are around 600 thousand riders. Opportunities for heli boarding in the states are good and the cost won't freak you out (not if you're a credit card rider that is). Snowboarders are monitored on the slopes by the ski patrols with some patrollers actually on a board. Insurance for riding in the US is a major. If you're found on the slope with out any you'll be kicked off so think on getting it before you go.

AMERICA

Getting there

Reaching the US from Europe is no problem, you can take international flights (remember to check charges for taking a snowboard on a plane), from Europe to all main American cities with many having options for domestic flights direct to resorts. Alternatively you can reach resorts by bus which is often a free shuttle service. If you want to connect by hire car note you will almost certainly need a credit card. If you have no-other option you could take a taxi from the airport to the resort, but it will sting you. If you are travelling with only a few bucks, and no credit card, then seek out a deal with a package tour operator. If you're touring around in the US for a while, then hitching and using Greyhound buses is a good idea, and cheap. Alternatively, before leaving, buy a go anywhere Amtrak train ticket. Visa requirements vary for different nationalities, however for EEC countries you are able to spend up to three months in the US without a visa, but you're not allowed to work 'officially', with out a work permit. This goes for any work, whether its snowboard teaching, or washing dishes. Check with your countries US immigration office on exact visa requirements.

Accommodation like any resort in the world includes Hotels etc., however Americans like things called Condo's (apartments), which are reasonably priced and of very high standard with gadgets all over the place. You will also find basic B&B's, easy-go-lucky bunk houses or Ski Dorms'. Alternatively check at a resort snowboard shop to see if anyone can offer you some floor space to kip down on. You can camp at resorts and there are areas for camper vans but remember in the winter time it's going to be damn cold. Youth hostels are another good cheap option.

You will be spoilt for eating and watering joints. Americans love their food and they like their portions big. Food is cheap but remember that you have to tip in restaurants. American beer is also cheap, but in general it's naff and weak. Proof of age is constantly asked when you're buying alcohol, whether in a restaurant or a store, so keep some form of ID on you where ever you go.

Americans are no different to the rest of the world when it comes to partying, you will have no problem in finding loads of good snowboard lifestyle places to play pool, hang out or even boogie. Yankee snowboarders like to ride hard during the day, and play hard at night, so just remember that hangovers and halfpipes the day after, don't go well together.

US tipping guide for snowboarders with a conscience

Hotels	$1 for the porters
	$1 for parking valets
	$2 a day for chambermaids
Taxi's	15% to 20%
Restaurants	15% of the bill (before taxes)
Coach tours	$1.50

US tipping guide for snowboarders without a conscience

Hotels	$0 for the porters - carry your own board and bags
	$0 for parking valets - the sad gits should get their own car.
	$0 a day for chambermaids - leave the room messy
Taxi's	0% - hitch or take a bus
Restaurants	eat out of supermarkets
Coach tours	$1.50 – if he plays the right sounds on the music system.

Photo: little ones in Aspen, by Mike Brinson

DIRECTORY

US Airlines (UK numbers)

American Airlines:	0181 572 8646
Continental Airlines:	0800 776 464

Main Airports (US numbers)

Boston	+00 1 617 569 7470
New York	+00 1 718 244 4444
Denver	+00 1 303 342 2000
San Francisco	+00 1 415 876 2377
Los Angles	+00 1 310 646 5252
Salt Lake City	+00 1 801 575 2400

Main US Snowboard Manufacturers

Aggression	+1 303 420 3990
Avalanche	+1 707 746 6982
Aunt Mables	+1 503 386 4446
Basic	+1 714 650 6656
Beyond	+1 604 687 8310
Barfoot	+1 410 213 0508
Body Glove	+1 310 374 4074
Burton	+1 802 862 4500
Burnt	+1 416 784 5884
Business	+1 208 397 4348
Caution	+1 801 977 1177
Circle O	+1 714 548 6107
Crap	+1 916 345 3290
Diesel	+1 415 789 9398
Division 23	+1 310 533 4838
Dog Town	+1 213 627 2641
Exit 32	+1 206 888 2391
40 Below	+1 818 966 7667
5150	+1 909 736 6540
G & S	+1 619 581 5166
GNU	+1 206 270 9792
Jobless	+1 401 682 2880
Joyride	+1 208 397 4348
K2	+1 206 463 3631
Kemper	+1 803 294 5370
Lamar	+1 619 550 0555
Lib Tech	+1 206 270 9792
Liquid	+1 206 222 6015
Morrow	+1 503 375 9300
Nitro	+1 503 386 4006
Only	+1 604 876 6044
Original Sin	+1 802 655 2413
Palmer	+1 702 831 7776
Peach	+1 415 882 9725
Reality	+1 714 969 4984
Ride	+1 206 222 6015
Santa Cruz	+1 408 459 7800
Sims	+1 604 525 9441
Smelly Tuna	+1 310 374 2279
Solid	+1 719 836 3548
T-Bone	+1 818 781 6946
Third Rail	+1 714 492 6272
Vision	+1 714 722 8556
Vortex	+1 415 435 2100
White Elephant	+1 403 278 3100
Widow Maker	+1 310 268 8428
World Ind.	+1 800 366 6670
Yellow Bus	+1 503 434 8922

Useful US numbers (US numbers)

Amtrak Railway Co.
Tel: 800 827 7245

Greyhound Buses
Tel: +1 214 419 3996

American Youth Hostels
Tel: +1 202 783 6161

Hosteling International
Tel: +1 310 393 1769

Transworld Snowboard Mag
Tel: +1 619 722 7777

Snowboarder Mag
Tel: +1 714 496 5922

US Amateur Snowboard Association (USASA)
P.O. Box 4400, Frisco, Colorado, 80443, USA
Tel & Fax: +1 303 668 3350

ISF North America (HQ)
PO Box 477, Colorado, 81658, USA.
Tel: +1 303 949 5473
Fax: +1 303 949 4949

US FACT FILE

AMERICA

UNITED STATES – INTRO

USA Statistics

Status	Federal Republic
No of states	50
Capital	Washington
Area	9,363,130 sq. km
Population	249,975,000
Density	27 people per sq. km
Language	English
Currency	Dollar
Neighbouring Countries	Canada & Mexico
Winter snowboard periods	October to April
Summer snowboarding	Between April & July
Highest Mountain	Mount McKinley 6194 m

Country Snowboard styles

Freeride/Freestyle	98%
Alpine/Caring	2%
Soft boots	85%
Hard boots	15%

Drugs	Cannabis and dope are illegal through out U.S.
Death penalty (legalised murder)	Exists in 38 states
Military Service	You can join the forces at 17 and kill for the country but unless you're 21 you can't have a beer to celebrate or drown your sorrows.
Alcohol drinking age	21
Age of consent for sex	The lowest is in Hawaii at 14
Prostitution	Legal in some states
Roads	Vehicles drive on the Right.

23

CRESTED BUTTE

Crested Butte in the Rockies is one of Colorado's ex mining haunts and well worth a visit. It's gained a major reputation as a snowboard friendly resort with some extreme top dog riding to be had in a no bullshit place that's not your typical dollar hungry Colorado destination. Having already successfully staged a series of national events, for 1997 Crested will be hosting the US Extreme Snowboarding Championships having some amazing terrain on which to be able to do so. Crested will appeal to those who like their mountains high with steeps, couloirs, trees and decent off-piste in big bowls. With some 80 runs spread over 1162 acres no one need feel left out on a relatively crowd free mountain that's got a good snow record.

Much of the terrain is best suited to riders who know how to handle a board and prefer off-piste. Wide arc carvers wanting just piste will feel a bit left out but not disappointed, check the flats out on the Paradise where you can crank few big ones. The area known as the Extreme Limits is a gnarly un-pisted heaven for extreme lovers wanting big hits and steeps that will make your eyes water if you bail. Check out the Headwall and North Face areas for some double blacks, which offer cliffs, couloirs and trees. The Banana Funnel is definitely not for wimps. Get a copy of the Crested Buttes extreme area map before heading off.

Intermediates beginning to turn on the style and wanting some cool freeriding piste or off-piste with trees, can give it a go with the runs from the side of Paradise lift, while beginners cutting their first runs would do best to hang out on the areas near the village, before trying out Poverty or Mineral Point off the Keystone lift.

Freetylers wanting to try out new tricks can get air in Crested Butte's gnarly fun park which has rails, logs, table tops and Qtr-pipes and is skier free. To get to the park take the Silver Queen or Keystone lift.

The village of Crested Butte is 3 miles from the slopes, with the usual assortment of beds etc. spread between the village and slopes which is serviced by a shuttle bus. Night time isn't too scary but you can drink till you drop in a number of Yankee style joints. Give the Talk of the Town a visit for booze which also has pool and table football. The main cool snowboard shop which is a good hangout is 'The Colorado Boarder' the shop which offers all things snowboarding and also sponsor the park.

Winter snowboard periods between Nov. and April.

No summer snowboarding

Top Station	3620m
Base	2774m
Vertical Drop	933m
Longest run	4km
Ride area	1160 acres
Snowmaking	238 acres

Terrain ability suits:

Beginner	13%
Intermediate	29%
Advanced	58%

Terrain Ride styles suits:

Freeride	60%
Freestyle	25%
Alpine/Carve	15%

Fun Park is sponsored by Colorado Boarder shop.

Photo : Tom Stillo. Crested Butte Mountain Resort Co

Lift Tickets

Kids pay their age

Adult Regular season

1/2 day	$32
1 day consecutive	$44
2 day consecutive	$87
4 out of 5 days	$157
5 out of 6 days	$197
6 out of 7 days	$229
7 out of 8 days	$260

Lifts open at 9.00-4.00pm

Chair lifts: 27

Drag lifts: 2

Leashes compulsory

No rear foot free rules

Photo : Tom Stillo. Crested Butte Mountain Resort Co

24

SNOWBOARD INSTRUCTION
2 hour lesson $35
4 hour lesson $45
2 hour lesson and hire $55
4 hour lesson and hire $55

SNOWBOARD REPAIR/SERVICE
Hot wax & edge service $20

SNOWBOARD SHOPS
Colorado Boarders
tel: +1 970 349 9828
Sales-Hire-Repair & Instruction
(independent snowboard shop)

Burt Snowmobiles Rentals
tel: + 1 970 349 2441

LIFE STYLE

Eat at: The Saloon where
a burger will cost $3.50

Night time hangouts
Talk Of The Town for some
punk music,
Pool and table football

Photo : Tom Stillo. Crested Butte Mountain Resort Co

Accommodation
Central Reservations tel:
+1 970 34 2222

Crested Butte Tourist Office
PO Box A-500-Gothic Rd
Mt. Crested Butte
CO-81225
www.cbinteractive.com/cbws
tel: +1 970 349 333
Snowphone tel: +1 970 349 2323

UNITED STATES – CRESTED BUTTE

By bus approximately 6 hour
journey to resort.

Fly to Denver International
airport with connection to
Gunnison domestic airport
30 miles from the resort.
Transfer by bus or taxi.

Transfer from Denver airport:

By car hire approximately 5
hours driving to resort. Use
as a map reference routes
US 285, 50, and 135.

Journey via the Monarch
Pass is about 230 miles.

25

COPPER MOUNTAIN

Of all the ski areas in Summit County, Colorado, Copper Mountain offers the largest acreage and the most trails. It is one of the most popular mountains where snowboarders hangout despite near-by Breckenridge with it's board park and half pipe. Copper's long trails and very few traverses appeal to fans of tree runs and those looking for something interesting to tackle and test themselves with. Among the most popular boarding lifts are Eagle, Flyer and E-Lift. For the die hard a short hike off S-lift will give you access to the extreme terrain of Union Bowl and Copper Bowl where you will find wind lips and rock jumps galore. Also off S-lift is 'Onion Roll' a huge natural roller, perfect for jibbers. Unfortunately Copper doesn't have any gondola lifts which, considering the size of the mountain is a real drag. Most of the main chairs take around the 10 minute mark, though it seems double that when you're dangling hundreds of feet up in the air with wind driving snow up your nose and down your neck. Copper has several work programmes of interest to the foreign traveller which enable you to legally earn either day tickets or a whole season pass instead of paying. There's also the generous gesture of a free board program, basically, apart from peak holiday dates you can use K and L lifts simply by going to a ticket office and asking for the free pass. K and L aren't of much interest to the experienced snowboarder but if your a beginner they're perfect. Surviving in Summit County with no money is surprisingly easy, although eating at Copper has the usual pitfalls - painfully expensive. The price of a burger and a coke at Copper Commons is about $6. The Summit Stage is a free bus system which serves all of summit county including all the mountains. If you spend more than two days on the mountain you are going to meet kids working the season who are usually more than happy to help out with floor space for a couple of nights.

The town of Breckenridge and Frisco have plenty of night spots but unless you're 21+ and have photo ID to prove it, your going to be seriously bored. On the skate scene is the excellent Big Fish, again in Breck, about 15 miles from Copper. It has two small ramps, back to back with a hip and a 6 foot ramp to vert wall. A cool night spot is Rasta Pasta with reggae and $1 for a beer or Eric's for Booze and pool.

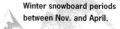

Winter snowboard periods between Nov. and April.

No summer snowboarding

Summit	3767m
Resort height	2926m
Vertical Drop	841m
Longest run	2.8 miles
Ride area	2000 acres
Snowmaking	270 acres

Terrain ability suits:

Beginner	22%
Intermediate	27%
Advanced	51%

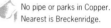

Terrain Ride styles suits

Freeride	50%
Freestyle	10%
Alpine/Carve	40%

No pipe or parks in Copper. Nearest is Breckenridge.

1996/97 Lift Pass price guide

	Adult	Child(14 under)
3 day	$108	$30
4 day	$144	$40
5 day	$180	$50
6 day	$216	$60

Lifts open at 9.00 am to 4.00pm
Weekends and Holidays.
Chair lifts: 27
Drag lifts: 4
Snowboard leashes required.

Photo : Copper Mountain resort

Page rider Sara Hall
Freelance writer and paint stripper

Snowboard instruction
1 day ride, lift and instruction $58
2 ½ lesson $46

Snowboard & Boot hire
1 day hire $25 -2 day $50
Demo boards $30 a day

Snowboard repair/service
Hot wax & edge service from $5

Snowboard shop/s
Powder Tools +1 970 968 2334
Sales-hire-repair.
(ski/snowboard shop)

Max Snowboard Rentals
+1 970 968 2323
Sales-hire-repair
(ski/snowboard shop)
Snowmobiles guided tours

Climbing wall

Sports centre
Opens at 6am for swimming and gym.

Life style

Skateboarding
Healthy skate scene in Breckenridge
with park and pipes

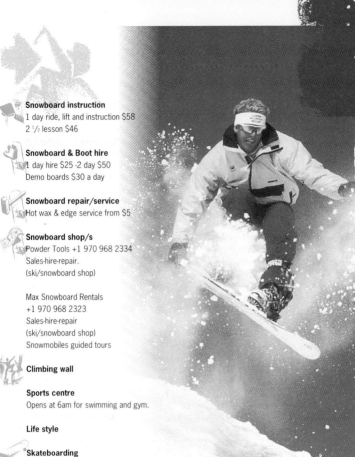

Rider :Ben Blankenbury, Copper Mountain Resort USA

Coppers hamburgers cost from $4.25, a hot
dog $3.50 or a slice of pizza $2.75 and a
regular coke $1.95.

Resort launderette: ✔

Night time hangouts
(all Breckenridge 15 mins)
Eric's Underworld: disco, acid & jazz
A glass of beer costs $2.50
The Brown: laid back snowboarders scene
A glass of beer costs $1.75
Rasta Pasta: reggae and cheap pasta
Glass of beer costs $1
For pool: Eric's
For pool and table football: The Brown

Accommodation
Alpen Hutte hostel
Cost from $13 to $ 27 per
person a night.
+1 970 468 6336

Copper Mountain Tourist office
PO box 3177
Co. 80443
+1 970 968 2882
http://www.Ski:copper.Com

Fly to Denver International

Transfer:

By bus approximately
3 hours journey to resort.

N/a

By car hire approximately 90 minutes
driving to resort. Use as a map reference
routes US I-70 west to exit 195.

Journey Denver via the Eisenhower
tunnel is about 75 miles.

JACKSON HOLE

This is a truly all American resort and comes with cowboys, saloon bars and high peaks. Not your typical rolling tree lined mountains found in a lot of US resorts. Jackson in fact is in a big valley some 10-40 miles wide and 50 miles long. At the base of the slopes is a small Village called Teton, 12 miles away from the main town of Jackson Hole which has the much smaller resort of Snow King rising out of it. Bird brains in nappies will find Jackson's mostly steep and testing terrain a bit daunting. No hope first timers on skis won't manage Jackson but most novices on a board should manage to get around after a few days although leave out the Rendezvous area. Freeriders should love it here, there are some 100 trails with the best stuff found on the Rendezvous mountain which has the biggest vert in the US - some 1261 meters. Once you get off Rendezvous' clapped out old tram you drop down into a cool playground offering chutes, jumps and big drop in's. There's also plenty of trees to flip through. Beginners should stick to the runs leading off the Teewinot chair and the Blues on the Apres mountain while intermediates should check out the areas around the Casper Bowl, Moran Face and around Upper Gros. As well as a half pipe and fun park, Jackson also runs women only snowboard camps with a high standard of snowboard instruction to all levels. A lift pass in Jackson also covers you for Snow King and Grand Targhee giving a combined snowboard acreage of over 4400 acres.

Off the mountain Jackson is all US with numpties strutting about in Stetsons and hanging out in sad saloon bars. There are dozens of drink and eating palaces and accommodation is spread around with the best options in Jackson town itself. Fortunately there is a free regular bus service that operates between Tope and Jackson which takes about 20 minutes. Baby face snowboarders beware. The drinking laws are strict here so make sure you have ID, fake or other wise where ever you go. To help get the best picture on Jackson check out the Hole in the Wall Snowboard shop, a full-on riders place.

Winter snowboard periods between Dec. and April.

No summer snowboarding

Top Station	3185m
Resort height	1924m
Vertical Drop	1261m
Longest run	3 km
Ride area	2500 acres
Snowmaking	80 acres

Terrain ability suits:

● Beginner	10%
● Intermediate	40%
● Advanced	50%

Terrain Ride styles suit:

Freeride	55%
Freestyle	25%
Alpine/Carve	20%

Jackson has 1 halfpipe and a Fun Park

Page Rider: Lesley Mckenna UK Burton Rider

Jackson lift pass guide

	Child	Adult
1 day	$22	$43
5 day	$100	$200
7 day	$133	$266

Lifts open at 9.30pm to 4pm daily.
Gondolas: 1
Chair lifts: 10
Drag lifts: 3
Snowboard leashes required.

Photo: Jackson Hole Resort

Snowboard instruction
¹/₂ day lesson $40, 1 day $50,
3 day lesson $130, 5 day $190

Snowboard & Boot hire
	1-3 days	7 days
Basic	$14	$12 per day
Demos	$25	$21 per day

Snowboard shop
Hole in the Wall +1 307 739 2689
Sales-hire-repair & interaction
(independent snowboard shop)

1 days heli-boarding from $465 per person
Includes 6 runs a guide and lunch
Tel, High Mountain +1 307 733 3274

Snowmobiles with a 350 mile trail to ride.

Sports centre
Open 7 days a week.

Climbing school ✔
Climbing wall ✔
Paragliding ✔

Life style

Eat at
Bubbais bar-b-que for decent nosh.
Cadillac grill for a burger from $4.50.

In supermarkets a loaf of bread
Will set you back $3, a carton of
Milk $1.50 and 10 beers $8.00

Night time hangouts
Mangy Moose, for live music and pool.
a glass of beer costs $1.50

Photo: Bob Woodal/ Wade Mckoy. Jackson Hole resort

Accommodation
The bunk house hostel,
from $18 a night slopes
12 miles away. +1-307 733 3668
The hostel, from $43 a night.
+1-307 733 3415

Hitching Post lodge from $33
a night +1-307 733 2606

El Rancho motel from $34 a night
+1-307 733 357

Jackson Hole tourist office
P.O box 982
Jackson Hole Wy 83001
+1-307 733 3316
Ttp://www./Jackson.Com/ski
Snowphone+1-307-733 5200

Fly to Salt Lake City international airport with connection to Jackson domestic

Airport 11 miles from the town of Jackson transfer by shuttle bus or taxi

Transfer from Salt Lake City airport;

By bus approximately 6 hours journey to resort.

n/a

By car hire approximately 5Ω hours driving to resort.

Driving use as a map reference routes interstate highway 80, route 189 and 89.

MAMMOTH MOUNTAIN

California has given us Hollywood, Daffy Duck and luckily Mammoth Mountain, a massive place and one of the biggest resorts in America with over 150 runs to check out. This great snowboarders haunt which is located in the Eastern Sierra, has welcomed riders for years offering some pretty cool terrain with a good snow record that allows snowboarding to last often until June each year. The terrain will give all levels of riders something to tackle but mainly suiting freeriders with big bowls in the Huevos Grande area and drops at Wipeout and Hangman's Hollow. Carvers will be able to put in a few big turns on the run known as Cornice Dave's Run. Beginners will be able to get going in the tree lined easy runs. The area known as Lower Dry Creek is a natural halfpipe to suit Freestylers but if you want the real thing plus a funpark then check out Mammoths new park and pipe reached from Chair 20 on the trail named 'Merry-Go-Round'. Alternatively if you travel to June Mountain, about 20 minutes away, you'll be able to try out it's well established park and pipe which has a selection rails, quarter pipes, logs and table tops. Mammoth has a good selection of open and tight trees to ride in plus some cliff jumps and extremes around Upper Dry Creek to keep advanced riders happy.

The slopes are about 4 miles from the main eating, sleeping and drinking hangouts, a free shuttle bus operates. There is accommodation available at the base of the slopes however it's a bit dollar hungry and usually frequented by family ski groups with heaps of credit cards, a point to note is that Mammoth does get busy at weekends when it fills up with California's finest. There's not much happening off the slopes but that doesn't mean you can't enjoy your self. Mammoth has a cool skate scene and is planning to open an indoor skate park. When it comes to eating and drinking you are spoilt for choices with dozens of places including Macdonalds. There are loads of shops to spend your bucks in with the normal array of banks and newsagents as well as supermarkets. To get the best low down on Mammoth check out Wave Rave snowboard shop who also offer skateboarding or Storm Riders, both are cool shops where you can rent demo boards with either soft or hard boots and get instruction.

Winter snowboard periods between Nov. and June.

No summer snowboarding

Top Station	3369m
Base	2424m
Vertical Drop	945m
Longest run	4.8km
Ride area	3500 acres
Snow cannon runs	22

Terrain ability suits:

Beginner	30%
Intermediate	40%
Advanced	30%

Terrain Ride styles suit:

Freeride	55%
Freestyle	25%
Alpine/Carve	20%

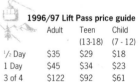

Mammoth has a new Halfpipe and 2 Fun Parks.
Park and pipe also at near by June Mountain (20 minutes away)

1996/97 Lift Pass price guide

	Adult	Teen (13-18)	Child (7 - 12)
½ Day	$35	$29	$18
1 Day	$45	$34	$23
3 of 4	$122	$92	$61
5 of 6	$191	$143	$96

Lifts open at 8.30-4.00pm week days
8.00-4.00pm weekends and holidays

2 gondolas - 28 chair lifts - 1 T-bar
Snowboard leashes required

Photo: Mammoth Mountain Resort

SNOWBOARD INSTRUCTION
$^1/_2$ day lesson $30, -1 day $41
One day package $71=lesson/hire/lifts

SNOWBOARD & BOOT HIRE
1 day hire for Standard B & B $23
1 day hire for Performance B&B $28
1 day hire for Demo B&B $30

SNOWBOARD REPAIR/SERVICE
Full base Tune service $20

SNOWBOARD SHOP/S
WAVE RAVE +1 619 934 2471
Sales-Hire-Repair & Instruction
(independent snowboard shop)

STORM RIDERS +1 619 934 5831
Sales-Hire-Repair & Instruction
(independent snowboard shop)

Mammoth has a Climbing school and Wall

Snowmobile rides

LIFE STYLE

SKATEBOARDING
Indoor park, outdoor ramps planned
summer 1996.
For decks etc check out Wave Rave.

Rider; Tarvis Browne: Photo Ken Hermer

Eat at- Macdonalds for Big Macs.
Bergers for Buffalo burger $5.

Resort launderette: 4 machines $1.50

NIGHT TIME HANGOUTS
THE CLOCK TOWER.
a glass of beer cost $2-3
WHISKEY CREEK - for Rock music
a glass of beer cost $2-3
KEGS N'CUES for pool & games & booze
a pool table cost $7 AN HOUR

ACCOMMODATION
PONDEROSA SPORTS LODGE
from $18 a night
+1 610 934 0629
BUDGET INN
from $50 a night
+1 619 934 8892
MAMMOTH INN,
from $80 a night-walk to slopes
+1 619 934 2581

MAMMOTH TOURIST OFFICE
1 Minaret Road,
Mammoth Lakes CA. 93546
+1 619 934 2712
http://www.rsn.com/mammoth
Snowphone +1 619 934 6166

Fly to Los Angeles International airport with
connection to Mammoth Lakes. Domestic airport 40 minutes from the resort. Transfer by
bus or taxi

N/A

Transfer from Los Angeles airport;

By bus approximately 8 hours journey to
resort. Single ticket cost from $40.75

By car hire approximately 5 hours driving to
resort. Use as a map reference routes 14 to
US highway 395 and 203. Journey from Los
Angeles is about 300 miles.

OKEMO

Okemo is located in the village of Ludlow, in the Eastern United States. There is tons of diverse terrain to ride at Okemo, with almost 90 trails, so plenty of room no matter what kind of rider you happen to be. Those who like the bumps must check out Ledges, Chief and The Plunge. Don't miss Sel's Choice, where a 400-watt sound system keeps bumphounds coming back for more. The gladed runs of choice are Double Diamond and Outrage. Both are long, steep and covered by snowmaking. This means that they open early and stay open late into the season. Okemo is expanding its gladed area for the 1996-97 season so there will be even more tree riding! Once you're clear of the trees and bumps, you'll never believe the huge, ultra-long, rolling trails that are Okemo's trademark. Sapphire, World Cup, Coleman Brook, and Tomahawk are just a few trails that are perfect for going fast and boosting huge airs. Be careful though. Many of the rolls that make these trails so much fun are blind when you're flying over them. For safety's sake you must use a spotter when jumping at Okemo. Freestylers won't want to miss Okemo's snowboard park, located at the bottom of Sel's Choice. Aside from the 420 foot halfpipe, there is an array of jumps, rails, spines and boxes for every ability. Every season there is at least one jump, usually a tabletop, that is so big that it takes a week or two for locals to clear it. For the coming season there will be a lift exclusively for snowboarders using the pipe and park. The lift system at Okemo is rarely busy, however if you haven't got a leash you won't be allowed on. If you need to brush up or learn something new, Okemo boasts an award-winning snowboard school catering for all levels and styles. The beginner terrain is easy to handle and serviced by two chairs and a pomma lift.

There are plenty of places to stay with the usual array of hotels, motels, youth hostels and restaurants to suit every budget whether it be slope side condo' or a giant bed and breakfast. If you need to purchase gear, there are a few options. There's a shop on the mountain, or check out Pit and Northern Ski Works at Okemo, (for board tuning, Bret at Northern Ski Works is your man). To fine dine then Niki's or DJ's is the place while Savannah's is the Burger joint. Booze with food then it's The Black River Brew Pub you should head for. Okemo in a nut shell: big mountain riding, small mountain atmosphere.

Winter snowboard periods between Nov and April.

No summer snowboarding

Top Station	1029m
Base	367m
Vertical Drop	662m
Longest run	7.2km
Ride area	485 acres
Snowmaking	95%

Terrain ability suits:

● Beginner	30%
● Intermediate	50%
● Advanced	20%

Terrain Ride styles suits:

Freeride	40%
Freestyle	20%
Alpine/Carve	40%

1 half pipe 2 fun parks with exclusive lift and pipe dragon. The pipe is to host the North American ISF Master World Cup on March 6-9 1997.

Page Rider : Mathew Beck – 22 year old freestyler from Vermont, sponsored by Limited and Swag.

Lift pass guide

	Low season		High season	
	Child	Adult	Child	Adult
½ day			$18	$30
1 day	$12	$20	$27	$43
5 days	$50	$90	$125	$198
7 days	NA	NA	$175	$267

Lifts open at 9.00-4.00pm week days, 8.00-4.00pm weekends and holidays

Chair lifts 10
Drag lifts 3

Lift policy is rear foot out of binding
Snowboard leashes are required

Rider : Mathew Beck

SNOWBOARD INSTRUCTION
¹/₂ day lesson $20, - 1 day $45
2 day lesson $80 - 5 day $120

SNOWBOARD & BOOT HIRE
1 day hire $30 - 2 day $56 - 5 day $131

SNOWBOARD REPAIR/SERVICE
Hot wax & edge service $30

SNOWBOARD SHOP/S
THE PIT +00 1 802 228 2001
Sales-Hire-Repair
SNOWBOARD SHOP/S
NORTHERN SKI +00 1 802 228 3344
Sales-Hire-Repair

Snowmobiles rides at Snow County
+00 1 802 226 7529

LIFE STYLE

SKATEBOARDING
Ramps, pipe and street rails.
For decks etc check out Sound Barrier

Eat at;
Brew Pub
DJs
Pub Niki's
Savannahs

In supermarkets a tin of beans $.69 cents.
Frozen pizza $1.99
10 pack of beer $7.99

NIGHT TIME HANGOUTS
Savannahs ,food booze and bands
Brew pub, food booze and bands
Christopher's, food booze, music and pool

Accommodation
Resort Properties
+00 1 802 228 5571

1, 2, 3 BEDROOM CONDOS
from $150 a night. Slopes 100m
Tel +00 1 802 228 5571
Cavendish Pointe Hotel
from $55 a night, slopes 3 miles
+00 1 802 226 7688
Best Western Hotel
from $47 a night, Slopes 1 mile
+00 1 802 228 8188

Okemo Tourist Office
RR 1 Box 106
Ludlow, VT 05149, USA
+00 1 802 228 5571
http://www.okemo.com/okemo

Fly Boston international with
connections to Rutland
domestic airport which is 25
miles from the resort
reached by bus.

Transfer from Boston airport;

By bus approximately 4
hours journey to resort.

By train to Pre-St-Didier 8
minutes away or to Chamonix
transfer by bus to resort
30km

By car hire approximately
3¹/₂ driving to resort via
nearest main city Hartford
which is 120 miles, or
Rutland which is 30 miles

UNITED STATES – OKEMO

33

SQUAW VALLEY

Squaw is full on, the dogs B's - a riders resort which has become very snowboard friendly. With its European alpine feel having hosted the 1960 Winter Olympics, Squaw is well used to looking after its visitors. 4000 acres of open bowl riding, 6 peaks, 33 lifts with a capacity of 49000 people an hour, a half pipe and 2 fun parks combined with an average of 450 inches of snow a year (with massive amounts of snowmaking too) make this place a great snowboarders hangout which features in countless snowboard videos. Crossing into two states and linked to Heavenly Valley there is simply heaps for terrain for all styles of rider to conquer with steeps, trees and long chutes along with easy flats for novices. A resort that serves the weekend city dweller, the slopes can be fairly quite during the week days leaving plenty of powder and open runs to shred. Hard boot carvers and piste loving freeriders will not want to leave the amazingly well groomed slopes. The runs of the Squaw and Siberia express are superb for laying some big carves and can be tackled by all levels. Freeriders wanting an adrenaline rush need to try out the runs off the KT-22 or Olympic Lady chairs (lose it up here and it's all over). Powder seekers will find offerings around the Headwall or over at Granite Chief which is a black graded area and not for wimps. If its trees you want then they are all over the place with some marked out of the Shirley Lake chair. Unlike so many resorts around the world Squaws main beginner stuff is found up the slopes rather than at the bottom, which is reached by either a gondola or a cable car ride and a number of chair lifts, there's no danger of T-Bar tackling as there are none and though the easy stuff is high up if you soon master the art of staying up there is a blue run that takes you back to the base. The local ski school here is good and knows how to look after any style or level of rider with a number of packages offered through the main snowboard shops.

Lodging, feeding and partying can be a bit mixed. There are loads of varying price places to kip down within easy reach of the slopes, check out the hostel for a cheap bed, it has bunks at happy prices (bring own sleeping bag). Food is available all over the place from cheap to steep, but if you want to party make for Tahoe or Truckee about six miles away. For your daily snowboard needs call in at Snow Wave snowboard shop, its cool.

Winter snowboard periods between Nov and May

No summer snowboarding

Top Station	2758m
Resort height	1890m
Vertical Drop	869m
Longest run	4.8km
Ride area	4000 acres
Snowmaking 200+ acres	

Terrain ability suits:

● Beginner	25%
● Intermediate	45%
● Advanced	30%

Terrain Ride styles suits:

Freeride	40%
Freestyle	30%
Alpine/Carve	30%

Half pipe
2 Fun parks

Lifts open at 9 am-4.00pm week days 8.30-4.00pm weekends and holidays. Night Riding from 4pm to 9 pm.

Cable cars	1
Gondolas	1
Chair lifts	29
Rope Tows	2

Leashes compulsory

Squaw Lift pass guide

	Child	Adult
1 day	$5	$46
2 day	$10	$86
5 day	$25	$200
7 day	$30	$266
Season	$300	$1299

SNOWBOARD INSTRUCTION
1/2 day lesson $26 group lesson
Private $60 an hour.
Kids $60 per day.

SNOWBOARD & BOOT HIRE
1/2 day $22 -1 day $33
Snowboard only $20 a day
Demo boards $39 a day

SNOWBOARD REPAIR/SERVICE
Hot wax & edge service $25

SNOWBOARD SHOP/S
SNOW WAVE 00 1 916 581 5705
Sales-Hire-Repair & Instruction
(independent snowboard shop)

SQUAW VALLEY SNOWBOARD SHOP
00 1 916 583 6935
Sales-Hire-Repair & Instruction
(Ski snowboard shop)

Snowmobile hire at Tahoe City

Bungee Jumping ✔

Climbing wall ✔

LIFE STYLE
Around town a Hot Dog will cost around $3,
a Pizza $11 and a ten pack of beer $8.

NIGHT TIME HANGOUTS:
RED DOG SALOON IN SQUAW
for Rock music, a glass of beer costs $3

Photo: Tom Day - Squaw Valley Resort

NAUGHTY DAUG SALOON IN TAHOE CITY
Rock music, a glass of beer costs $2.50

PETE N PETERS IN TAHOE CITY
for pool with rock music
a beer cost $2.50

PIER STREET IN TAHOE
Disco, a beer costs $2.50

ACCOMMODATION
THE HOSTEL AT SQUAW VALLEY
From $20 a night per person
00 1 1800 545 4350

River Ranch
from $59 a night per person
00 1 1800 545 4350

Squaw Valley Tourist Office
Squaw Valley CA-96146
00 1 916 583 3494
Reservations: 00 1 1800 545 4350
Snowphone: 00 1 916 583 6955

By bus approximately 1 1/2
hours journey to resort.
A single ticket cost $15

n/a

By car hire approximately
1 hours driving to resort.

Fly to Reno Tahoe
International airport or San
Francisco International which
is 3 1/2 hours car drive or
8 hours and $40 bus ride to
the resort.

Transfer from Reno airport;

Driving use as a map
reference routes interstate
80 and US highway 89

Journey from Reno is
45 miles and from San
Francisco 200 miles.

STOWE

If you want some serious East Coast snowboarding, then they don't come much more serious than Stowe. It has a proper mountain and the history of over six decades going for it. Spread over three distinct areas, each one lends itself to a different ability: Spruce Peaks, the beginners to intermediate area but a bit isolated from the main part of the ride area; Mount Mansfield area is accessed by the 8 person gondola, the fastest one in the world. This area is an intermediate paradise with some great cruising terrain, it is also perfect for those who like to arc'em. The final area is the largest with a mix of all terrain types, and where the advanced terrain is. Hit Goat or Starr if you are good or conditions are awesome. Both of these trails are narrow and steep. Liftline and National on the other hand are tamer, having been widened over the years and you can occasionally find them groomed. But generally unless you are into bumps steer clear of these four runs. Nosedive is good for freeride and carving, and the rest of Mansfield area consists of intermediate terrain, a few of these trails have good natural hits and jumps on the trail edge. Under the gondola is cruise freeride terrain and like many of the areas there are heaps of tracks through the trees and plenty of places within the main area to disappear into. Freestylers are going to kick arse on any mountain after a session in Stowe's specially designed fun park called the Jungle located on the Lower Lord area easily reached from lift 4. Stowe also has a pipe, the local ski school actually offers 20 minute lessons called the Quick Trick for about $15. The school also caters for new dudes and those who think they know it already with advanced clinics.

The Stowe village, famed for it's ice cream factory, is about six miles from the main slopes, which is reached by a free shuttle bus. There are plenty of places to lay your head all along the road to the slopes with the usual choice of condos and B&Bs, however Stowe doesn't have the most radical night life though you can drink yourself stupid in a number of bars. Check out The Shed for the best goings on, or for nosh try Miguels. If you're a sad git that wants to pump iron, then there is a fitness centre just for you, (go drinking instead).

For snowboarding needs visit the Spruce Mountain shop or Snowboard Addic.

Winter snowboard periods between Nov and April.

No summer snowboarding

Top Station	1109m
Base elevation	475m
Vertical Drop	720m
Longest run	6km
Ride area	480 acres
Snowmaking coverage	73%

Terrain ability suits:

Beginner	16%
Intermediate	59%
Advanced	25%

Terrain Ride styles suits:

Freeride	40%
Freestyle	25%
Alpine/Carve	35%

Fun park; is reached by using lift number 4.
Halfpipe; is off lift 2 and down Nose Dive to Midway.

Rider: Ted Fleischer, Stowe Mountain Resort

1996/97 lift pass guide;

US $	Early/Late season	
	Child	Adult
1/2 day	$10	$20
1 day	$15	$30
5 day	$60	$125

Night riding from 4pm to 10pm Wed to Sat. Adults $20 - Child $16

Lifts open at 8am to 4 pm week days and 7.30am to 4pm weekends.

Chairlifts 9
Drag lifts 2
Snowboard leashes required.

Photo: Stowe Mountain Resort

SNOWBOARD INSTRUCTION
1 day hire + lesson & pass $70.
Quick 20 minute day lesson $15
Advanced ride clinic, 3 hours $25.

SNOWBOARD & BOOT HIRE
1 day hire $20, 2 day $35, 5 day
$80

SNOWBOARD REPAIR/SERVICE
Hot wax & edge service $25

SNOWBOARD SHOP/S
THE SPRUCE MOUNTAIN
Sales-Hire
SNOWBOARD ADDIC
Sales-Hire

**Snowmobile rides at the Nichols
snowmobile park.**

Stowe has a number of fitness centres with day passes, for swimming,
Treadmills, rowing, weights, mas-
sage and whirlpools.

LIFE STYLE

Eat at
Miguels for Mexican and Corona.
Pie in the Sky for Pizza and Pasta
(cheap)

Stowe's big attraction.
Ben & Jerrys Ice Cream Factory at
nearby Waterbury also the location
of Cold Hollow Cider Mill.

NIGHT TIME HANGOUTS
THE SHED
for home brew and food from
$5 a head
STOWE INN & TAVERN
easy place for a beer and
Yankee food.

Rider Lowell Hart: Photo: Stowe Mountain Resort

Accommodation
The Round Hearth - (slopes 4 miles)
00 1 800 829 7629

2 nights	$97
3 nights	$119
5 nights	$151

Ski Dorm - slopes (3 miles)
00 1 800 253 4882

2 nights	$65
3 nights	$88
5 nights	$129

Rates are per person.
For lower seasonal rates call.

Stowe Tourist Office
5781 Mountain RD Stowe
Vermont - 05672
Web   00 1 802 253 3000
http://www.stowe.com/smr
Snowphone: 00 1 802 253 3600

Transfer from Boston airport;

By bus approximately 4 hours
journey to resort.

By car hire approximately
3¹/₄ hours driving to resort.

Fly to Boston International airport with connection to
Burlington domestic airport 40
minutes from the resort transfer by bus or taxi.

By train approximately 3¹/₂
hours journey to Waterbury
station, 15 minutes from Stowe

Driving use as a map reference
routes Interstate 89 exit 10.

Journey from Boston is
205 miles.

STRATTON MOUNTAIN

This is it! This is where it all began! Located in South Vermont, Stratton Mountain is generally recognised as the home of snowboarding. A decent sized resort, Stratton was one of the first areas to give snowboarders access to the mountain & Jake Burton Carpenter used to test his early boards here. Stratton is also where the states first pro snowboard school was set up, and is also home to the worlds longest running snowboard competition - The US Open, which uses what is reputed to be the best halfpipe on the planet. The Green Mountain race series also comes to Stratton for a couple of events.

Terrain at Stratton will suit all but those riders who look for extreme & cliff jumps. Beginners & novice riders will have the whole of the lower mountain to explore plus easy routes from the summit. Freetylers hanging around the lower mountain can use the high speed six-person chair to access the snowboard only park and the 120m long pipe. The park has table tops, gaps and ramps. For this coming season the pipe will have sounds and floodlights. On the lower mountain there is also a terrain park for boarders and skiers which is not such a good idea as the skiers have no etiquette & show a complete lack of patience.

The North American/Upper Standard & Lifeline will grab the Alpine rider for big turns. Freeriders will like the rolls & banks on the intermediate & novice terrain of Black Bear & The Meadows. Riders with some know-how should check out the Upper Tamarack and if you are looking for some open trees Freefall is the place. The snow record here is pretty good and is backed up with a full snowmaking covering all the major trails.

Midweek you are up & down the mountain in a flash, but at the weekend lines for the lifts appear as everybody from NYC & Boston arrive.

At the base of the mountain is a compact alpine village with more or less everything you need. The scene couldn't be described as wild and in your face but it's out there and there's plenty going on. The Base Lodge is the first stop with a pool table, pinball and a juke box. Later on check out the Green Door Pub. For snowboard needs, take a look at Syd & Dusty's Snowboard Shop or Mountain Riders and Bonkers Board Room. You can rent demos as well as standard kit.

Winter snowboard periods between Nov and April.

No summer snowboarding

Top Station	1200m
Base station	589m
Vertical Drop	611m
Longest run	5km
Ride area	478 acres
Snowmaking	70%

Terrain ability suits

● Beginner	35%
● Intermediate	37%
● Advanced	28%

Terrain Ride styles suits

Freeride	45%
Freestyle	25%
Alpine/Carve	30%

400 ft Halfpipe & 2 Fun parks

Page ride Paul Bernie Sims, UK snowboard instructor based in the US.

1996/97 lift pass guide from;

US $	Adult	Child
2 day	$79	$57
5 day	$154	$120
6 day	$179	$141

*Children under 6 ride free.

Lifts open at 8.30-4.00pm week days, 8.00-4.00pm weekends and holidays

Gondolas	1
Chair lifts	9
Drag lifts	9

Rear foot no rules, Leashes Compulsory

SNOWBOARD INSTRUCTION
1 hour lesson $25
Ride package
1 day hire with 3 ½ hour lesson and pass $59
Night Rider - Lift Hire & Lesson $39

SNOWBOARD & BOOT HIRE
1 day hire $31 - Additional day $22

SNOWBOARD SHOPS
SYD + DUSTYS + 1 802 297 2200
Sales-Hire-Repair & Instruction
(independent snowboard shop)
MOUNTAIN RIDERS + 1 802 297 2200
Sales-Hire-Repair & Instruction
(independent snowboard shop)

Snowmobiles: ✔

SPORTS CENTRE
Open 7 days a week from 7am to 9pm

LIFE STYLE

SKATEBOARDING
Nearest ramps and pipe: Bennington 45 min
Indoor pipe,
outdoor street Course

A hamburger costs from $3.00
A hot dog costs from $2.50

In supermarkets a carton of milk is $1.50
Loaf of bread 75c
12 beers $8.

Nearest laundrette 15 minutes drive away.

Rider- Lee : Photo Barrie Fisher. Stratton Mountain

NIGHT TIME HANGOUTS

PIZZARIA, for progressive Rock
a glass of beer cost $2-4
OUTBACK, For a bit of everything
a bottle of Bud cost $2.50
PIZZARIA, for pool & games
a pool table cost 25C

Accommodation
Central reservations +1 802 297 4000

VAGABOND SKI DORM
from $20 a night, slopes 2 miles
BEAR CREEK HOTEL
from $55-65 a night, slopes 10 min
AVALANCHE MOTOR LODGE
from $65-80 a night, slopes 15 mins
THE CHALET MOTEL
from $55-100 a night, slopes 15 mins

Stratton Welcome Centre
RR1 Box 145
Stratton Mt., Vermont
+1 802 297 2200
http://www.genghis.com/stratton.htm
Snowphone + 802 297 4211

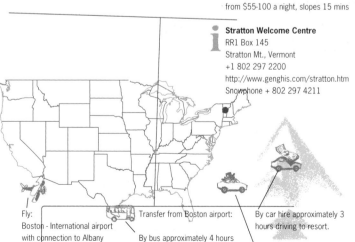

Fly:
Boston - International airport
with connection to Albany
domestic airport 1 1/2 hours
transfer by bus or taxi.

Transfer from Boston airport:

By bus approximately 4 hours
journey to resort

By train to White River Junction,
then bus to resort.

By car hire approximately 3
hours driving to resort.

Driving use as a map reference
routes Interstate 89 exit 10,
journey from Boston is 205
miles.

UNITED STATES – STRATTON MOUNTAIN

VAIL

Vail has the reputation of being one of America's most prestigious (read - snobbery) ski resorts and in some respects it's true. The town of Vail, a bizarre imitation of a 'typical' Swiss alpine village is centred around the base of the resort and is hellishly expensive. However there are plenty of good reasons to at least visit Vail if in Colorado. Vails attitude towards snowboarding is extremely positive, it has 2 half pipes and 3 funparks which although open to everyone, are frequented almost exclusively by snowboarders. The natural terrain is awesome. They even produce a special pocket sized Snowboarding mountain map which points you in the direction of the best boarding trails and spots. Popular back country includes Ptarmigan Ridge, a 25ft cornice jump and Kengis Khan, another cornice not suitable for sufferers of vertigo. The cliffs under Chair 4 are easier to access as long as you don't mind your slams being applauded by everyone on the lift. The tree run 'Cheeta Gully' has been marked as one of the special 'snowboard appropriate' trails and will test the tree avoiding abilities of the most proficient rider.

Vail Resort is made up of three mountains: Vail, Beaver Creek and Arrow Head Mountain. Plans are that for the '97 season all of the mountains will be connected so you will be able to ride a chair from one mountain to the next. A good time to ride Vail is late season, the snow is soft, the lift tickets drop dramatically in price and you don't have to put up with millions of day-glow vacationers. Another useful tactic for avoiding the mob is by staying out of mid-Vale which gets insanely busy on holidays. For some unknown reason the Lionshead area is generally less crowded and has more to offer the 'boarder.

Eating at the resort will destroy your bank balance but there is a near-by supermarket and a Subway right in the village where you can get a reasonably priced sandwich.

Because the resort is the entire town finding cheap accommodation is hard. Many of the locals avoid this by living out in one of the nearby towns which have cheaper housing but this has the annoying draw back of a 20 minute 'commute' to ride. The main snowboard shops to check out are Board Riders Club and One Track Mind both located at Linseed Vail.

Winter snowboard periods between Nov and May.

No summer snowboarding

Top Station	3490m
Resort height	2475m
Vertical Drop	1015m
Longest run	7.2km
Ride area	4112 acres
Snow cannon runs	347 acres

Terrain ability suits:

● Beginner	32%
● Intermediate	36%
● Advanced	32%

Terrain Ride styles suits

Freeride	70%
Freestyle	10%
Alpine/Carve	20%

2 halfpipes and 3 fun parks

Photo: Jack Affleck. Vail Resort

1996/97 lift pass price guide:

US$	Reg Season		Holiday	
	Child	Adult	Child	Adult
1 day	$35	$48	$35	$48
3 day	$105	$144	$105	$144
5 day	$160	&225	$165	$230

Lifts open at 9am to 4pm all periods

Chair lifts 25
Drag lifts 6
Rear foot free on drag lifts and snowboard leashes required.

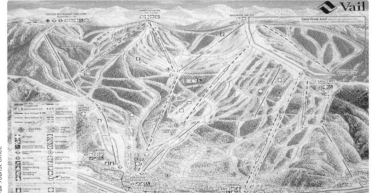

Photo: Vail Tourist Office

Page rider: Sara Hall

Photo: Jack Affleck. Vail Resort

SNOWBOARD INSTRUCTION
Discover Boarding levels 1-3
1/2 day lesson/lift/hire $60
1 day lesson/lift/hire $90
3 day lesson/lift/hire $270
Kevin Delany snowboard camps
7 days full board/hire/lifts/
instruction available

SNOWBOARD & BOOT HIRE
1/2 day hire $18, 1 day $25, 2 day $50
Demo boards $22 per day board only
Junior boards 98cm up - 1 day $18

SNOWBOARD REPAIR/SERVICE
Hot wax & edge service $15

SNOWBOARD SHOPS
ONE TRACK MIND +1 970 476 139?
Sales-Hire-Repair
(Ski/Snowboard shop)
BOARD RIDERS CLUB +1 970 476 1?5?
Sales-Hire-Repair & Instruction
(independent snowboard shop)

Heli-boarding

Snowmobiles cost $100 per day

Climbing wall ✓

LIFE STYLE

SKATEBOARDING
No Ramps in Vail, nearest Breckenridge
For decks etc. check out Board Riders Club

Vails Hot Dogs cost from $3.25
and a Pizza $3.35.

In supermarkets a Loaf of bread $1.90.
10 pkt of beers $6.

NIGHT TIME HANGOUTS
SHIEKA, for techno
a glass of beer cost $2.50
GARFUNKELS, mixed scene and Pool
a glass of beer cost $2.00

Accommodation
+1 970 949 5750

Vail Tourist Office
Po Box 7
Vail Co. 81658
http://Vail.net
+1 970 476 5601
Snowphone: +1 970 476 4888

Fly to Denver International airport with connection to Eagle
County domestic airport 35
miles from the resort. Transfer
by bus or taxi

Transfer from Denver airport:

By bus approximately 3 hours
journey to resort.

N/A

By car hire approximately 2
hours driving to resort.

Driving use as a map reference
routes Interstate 70 exit 173,
176 and 180.

Journey from Denver is
100 miles.

WATERVILLE VALLEY

This is an easy go laid back place that forms part of a programme called the "Peaks of Excitement" which is a group of resorts working together that include Killington, Mount Snow/Haystack, Sugarloaf and Bromley. Waterville Valley which was helped out with a bit of cash back in the sixties by Robert Kennedy a member of that family! has helped the place become a pretty cool snowboard haunt. Situated in New Hampshire's White Mountain National Forest, the resort is only 2 hours from Boston and can be reached with no bother by either bus or car from major airports and cities. The slopes are about a mile and a half from the village which is serviced by a regular shuttle bus to the lifts. Waterville Valley really tries hard for snowboarders, it even has what it claims to be the only all snowboard mountain in the east with an area called, 'Snow's Mountain' that has its own lift and 5 runs which are not open to the two plankers. Snow's Mountain area is actually only set aside for snowboarders on weekends and during holidays but that's no big deal. The area is fairly tame and will suit beginners and intermediates most. Hard-core freeriders may not be to tested at Waterville but you still have something to cut on with plenty of trees to shred. Air heads and trick merchants however are going to like this place with it's massive halfpipe and funpark area known as The Boneyard. As one would expect The Boneyard is closed to skiers and features quarter pipes, rail slides and table tops. Being part of the "Peaks of Excitement programme means that you can use your lift pass at the other resorts should you want to move around, giving access to a combined area of over 2000 acres of boarding terrain.

Off the slopes Waterville is a simple and no big drama place, not the most happening hangout, but what the hell, you can make things happen if you wish. For some decent grub at reasonable prices check out Jugtown Deli or Alpine Pizza. If you want pool or games then go along to the Zoo Station. For a beer and night time hang out give Legends 1291 a look in. Waterville doesn't have much for skateboards in the winter unlike the summer where they have a new indoor skate park at the Sport Dome.

For all your snowboard needs go visit Ride-On snowboard shop located at the base of the slopes.

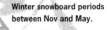

Winter snowboard periods between Nov and May.

No summer snowboarding

Summit	1220m
Base	
Vertical Drop	616m
Longest run	4.8km
Ride area	255 acres
Snowmaking cover	96%

Terrain ability suits

● Beginner	20%
● Intermediate	60%
● Advanced	20%

Terrain Ride styles suits

Freeride	45%
Freestyle	30%
Alpine/Carve	25%

**Half pipe
3 fun parks**

Photo: Waterville Valley Resort

Daily lift ticket rates;

	Mid week	Weekends
Adult	$39	$43
Teen	$34	$39
Youth	$24	$29

Lifts open at 9.00-4.00pm week days, 8.00-4.00pm weekends and holidays

Chair lifts:	8
Drag lifts:	10

No rear foot rules on drags but foot must be free on chair lifts
Snowboard leashes recommended

Photo: Ed Sawyer, Waterville Valley

SNOWBOARD INSTRUCTION
Learn to ride package
1 day hire & 1 lesson & pass $49
1 day lesson $30, 2 day $55

SNOWBOARD & BOOT HIRE
1 day hire $30, 2 day $55, 7 day $180

SNOWBOARD SHOPS
RIDE ON + 1 603 236 8311
Sales & Hire
*Located at base of slopes.

SPORTS CENTRE
Open 7 days for swim/squash/tennis/Gym.
*Open session entrance fee.

Sports Dome open in summer for Climbing wall
Climbing wall also at Rock Barn 35 mile drive.

LIFE STYLE

SKATEBOARDING
Indoor park at the new Sport Dome.
*summer time only.

Eating at Jugtown Deli for Breakfast.
A hamburger in Waterville Valley will cost from $4

In supermarkets
A carton of milk $1.50.
A packet of pasta $1.50
12 beers $11

Resort launderette ✔ a machine is $.75c

NIGHT TIME HANGOUTS
LEGENDS 1291
for live music, booze and dancing
a glass of beer cost $3
ZOO STATION
for pool & games
*Under 21 club.

Photos: Ed Sawyer, Waterville Valley

Waterville Tourist Office
Waterville Valley
NH-03215 USA
+1 603 236 8311
http://www.waterville.com/biz/waterville
Reservations +1 603 236 8371
Snowphone +1 603 236 4144

Fly to Boston International airport with
connection to Manchester domestic airport 70
miles from the resort. Transfer by bus or taxi.
Transfer from Boston airport;

By bus approximately 3 hours journey to resort.

N/A

By car hire approximately 2 hours driving
to resort.

Driving use as a map reference routes
Interstate 93 exit 28

Journey from Boston is 130 miles.
From New York 325 miles.

UNITED STATES – WATERVILLE VALLEY

WINTER PARK

Winter Park sits nestled at the base of Berthoud Pass, at an altitude of 9000ft and a mere 67 miles from Denver making it the closest major resort to Denver International Airport. Winter Park is the 5th largest resort in the USA with over 1373 acres of terrain.

Colorado is famous for its powder snow and Winter Park snags more than its fair share of it, with average annual snowfall of 350". Last season 95/96 saw a record 420" of white fun! Although there's a vast amount of snowfall, there's still plenty of blue sky days as Colorado has (on average) 300 days a year of sunshine. The high treeline of Winter Park means that even when there is low cloud, visibility is still good.

Winter Park is actually two mountains, Winter Park and Mary Jane. Winter Park has runs for all standards of rider and is well groomed for speed merchants and carvers alike. Mary Jane is almost totally for experienced skiers and snowboarders and it's terrain is allowed to mature naturally (i.e. skiers fuck it up and make huge moguls). There's plenty of tree runs around both mountains which are amazing, with near perfectly spaced trees.

Although the whole resort is super snowboard friendly, Winter Park have recognised the advantages of a snowboard park and have built two. One runs through a wooded glade and is an interesting idea, but you need to be wary of going to fast as trees can stop you fast as painfully. The other snowboard park is quite compact in area, but instead of having a standard layout of jump following jump, there is a far more "line" oriented layout, similar to a skatepark. There are lots of different lines through the park with experimental riders getting the most out of it.

The town of Winter Park sits approximately six miles down the valley from the resort and is a relatively sparsely populated, stretched out affair. A free bus service runs all day and most of the night from the lifts and throughout the resort. The evening are not as hectic as those in resorts such as Breckenridge or Aspen, but if you want to party there is usually something going on somewhere, such as line dancing at Rome on the Range (more fun than you might think) or the Sunday night disco at The Pub. The local snowboarders bar is located in the basement of The Lord Gore Arms and they show videos every night as well as playing music, DJ's and bands. Beer is cheap at Happy Hours throughout the resort.

Winter snowboard periods between Nov and May

No summer snowboarding

Top Station	3670m
Base	2730m
Vert drop	930m
Longest run	8km
Ride area	1373 acres
Snowmaking cover	274 acres

Terrain ability suits

● Beginner	22%
● Intermediate	58%
● Advanced	20%

Terrain Ride styles suits

Freeride	42%
Freestyle	30%
Alpine/Carve	28%

2 Parks and a pipe

Photo: Byron Hetzler Winter Park, Colorado

1996/97 lift pass rates from US$; Low season
1 day Adult $15, Child & $18

Lifts open daily at 9am to 4pm weekdays and 8.30am to 4pm holidays.

Chair lifts 20.

Photo: Winter Park, Colorado

SNOWBOARD INSTRUCTION
Beginners ¹/₂ day lesson $15, 1 day $25
Intermediates ¹/₂ day lesson $35.

SNOWBOARD & BOOT HIRE
1 day hire $18, 2 day $30, 5 day $75
Demo boards 1 day hire $20
Junior boards 1 day hire $18

SNOWBOARD REPAIR/SERVICE
Hot wax & edge service $15

SNOWBOARD SHOP
POWER PLAY SPORTS
+1 970 726 5359
Sales-Hire-Repair

Snowmobiles cost $55 for 2 hours

Swimming at YMCA.

Climbing wall ✔

LIFE STYLE

SKATEBOARDING
No ramps – but some street rails,
nearest halfpipe - Steamboat Springs

A hamburger in Winter Park will cost
from $3.50, a hot dog $2.75, or a pizza $10.

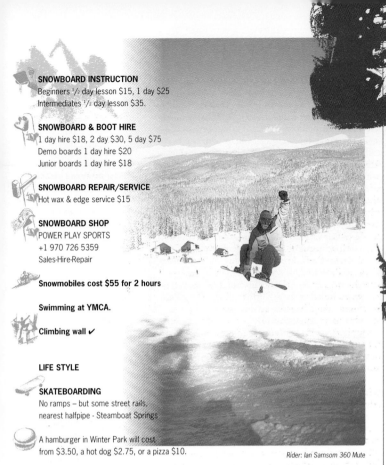

Rider: Ian Samsom 360 Mute

In supermarkets a can of coke $1, a carton of milk $1,
a loaf of bread $.99c. 10 pack of beer $5

Resort laundrettes: ✔

NIGHT TIME HANGOUTS
THE PUB
for snowboarders scene and pool
a glass of beer cost $1
THE CROOKED CREEK SALOON
alternative music
a glass of beer cost $3

Accommodation
ROCKY MOUNTAIN SNOWBOARD TOURS
Chalet accommodation
cost from $700 per person for 10 days
with full board.- Slopes 2 miles
UK: 0151 733 7593
USA + 1 603 236 8301

Winter Park Tourist Office
PO Box 3236
Winter Park CO-80482
+1 970 726 4221

Fly to Denver International airport

Transfer from the airport;

By bus approximately 2 hours journey to resort.
Return ticket $68

By train approximately 2 hours journey

By car hire approximately 2 hours driving to
resort.

Driving use as a map reference Interstate 70,
exit 232 to highway 40. Journey from Denver is
67 miles.

SUNDAY RIVER

Sunday River in the State of Maine is another big area in New England and a cool snowboard friendly resort. 'Sunday' has rapidly grown from a bit of a no hope locals haunt to a fairly happening place in a very short space of time with some major snowmaking facilities to help with the real stuff. Like most of the east coast this place is thick with trees with its trails hacked out from the pine to form runs suitable for all levels of rider particular freeriders who know how to go for it. Sunday Rivers impressive 8 mountain peaks are all open to snowboarders with over 70 runs to try out. Freestylers will find lots of natural hits to get air and plenty of places for jibbing and bonking as well as 10 mini parks some of which are open to skiers (disgraceful). Freeriders going for it should check out the double blacks on the OZ peak and Jordan Bowl, the Double black Caramba especially, however beware of Kansas a long flat muscle pumping traverse used to get you back to the main area. Advanced riders should head over to White Cap peak if you're looking for some bumps, steeps and trees to play in. For freeriders with balls and who like speed and steeps mixed together then go crank some fast turns on the White Heat run said to be one of the steepest runs on the east coast which will bring you out near lift number 11 which is also the best access lift to reach Sundays snowboard park or the trail called the Starlight. Beginners will find plenty of easy terrain to deal with especially around lifts 7 & 2 before progressing up to check out the American Express novice run. The local Ski school offers a number of teaching programs one of which they call the Perfect Turn Snowboard Clinic where they guarantee to teach you in a day with a maximum of six people in a class.

Off the slopes the village of Bethel plays host to your needs which is an easy going and laid back place. If you're a hard core party animal wanting dozens of discos etc. then you'll soon get bored, the night life isn't the most happening but still OK. The Brewpub, a micro brewery, is a great place to get a beer as well as the Foggy Goggle. There is accommodation at the base of Sundays slopes or within a six mile radius. The Snow Cap Lodge Dorm is set aside for groups and worth bedding down in at prices from $25 a night.

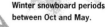

Winter snowboard periods between Oct and May.

No summer snowboarding

Top Station	945m
Vertical Drop	700m
Longest run	3km
Ride area	640 acres
Snowmaking	90%

Terrain ability suits

● Beginner	25%
● Intermediate	40%
● Advanced	35%

Terrain Ride styles suits

Freeride	70%
Freestyle	10%
Alpine/Carve	20%

1 Halfpipe
1 Fun Park
10 mini parks

Lifts open 9am -4pm week days,
8am-4pm W/ends and holidays
*Rear foot free on drag lifts
*Leashes compulsory

Sunday River Tourist Office
PO Box 450,
Bethel. ME. 04217
+1 207 824 3000
http://Sundayriver.com/
www/Sunday-river/
Reservations: + 1 800 543 2 SKI
Snowphone: + 1 207 824 6400

Fly to Portland International airport

Transfer from the airport;

By bus approximately 2 1/2 hours journey to resort.

N/A

By car hire approximately 1 1/2 hours driving to resort.

Driving use as a map reference Portland which is 70 miles to Sunday River.

LOON MOUNTAIN

Located in the state of New Hampshire in the White Mountain National Park, Loon is a small mountain about half the size of Stratton but very OK to ride with good and varied terrain to appeal to most recreational boarders. The mountain really feels like a freeride mountain but that said freestylers have a full on major park approximately 2000ft in length running right under the detachable quad that snowboarders come a long way for with the usual selection of hits including some great gap jumps. The best place for laying out a big carve is on the Upper and Lower Walking Bos. For novices and intermediate alpine riders the lower mountain has plenty to keep you busy. Angel Street is a fun but short Black Diamond with the opportunity to get some big air off the ledge at the top.

Loon has a good choice of accommodation some 13,000 beds within 16 kms of the slopes. There is some slopeside accommodation but most of the beds are 15 to 10 minutes away in the towns of Lincoln & Woodstock. For hangouts and food the places to check out are Woodard Inn for the booze and games room and the Woodstock Inn for nosh at good prices.

Lift pass Guide regular season

	1/2	1
Day		
Child (13-21)	$20	$25
Adult	$20	$27

Winter snowboard periods between Nov and April.

No summer snowboarding

Top Station	930m
Base	290m
Vertical Drop	640m
Longest run	2 1/2 miles
Ride area	250 acres
Snowmaking	97% of terrain

Terrain ability suits

● Beginner	20%
● Intermediate	64%
● Advanced	16%

Terrain Ride styles suits:

Freeride	60%
Freestyle	25%
Alpine/Carve	15%

Loon has a Halfpipe and a 600m long Fun Park

Snowboard shop for Sales/hire/repair
The Pit +1 802 228 2001
(Independent snowboard shop)

Snowboard Instruction

1 day/hire/lift/lesson	$52
1/2 day/hire/lift/lesson	$42

Chair lifts	7
Drag lifts	1

Loon Mountain Tourist Office
RR 1 Box 41,
Kancamagus Highway
Lincoln, NH-03251-9711
+1 603 745 8111
http://www.mainstream.com/loon
Reservations +1 800 227 4191
Snowphone +1 603 745 8100

Photo: Dennis Welsh . Loon Mountain Resort

 N/A

By car hire approximately 2 hours driving to resort.

Fly to Boston International airport

Transfer from the airport;

By bus approximately 3 1/2 hours journey to resort. Return ticket $68

Driving use as a map reference Interstate 93 exit 32 to highway 112

Loon Mountain is 80 miles from Manchester.

UNITED STATES – SUNDAY RIVER & LOON MOUNTAIN

SUN VALLEY

The white settlers of the 19th century invaded this former camp site of the Indians for a fast dollar in mining. Now a days the money rolls in from the mountain sliders on what is said to be Americas oldest resort dating back to 1935.

Sun Valley is a bit of a poncy resort having catered over the years for the rich and famous. In the early days Gable and Monroe hung out here, while today sad actors like Schwarzrnegger can be seen loitering around. However don't be put off, because the boarding terrain is pretty extensive and will appeal to those who like long descending open flats for cranking turns. Spread out over two mountains known as Bald, and Dollar, there are plenty of places to ride which are free of the stars and posers. Spring Cut-off which is a bit of a natural halfpipe is a good area for freeriders to shred while the Mid River and Mid Warm Runs will suit the piste carving speed dudes. There are a number of bowls to check out such as College South and Mayday which can have some fairly good powder to cut. Beginners should check the Seattle Ridge area, especially the Broadway and Christins Silver run which should sort you out before going on to more trying terrain. For the nutters who want to test themselves check out the Upper Greyhawk run, it's steep and could be mean, though it's not massive and does get easy half way down. For those who can afford it Sun Valley offers heli boarding trips into the Smoky Mountain ranges which has powder terrain for beginners to advanced riders. A days heli boarding includes the off piste guides. If you fancy giving snowmobiling a try, there are mile of trails in the National Recreation area which allows you to roam freely.

Any town that attracts the so called elite is bound to be dollar hungry and Sun Valley is no exception. Most of the accommodation close to the slopes is pricey, however the area offers several locations to lodge with beds for credit card-ers, and scam merchants, a shuttle bus runs between sites. There's also loads of places to eat and drink, and dozens of shops most of which are pointless. Shops that are worth checking out for snowboard needs are The Board Bin, and, Boards and Blades both offer a good snowboard rental service. For snowboard instruction go along to the local ski school on Dollar mountain. For a beer you could check out Dy-No-Mite, a joint owned by Bruce Willis.

Winter snowboard periods between Nov and May.

No summer snowboarding

Top Station	2789m
Resort height	1753m
Vertical Drop	1036m
Longest run	4.8km
Ride area	2067 acres
Snowmaking	600 acres

Terrain ability suits

● Beginner	38%
● Intermediate	45%
● Advanced	17%

Terrain Ride styles suits

Freeride	60%
Freestyle	15%
Alpine/Carve	25%

Heli-Boarding to the out back.
Tel +1 208 622 3108

Snowboard Clinic
One day (2 hours)
$40.00 per person

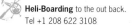

Lift pass Guide

Day	½	1	5
Child	$20	$28	$120
Adult	$36	$50	$240

Lifts open 9 am - 4.00pm

Snowboard shop; for
Sales/hire/repair
The Board Bin
+ 1 208 726 1222

Sun Valley Tourist Office
Po Box 2420
Sun Valley. ID 83353 USA
+1 208 622 4111
e.mail:sunval@micron.net
Reservations +1 208 726 3423
Snowphone +1 208 622 2093

Fly to Salt Lake City International airport

Transfer from the airport;

By bus approximately
5 hours journey to resort.

N/A

By car hire approximately
3 ½ hours driving to resort.

Driving use as a map
reference. Twin Falls 82 miles away,
or Bose 154 miles

HEAVENLY

With over 40 years under it's belt Heavenly knows how to show snowboarders a good time. This is a big resort that lies across two states with one of the largest snowboard/ski acreage's in the US. Most of the trails are set inside the tree lines which will appeal to freeridng intermediates. There are plenty of well prepared pistes for carvers to get to grips with on runs like Lizs's or the Olympic on the Milky Way. Freeriders basically get a mountain with bit of everything from powder in the Milky Way to double black steeps and trees at Mott & Killebrew Canyons. The Airport funpark located on the Nevada north side will keep freestylers happy for hours. Both beginners and novices get the chance to start out at the top as a lot of easy stuff starts high up and continues town to the base. To get the basics sorted out beginners should see the guys at the Shred Ready snowboard School; they know their stuff.

Eating, sleeping, and drinking in Heavenly and nearby Lake Tahoe, is OK, no dramas, can be lively but also heavy on the pocket. Check out McPS for a beer and Pool.

Visit The Boardinghouse snowboard shop for Sales/hire/repair +1 802 228 2001.

Winter snowboard periods between Nov and April.

No summer snowboarding

Top Station	3060m
Base	2195m
Vertical Drop	1067m
Longest run	8.8 km
Ride area	4800 acres
Snowmaking	66% of terrain

Terrain ability suits
- Beginner — 20%
- Intermediate — 45%
- Advanced — 35%

Terrain Ride styles suits

Freeride	60%
Freestyle	15%
Alpine/Carve	15%

The Airport fun park is located on the Nevada side slopes.

1 tram, 18 chairs, 5 drags, leashes compulsory.
lifts open 8.30am to 4.pm
1 day adult pass $47, 5 day $210

Snowboard Instruction
2 hour lesson with lift and hire $69.

Photos: Heavenly Resort

Fly to San Franscio international airport with connections to South Lake Tahoe domestic airport six miles from the resort

Transfer from San Francs airport;

By bus approximately 5 ¹/₂ hours journey to resort.

N/A

By car hire approximately 4 hours driving to resort.

Driving use as a map reference US route 50

Heavenly Valley is 198 miles from San Francs or 58 miles from Reno.

Heavenly Tourist Office
PO Box 2180
Heavenly, Stateline
CA -89449
+1 702 586 7000
http://www.skiheavenly.com
Reservations +1 702 586 7050
Snowphone +1.702 586 7000

KILLINGTON

Killington is big, the Beast of the East. Lots of bumps - Superstar on Skye Peak and Outer Limits on Bear Mountain and lots of trees to ride in with numerous 'secret' trails. The pipe is good but for its location. Unfortunately on sunny days one side of the pipe becomes very soft and the other hard, however there are lots of parks and mini parks (some of which are shamefully open to skiers as well as boarders). There's plenty of good cruising in Killington but particularly Ramshead and Snowdon area also on Skye peak. Killingtons steep terrain ranges from modern ultra-wide straight down the falline trails like Double Dipper which is good for big carves to narrower more traditional runs like the East Fall and Royal Flush. Ovation and Cascade are also decent steeps. The beginner areas are excellent, however like a lot of New England these areas can get busy at weekends with New Yorkers and Bostonians. Stick to mid week if possible - no crowd and empty runs. One thing for boarders to be aware of is traversing. It's very easy to end up spending a lot of time travelling across the mountain, trying to get to another part of Killington.

Lodging in Killington is a bit hit and miss with no real town. Accommodation is spread over a 5 mile stretch. For a beer etc. check out the Pickle Barrel or Wobbly Barn.

Winter snowboard periods between Oct and June.
No summer snowboarding

Top Station	1293m
Resort height	319m
Vertical Drop	960m
Longest run	10.2 miles
Ride area	843 acres
Snowmaking acres	74% acres

Terrain ability suits
- Beginner 45%
- Intermediate 20%
- Advanced 35%

Lots of Fun Parks & a Halfpipe

Number of lifts 20
*Rear foot free and Leashes compulsory
3 day adult pass $121; 5 day $181

Killington Tourist Office
104 Killington Rd, Vt-05751
+ 1 802 422 3333
http://killington.com/biz/killington
Reservations: + 1 802 747 4419
Snowphone: + 1 802 422 3261

Nearest international Airport Boston
Transfer time 3 hours

BRECKENRIDGE

Breckenridge is a true US classic, having played a leading role in the development of snowboarding in the US. Breckenridge, west of Denver and part of the Ten Mile Range, is a fairly big place with terrain that spreads over four main peaks all offering different elements, with some saying that 'New SKool' started here. Whether your new or old school you should have no bother cutting some big turns on the mainly wide open flats. All the runs which cover some 1900 acres making up 125 trails are serviced by fast chair lifts and a few drags. Intermediates and nappy wearers (beginners) will find the runs of Peak 9 the place to head, while freeriders looking for bumps, bowls and hits should check out the stuff of peak 8. Nutters looking for speed, take a look at peak 10, while the extreme bods will be able to fill their pants at peak 7. Freestylers can play for hours in the full on park and big pipe.

Breckenridge's town is a large affair with the customary dozens of silly and pointless boutiques etc., as well as normal shops. The town which nestles at the base of the four peaks boasts at having some 23,000 places to sleep spread out in hotels, chalets and Inns with beds for all financial pockets. With the amount of food joints here no one should go hungry and for lifestyle there's plenty of beer and dancing to be had at a few notable hangouts.

Winter snowboard periods between Dec. and June.
No summer snowboarding

Summit	3962m
Base	2926m
Vertical Drop	1036m
Longest run	3.5 miles
Ride area	1915 acres
Snowmaking	335 acres

Terrain ability suits:
- Beginner 15%
- Intermediate 27%
- Advanced 58%

Fun Parks and Halfpipe

Number of lifts 17
*Rear foot free and Leashes compulsory
1 day adult pass $40- 6 day $192

Breckenridge Tourist Office
1599 Summit County Road #3
PO Box 1058
Breckenridge Co. 80424
+ 1 970 453 5000
Reservations +1 303 453 2918

Nearest main Airport Denver
Transfer time 2 hours

SNOWMASS

Snowmass is the biggest of the resorts that make up the Aspen area, with lots going for it though mainly suiting riders who can handle a board moderately well, there's double black diamonds runs, and trails through trees, steeps and awesome powder. Intermediates wanting wide motorway flats to put in big carves should get up to the Big Burn reached off lift number 4. Freeriders wanting to cut some serious terrain should check out Hanging Valley and Cirque for some double black steeps and powder bowls. Snowmass is riddled with natural hits as well as a 500ft+ half pipe for freestylers wanting to get air. Beginners cutting their first snow should start at the base area serviced by the Fanny Hill chair lift, before trying out the steeper stuff on the Big Burn. The local ski school has a 3 day beginners programme that guarantees to teach you to ride down from Two Creeks Quad, if you don't you get an extra day free.

The village at the base of the slopes has dozens of places to kip with affordable beds within easy reach of the slopes. For a drink check out the Copper Street Pier with rock music and beer at $1, or Eric's for pool and a beer at $3.

Winter snowboard periods between Nov. and April. No summer snowboarding

Top Station	3753m
Resort height	2470m
Vertical Drop	1283m
Longest run	4.6 miles
Ride area	88km
Snowmaking:	130 acres

Terrain ability suit's

● Beginner	10%
● Intermediate	70%
● Advanced	20%

Fun Park 500ft halfpipe

Number of lifts 17 *Rear foot free and Leashes compulsory
1 day adult pass low season $39, 5 day $175.

Snowmass-Aspen Tourist office
425 RIO Grande Place,
Aspen-Co 81612
+1-970 923 7736..
Reservations +1-970 923 1221
Snowphone +1-970 925 1221
http://s2.com/skiaspen

Fly to Denver airport, transfer 4 hours

MOUNT SNOW / HAYSTACK

Mount Snow/Haystack in the Green Mountains National Forest is a regular spot for New Yorkers being just a couple of hundred miles just up the road. Basically two areas are sold as one and together they form a mostly cruising mountain to best suit intermediates and novices with some decent size runs and interesting terrain features with lots of hits, rolls, flats and trees to check out. For freestylers the Un Blanco Gulch is a full on 3000ft fun park with excellent rails, table tops and hits, there's also a series of mini parks dotted over the mountain and a cool half pipe for grommets to get air from. Advanced riders should check out the North Face, with a series of blacks and double blacks, not massive but OK and will test you with a mix of bumps and groomed terrain. Freeriders roaming all over the mountain should give Haystack's 'The Witches' double blacks a look. Like the North face their small but worth a go. Intermediates wanting to carve some arcs can do so with ease on Snowdance one of the blue runs down from the Summit Cafe. Beginners can also tackle some green runs leading down from the Summit which are no big problem.

Lodging in and around the area is simple with a selection of Lodges between both areas offering walk to the slope options. Night time booze and music at The Snow Barn, Deacons Den or the Silo.

Winter snowboard periods between Nov. and April. No summer snowboarding

Top Station	1097m
Base	579m
Vertical Drop	518m
Longest run	
Ride area	643 acres
Snowmaking	80%

Terrain ability suit's

● Beginner	21%
● Intermediate	62%
● Advanced	17%

3000ft Fun Park, 2 pipes

Number of lifts 24
*Rear foot free and Leashes compulsory
5 day pass $168

Mount Snow Tourist Office
400 Mountain Rd
Mount Snow, VT-05356
+ 1 802 464 8501
Reservations + 1 800-245-SNOW
Snowphone: +1 802 464 2151

Nearest main Airport Boston
Transfer time 2 1/2 hours

QUICK RIDE AROUND TWELVE OTHER US SNOWBOARD RESORTS

Resort	Mountain Information and Travel.

	Summit	Resort	Vert. Drop	Ride Acres
Arrowhead	2774m	2256m	518m	180
Colorado	●Beg 30%	●Int 50%	●Adv 20%	

Tiny resort, good easy flats in trees. longest run 3.5km, serviced by 2 lifts.
Information Tel: + 1 970 476 5601.　Fly to Denver 2^1/$_2$ hours transfer.

	Summit	Resort	Vert. Drop	Ride Acres
Beaver Creek	3486m	2469m	1018m	1191
Colorado	●Beg 18%	●Int 40%	●Adv 42%	Half Pipe ✔ Park ✔

Major mountain great freeriding heaps of trees. Full on fun park. 11 lifts.
Information Tel: + 1 970 476 5601.　Fly to Denver 2^1/$_2$ hour transfer.

	Summit	Resort	Vert. Drop	Ride Acres
Big Sky	3398m	2124m	1274m	3500
Montana	●Beg 10%	●Int 47%	●Adv 43%	Half Pipe No Park No

Big vert with steep, deeps, bowls and perfect terrain for all levels. 16 lifts.
Information Tel: + 1 406 995 5000.　Fly to Bozeman 1 hour transfer.

	Summit	Resort	Vert. Drop	Ride Acres
Bretton Woods	945m	457m		30 trail27
N/Hampshire	●Beg 30%	●Int 43%	●Adv 42%	Half Pipe ✔ Park ✔

Cool place with US family appeal. Tree lined flats, 400ft Pipe. 30 runs 5 lifts.
Information Tel: + 1 603 278 5000.　Fly to Boston 3 hours transfer.

	Summit	Resort	Vert. Drop	Ride Acres
Brian Head	3445m	2926m	654	110
Utah	●Beg 30%	●Int 40%	●Adv 30%	Half Pipe ✔ Park ✔

Perfect for beginners, great freestylers place with well equipped park. 5 lifts.
Information Tel: + 1 801 677 2035.　Fly to Salt Lake city. 5 hours transfer.

	Summit	Resort	Vert. Drop	Ride Acres
Buttermilk	3018m	2399m	619	410
Colorado	●Beg 35%	●Int 39%	●Adv 26%	Half Pipe ✔ Park ✔

Novices will love it with loads of easy terrain. Good freestylers pipe. 6 lifts.
Information Tel: + 1 970 925 1220.　Fly to Eagle County 75min transfer.

	Summit	Resort	Vert. Drop	Ride Acres
Cannon Mt.	1274m	590m	654m	38 trails
N/Hampshire	●Beg 20%	●Int 70%	●Adv 10%	Half Pipe ✔ Park ✔

Lots of trees, suit intermediate piste riders in softs or hards. 6 Lifts.
Information Tel: + 1 603 823 5563.　Fly to Boston 2^1/$_2$ hours transfer.

	Summit	Resort	Vert. Drop	Ride Acres
Smugglers Notch	1109m	314m	795m	58 trails
Vermont	●Beg 21%	●Int 56%	●Adv 23%	Half Pipe ✔ Park ✔

Small resort attracting lots of families to easy terrain. Not testing at all. 6 lifts.
Information Tel: + 1 802 644 8851.　Fly to Boston 2 hours transfer.

	Summit	Resort	Vert. Drop	Ride Acres
Snowbird	3353m	2365m	988m	2000
Colorado	●Beg 25%	●Int 30%	●Adv 45%	Half Pipe No Park No

Long season resort for freeriders and carvers with good steeps and piste. 9 lifts,
leashes and back foot free in lift lines compulsory.
1 day pass $45. 1 full day lesson $59, 5 day rate is $270.
Information Tel: + 1 801 742 2222. http://www.snowbird.com. Fly to Salt Lake 45 mins transfer.

	Summit	Resort	Vert. Drop	Ride Acres
Steamboat	3221m	2103m	1118m	2679
Colorado	●Beg 14%	●Int 56%	●Adv 30%	Half Pipe ✔ Park ✔

Cool place for freeriders and freestylers to ride with good parks and loads of natural hits.
There's also a kids park 'Spike' to get the first small air from. Longest run 5km. 20 lifts
where leashes are compulsory. 1 day adult pass $46, 5 days $205.
Information Tel: + 1 970 879 6111.　Fly to Denver 3 hours transfer.

	Summit	Resort	Vert. Drop	Ride Acres
Telluride	3735m	2659m	1074m	1050
Colorado	●Beg 21%	●Int 47%	●Adv 32%	Half Pipe ✔ Park ✔

Freeriders place with steeps and deeps. Plenty of easy stuff. 13 lifts
Information Tel: + 1 970 728 4431.　Fly to Denver 3 hours transfer.

	Summit	Resort	Vert. Drop	Ride Acres
Wolf Mountain	2743m	2073m	670m	1400
Utah	●Beg 24%	●Int 34%	●Adv 42%	5 Half Pipes Park ✔

5 pipes, night riding in the park over table tops. Good off piste. 7 lifts.
Information Tel + 1 801 649 5400.　Fly to Salt Lake 40 mins transfer.

SUMMER SNOWBOARDING ON MOUNT HOOD, OREGON

Rider; Terje Haakonsen,Photo: Vincent Skoglund

There are a number of resorts that offer a limited period of summer snowboarding in the US, but unlike many European glacier resorts, summer boarding in the US takes place in areas that tends to keep winter snow longer rather than be on high glaciers. The result is the areas are fairly small and don't usually last all summer long. This aside you can find some good snow to ride mainly during the months of June and July some times going into August. A lot of pro riders run summer camps and build half pipes tailoring their camps towards freestyle. These camps are worth doing and offer the best chance to pick up some new tricks in short sleeves with a lot of pros. The most popular summer destination is Mt. Hood in Oregon. This is where you will see the largest cluster of US pro's hanging out. It has a number snowboard camps, Tim Windells High Cascade and Mount Hood Snowboard camp are just two. As for the slopes, Hood is more like a mile long patch. The upper patch is all race lanes for the ski teams but after 1pm they all sod off and go roller blading or something just as sad. The lower patch is a multitude of big gaps, half pipes, kickers and rails, but be warned if you're not on a camp you can't ride them, you will have to make do with the disused pipes and hits. The up lift facilities are '1' and that's your lot. A one mile long, very old single person chair that will cost you around $25 to get your arse up, yet you will only use it once as it shuts at 3pm and its not worth going up until after 1pm. Don't think about hiking up as its longer than you think and the ski patrol will watch you walk the whole way then send you away. After a day on the hill, the night time is spent in the Rats Skeller Bar in Government Camp which is the closest town to the hill. The bar is full of snowboarders from all over the world who all look the same. Beware of the Orientals they drink beer in scary amounts. The best place to eat is Huckleberrys, the nearest Taco Bell and Macdonalds is at Dairy Queen (15 miles away). Government Camp has loads of street skate boarding. General advice for Hood - hire a car, learn Japanese, don't ride in the morning (its bullet) and drink shorts as the beer is weak on alcohol content.

ℹ Mt Hood Meadows Resort.
Po Box 470. Mt Hood
OR 97041
+1 503 337 2222
Snowphone +1 503 227-Snow (7669)

Portland Airport 67 miles

Seattle airport 243 miles

RIDER'S OWN NOTES ON AMERICA

CANADA

Work this one out? Canada, a country that speaks English as it's main language with a washed downed American accent, a country that uses Dollars as it's currency, a country that has a large section of it's population speaking just French and fighting for its independence, and a country that is the largest to be headed by a stupid sounding British lady who resides in a number of castles and who thinks the world smells of fresh paint.

Mixed up or what? Perhaps, but what is not in doubt is Canada's contribution to the world of snowboarding. Canada is a great place to ride and more laid back than it's neighbours the Yanks though it is more expensive. Canadian snowboard culture is much the same as across the border, mostly freeriding and freestyle oriented. Some of the early riders such as Keith Duck Boy Wallace an ex Burton pro rider hail from this massive country. Today Canada's top dogs are the likes of male pro's Mark Fawcett and Jasey Jay Anderson while Ivana Trudel does her bit for the girls.

Canada is the Second largest country in the world with coast lines joining three oceans (the Atlantic, Pacific and Arctic), its climate can often be unreal with amazingly hot summers in some areas and unbelievable scary cold winters in other's. Recorded temperatures of 75°F below have been made (try riding with just a tee shirt in that!). As a federal state there are ten provinces with some 270 resorts spread throughout the country. As in the US, Canada's resorts are split basically to east and west coast, with some major mountains that are a match for anything found in the European Alps. Blackcomb/Whistler with its glacier and Banff and Lake Louise are no piddley little hills. Like the States, Canada claim a number of fore runners and major names in snowboard manufacturing and snowboard clothing brands, but unlike America, Canada can boast lots of summer snowboarding on glaciers.

The Eastern side of Ontario offers a number or areas to board, but the vast majority of snowboarding takes place in French Canada. Quebec has 100 plus resorts that resemble much of the stuff on the eastern side of America. Getting to the Eastern side resorts is a doddle with gate way cities and international flights to Montreal, Quebec and Toronto that all have good onward travel services.

On the Western side of Canada the story is different all together, for this is where you get the best of all of Canadian snowboarding in the Provinces of Alberta and British Columbia. Alberta is also known for its oil wells as well as having four main snowboard resorts. However in British Columbia the jewel in the crown are the twined resort of Blackcomb and Whistler which has the highest vert anywhere in Canada or the US. Gate way city's for international flights to reach all the western areas are Calgary and Edmonton for Alberta and Vancouver for British Columbia. The one thing that Canada can boast at offering better than anyone else in the world is the amount and standard of heli boarding you can do full-on. You can do thousands of miles and hundreds of thousands of vert from a helicopter and the Canadians know where the best spots are.

Getting around Canada is as easy as in America, travelling by train on VIA Rail, Canadas rail net work or on Greyhound buses. Accommodation facilities in Canada are the same as in the US, condos, snazzy and often over priced although high quality hotels, as well as B&Bs and lodges. Prices vary from place to place and in general are higher than in the US (unless you can bunk on a floor and over load with people). Entry into Canada is liberal but in most cases you will need a passport and nationals outside the EEC may need visas. Be advised you can't work officially without a work permit and rules are strict, get caught scrubbing dishes in a hotel without the correct paper work and be on your way home quick style.

Canadian snowboard styles favour
Freestyle 40%, Freeride 50% and Alpine 10%.
Soft boots 95$ - Hard boots 5%.

Canadian Snowboard Federation (CSF)
204 -1290 Homer Street, Vancouver BC V6B 2V5,
British Columbia
Tel +1.604 662 7444

Canadian Airlines
Tel + 0345 616 767

Snowboard Canada magazine
Tel - +1 -416 698 0138

FACT FILE

Photo: Tyax Heli of Mika Enroth at Whistler

Status	Federal Parliamentary Monarchy
No of Provinces	10
Capital	Ottawa
Area	9,970,610 sq. km
Population	27,561,700
Density	3 people per sq. km
Language	English & French
Currency	Canadian Dollar
Neighbouring Countries	America
Winter snowboard periods	October to May
Summer snowboarding	Between May & September
Highest Mountain	Mount Logan 6050m
Country Snowboard styles	Freeride/Freestyle 85%, Alpine/Carving 15%
Soft boots	85%
Hard boots	15%
Drugs	Cannabis is illegal through out Canada
Death penalty (legalised murder)	None in Canada
Military Service	Nationals are free to join the services
Alcohol drinking age	Age 18.
Age of consent for sex	Male 16, Female 16

Map labels: Artic Ocean, Beaufort Sea, U.S.A., Anchorage, Valdez, Juneau, Great Bear Lake, Great Slave Lake, Lake Athabasca, B.C., ALBERTA, Jasper, Edmonton, Banff/Lake Louise, Calgary, Fernie Snowvalley, Silver Star, Red Mountain, Blackcomb/Whistler, Vancouver, Victoria, Pacific Ocean, Hudson Bay, Lake Winnipeg, Winnipeg, Regina, Brandon, Thunder Bay, ONTARIO, Lake Superior, Lake Michigan, Lake Huron, Lake Ontario, Lake Erie, Toronto, Ottawa, Laurentian Mountains, Mont Tremblant, Montreal, QUEBEC, Quebec, Ifnukjuak, Labrador City, Corner Brook, Gulf of St. Lawrence, Mont Sainte Anne, St. John's, Atlantic Ocean

57

BANFF

They say heaven is a place on earth. Well try about 112 miles west of Calgary Alberta and you find Canada's largest resort, Lake Louise. Spread over 4 mountain faces with 4000 acres of snowboard terrain, there are a huge proportion of snowboarders at Lake Louise, largely due to the high numbers who work and live in the area. The terrain will suit all levels and is serviced by a well connected lift system. Louise can load more than 15,500 people per hour. High speed quads whisk you from the base to 'The Top of the World' in under eleven minutes where you can access the back bowls. Unlimited and unbelievably long tree lined powder runs lie in wait at every turn. For a fast but easy run try Wiwaxy which is the longest run on the mountain at 5 miles long, while freeriders will find the West Bowl or Purple Bowl a good bet offering a mixture of extreme and easier runs. For plenty of hits, a knee deep hike up to the double black Elevator Shaft is worth the slog. There's also a host of black runs, cornice drops and rock jumps to try out, in particular go collect some bruises on Summit Platter. Alternatively beginners will find the runs of the Eagle chair will suit all their needs before progressing onto some of the more challenging areas on the back side of the mountain. Freestyle Grommets should head straight for the Evians fun park hidden in the trees just off the Wiwaxy. Here you'll find a big pipe and as many hits as you can handle, Greg Todds (sponsored by K2) who lives locally helped to build the park and is often seen riding it. It's illegal to ride in the Avalanche danger areas and if you're caught you will be ejected from the hill and your pass confiscated so be warned because you could be prosecuted. Anyway the mountain is so vast there are plenty of powder runs without venturing out of bounds.

The village of Louise is a couple of Km from the slopes which is served by a free shuttle bus every half hour, but hitching is common and often just as quick. One of the best places to sleep and the only cheap accommodation is at the Youth Hostel. It's a good hangout with a licensed cafe and the best value food. Night time hangouts are limited with 'Stables' being the busy Saturday night spot. While 'Charles' or 'The Grill' is good for a beer and pool. A trip to Banff is a good idea if you want a more lively choice, Banff is also the location of the only full on snowboard shop, 'Rude Boys' which has heaps of gear to check out, or you can simply chill back on the couch.

Winter snowboard periods between Nov. and May

No summer snowboarding

Top Station	2637m
Base	1645m
Vertical Drop	1000m
Longest run	5 miles
Ride area	4000 acres
Snowmaking acres	40%

Terrain ability suits:

● Beginner	25%
● Intermediate	45%
● Advanced	30%

Terrain Ride styles suits:

Freeride	50%
Freestyle	30%
Alpine/Carve	20%

1 half pipe and a fun park of the Olympic chair lift

1996/97 Lift Pass price guide (C$)

	Adult
1 Day	$45
2 Day	$88
5 Day	$205

Lifts open at 9am to 4pm daily
Chair lifts	8
Drag lifts	3

Lift policy is rear foot free on drag
Snowboard Leashes Compulsory

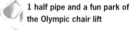

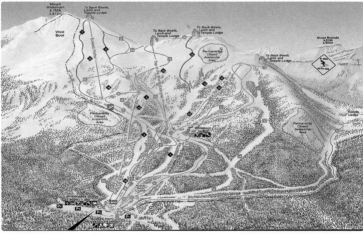

Page riders: Dot Tsikou, Ali Coates

Rider Greg Todd: Photo: Derek Kettela

SNOWBOARD INSTRUCTION
½ day $25 - 1 day $45
Private $48 per hour.
Snowboard Week – includes
3 hours instruction a day, Video session,
½ pipe, park and carving training = $165

SNOWBOARD & BOOT HIRE
1 day $36.50, 3 day $87.25,
5 day $145.50. Demo boards $40 per day

SNOWBOARD REPAIR/SERVICE
Hot wax & edge service $28.00

SNOWBOARD SHOPS
RUDE BOYS + 1 403 762 8480
Sales-Hire-Repair
(independent snowboard shop)

Snowmobiles Tours
Kinbasket Adventures
Golden BC, + 1 604 344 6012

Heli-boarding, Tel +1 403 762 7100
1 day flight from $570 per person

CLIMBING SCHOOL at Banff: ✔
Climbing wall at Banff: ✔

LIFE STYLE

Skateboarding ramps at Banff
For decks & gear check out Rude Boys

Eat at:
The Youth Hostel for good cheap grub.
Beeline for burgers and pizzas.
Laggans for bagels and brownies.
Around the area a burger costs from $5,
a pizza from $7 and a 6 pack of beer $7.

NIGHT TIME HANGOUTS
CHARLIE'S (LAKE LOUISE), for alternative stuff
a glass of beer costs $3.50.
THE BAR & GRILL, for everything including pool
a glass of beer cost $3.50.
Stables for the Saturday night scene
a glass of beer cost $3.50.

Accommodation
Central Reservations
+1 403 522 3833

THE INTERNATIONAL YOUTH HOSTEL
from $18 a night
+1 403 522 2200

Lake Louise Tourist Office
505, 1550 - 8th Street SW
Calgary, Alberta, T2R 1K1
+1 403 256 8473
http://skilouise.softnc.com/louise.html
Snowphone: +1 403 244 6665

Fly to Calgary International Airport

Transfer:

By bus approximately 2 hours journey
to resort. A single ticket cost from $24

N/A

By car hire approximately 1 ½ hours
driving to resort.

Driving use as a map reference
Route Highway 1 from Calgary being
approximately 128km from the resort.

BLACKCOMB/ WHISTLER

Most agree that Blackcomb and Whistler are the best in North America and it's easy to see why. The two mountains that base out together are the cojones. If you don't get a buzz out of snowboarding here take up knitting as you'll be better suited to it. Whistler is the oldest of the two resorts having opened back in 1966. It offers 6998 acres of terrain. Blackcomb with its 3341 acres opened in 1980 and boasts two major $^1/_2$ pipes, a $^1/_4$ pipe and a full-on park with sounds and a DJ. Yep, this place is it. You can try out all your ground tricks, down loads of easy no nonsense green and blues or head off piste for some pure freeriding before returning to cut up some well groomed double blacks. Freeriders wanting powder will fill their pants when the see what's on offer in Blackcomb's Glacier bowls or in Whistlers Harmony bowl. Riders who have made the grade should check out the double blacks at West Bowl on Whistler or the Couloir Extreme on Blackcomb - bail this and your eyes will water. Carvers wanting big acres check out the Dave Murray downhill run on Whistlers Creekside, while on Blackcomb novices just finding out what a carve is can practice with ease down the Springboard or Grundy before trying out the more testing Arthurs Choice or Black Sandwich, cut out through trees. Freestylers can go for big air in the 1/2 pipe near Rendevou Lodge before dropping down to the Kokanee Snowboard Park, which is where the New school grommets can boogie around on rails and 'tops to the sounds of the DJ's favourite tunes. Total beginners should get on really well on either mountain with easy runs at the base, mid-way and upper sections. The local ski school offers a number of instruction packages including two day camps. If you want to do some major off piste back country stuff then try heli boarding, and if you can't get here in the winter don't fret the glaciers are open from June to August and you also have the chance to go on one of Craig Kellys camps.

Off the slopes there's heaps going on and loads of places to go, check out the best happenings at one of the main snowboard shops -the famous 'Snoboard Shop', or Westbeach in Whistler and World Pro, all three do it all and know their stuff. For a cheap meal give MacDonalds the usual visit but also try Subway or Tex-Mex. Booze and music happens all over the place. For a cheap bed stay at The Whistler Hostel for around $20canadian, or one of the Dorms.

Winter snowboard periods between Nov and June.

Summer snowboarding Between June & Auguste

Blackcomb
Top Station	2284m
Base	675m
Vertical Drop	1609m
Longest run	7 miles
Ride area	3341 acres
Snow cannons	48

Whistler
Top Station	2790m
Base	685
Vertical Drop	1530m
Longest run	7 miles
Ride area	3675 acres
Snow cannons	22

Total Terrain ability suits
● Beginner	20%
● Intermediate	55%
● Advanced	25%

Terrain Ride styles suits
Freeride	50%
Freestyle	25%
Alpine/Carve	25%

2 Half pipes
1 $^1/_4$ pipe
1 fun park with DJ
and sounds

1996/97 Lift Pass price guide
(Covers Blackcomb and Whistler)
Canadian $	Youth	Adult
1 day	$15	$38
5 days	$133	$245
Season	$442	$1295

Lifts open 9am to 3.30pm week days, 8.30am to3.30pm weekends and holidays.
Night riding Wed & Sat 5 to 9pm
Gondolas	3
Chair lifts	17
Drag lifts	10

DUAL MOUNTAIN MAP

SNOWBOARD INSTRUCTION

One day package C$70=lesson/hire/lifts
Arc Adult Snowboard Camps
2 day camps, includes Video analysing
Hire, Breakfast, Tee shirt = C$160
+1 604 938 7720
Freeride Camps
2 day camp includes all mountain riding.
Video analysing, party and prizes = C$185
+1 604 938 7720
Junior Jibbers (7 to 12 years)
Full day lesson C$45
Ride Tribe (13 to 17 years)
Full day lesson C$48
+1 604 938 7720

SNOWBOARD & BOOT HIRE

1 day hire for standard B&B C$35
5 day hire for standard B&B C$103

SNOWBOARD REPAIR/SERVICE

Full base Tune service $20

SNOWBOARD SHOPS

BLACKCOMB MOUNTAIN +1 604 938 7720
Sales-Hire-Repair & Instruction
(independent snowboard shop)
SHOWCASE SNOWBOARDS
+1 604 938 7720 Sales-Hire-Repair

Snowmobile rides +1 604 932 4086

Heli Boarding
Mountain Heli-Sports +1 604 932 2370
6 hours with guide C$390

Paragliding cost from C$125 an hour

Photo: Mike Orr by Tyax Heli at Whistler

LIFE STYLE

Eat at:
Macdonalds for big Macs.
Tex-Mex for Tacos
Misty Mountain Pizza for Pizza.

NIGHT TIME HANGOUTS

GARFUNKELS
Tommy Africas
Savage Beagle

Accommodation
WHISTLER YOUTH HOSTEL
from C$20 a night.
+1-604 932 5492
FIRESIDE LODGE
from C$20 a night.
+1-604 932 4545
UBC Lodge
from C$20 a night.
+1-604 932 6604

Blackcomb Tourist Office
4545 Blackcomb Way
Whistler, BC Canada. VON 1B4
+1-604 932 3141
http://www.whistler.net/blackcomb/

Whistler Tourist Office
4010 Whistler Way
Whistler, BC, Canada
+1-604 664 5625
http://www.whistler.travel.bc.ca

By Train approximately 2¹/₂ hours journey
to resort. A single ticket cost from $17

By car hire approximately 1¹/₂ hours
driving to resort.

Fly Vancouver International Airport

Transfer;

By bus approximately 2¹/₂ hours journey
to resort. A single ticket cost from $13

Driving from home use as a map
reference Highway 99.

FERNIE SNOW VALLEY

Fernie Snow Valley is another of Canada's little talked of powder haunts located beneath the peaks of Trinity Mountain. They don't have snowmaking here because they don't need it, the real stuff falls deep and on a regular basis averaging some 800cm a season. What's more if you're not happy with conditions during your first hour you can get you money back. The town of Fernie has developed from a history related to coal and lumber along with a local legendary character called Griz who is said to be responsible for the amazing amounts of snow. However, whether you believe in numpty fairy tales or not what's for sure is the terrain, which is ideal for beginners and intermediates, and top's for powder hunting freeriders. Advanced riders wanting to go knee deep in powder can take the El Quad Chair and Bear T-bar to reach the easy stuff in the Lizard Bowl. Freeriders wanting a mixture should check out the Cedar Bowl area which is a wide open expanse offering some major stuff, then pump it down the Cruiser a no dramas wide blue before dropping down to the KC Chute a double black that should hold your attention with banks and gullies to look out for. At the end of this section take the Haul Back T-Bar to reach the Kangaroo, a decent black cut through some trees. From the bottom you can take Boomerang chair to reach some gnarly stuff off North Ridge which is not for the faint hearted. Carvers wanting to lay out some big one's can do so with ease down the Bear or the flats on the Cruiser. Beginners and novices just getting to grips with things are best suited to the runs from the Deer chair before trying the Bear and Elk runs which link together to give new bods a long run down to the Day lodge. Freestylers are going to find the natural pipes, gullies and hits full on and if that's not enough then Fernie has a man made pipe and park to keep new school grommets more than content all day long.

You can bed down near the slopes but its pricey. The better option is to stay in the town of Fernie which sits down in the valley just 3 miles from the slopes. Here you get a number of options to lodge at prices that aren't too freaky. Fernie is a laid back very friendly place that tries hard to look after you, with a few night spots and a good selection of joints to pig out in. Libby's offers cheap pizza while Papa Johns is the place for a beer. There is no main snowboard shop but the guys at Frozen Ocean will look after you.

Winter snowboard periods between Nov and April.

No summer snowboarding

Top Station	1798m
Base	1067m
Vertical Drop	732m
Longest run	5 Km
Ride area	1000 acres
Snowmaking acres	0

Terrain ability suits

● Beginner	30%
● Intermediate	40%
● Advanced	30%

Terrain Ride styles suits

Freeride	45%
Freestyle	25%
Alpine/Carve	30%

Halfpipe and a Fun Park located near the Deer chair

Shuttle bus operates daily from 8.45am.
A one way journey costs $2

1996/97 Lift Pass price guide (C

	Junior	Adult
½ Day	$20	$27
1 Day	$26	$34
3 Days +	$30/day	$22/day
One month pass $285.00		

Lifts open at 8.30 to 4pm daily
Chair lifts	3
Drag lifts	4

Lift policy is rear foot free on drag lifts Snowboard leashes required.

SNOWBOARD & BOOT HIRE
The Ski Base
423 -2nd Ave., Fernie
Snowboard hire $28

Fernie Sports
1191 7th Ave
Snowboard hire $28

Frozen Ocean
Snowboard hire $25

Snowmobiles contact
Island Lake Lodge,
Tel (604) 423 3700
Sno-Much-Fun,
Tel (604) 426 5303

LIFE STYLE

Eat at:
Subway and A&W for fast food

Night time hangouts
The Royal Hotel
The Pub

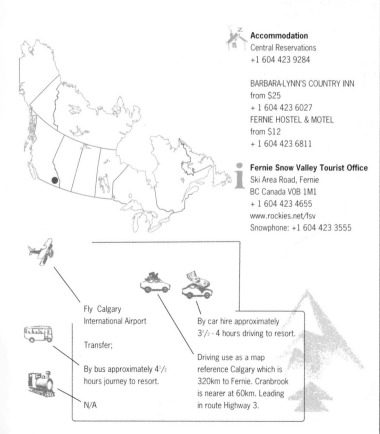

Accommodation
Central Reservations
+1 604 423 9284

BARBARA-LYNN'S COUNTRY INN
from $25
+ 1 604 423 6027
FERNIE HOSTEL & MOTEL
from $12
+ 1 604 423 6811

Fernie Snow Valley Tourist Office
Ski Area Road, Fernie
BC Canada V0B 1M1
+ 1 604 423 4655
www.rockies.net/fsv
Snowphone: +1 604 423 3555

Fly Calgary
International Airport

Transfer;

By bus approximately 4$^{1}/_{2}$
hours journey to resort.

N/A

By car hire approximately
3$^{1}/_{2}$ - 4 hours driving to resort.

Driving use as a map
reference Calgary which is
320km to Fernie. Cranbrook
is nearer at 60km. Leading
in route Highway 3.

RED MOUNTAIN

Red Mountain and the town of Rossland go back to the days of the Canadian gold rush being established in 1896. One of the oldest resorts in Canada, Red Mountain is a powder heaven and home of some of the best extreme riding in Canada. It has been operating as a resort since 1947 when it first put in a chair lift. One of Canada's dark horses, this place has a lot going for it with quite runs, free of large crowds, with powder left un-spoilt by the morning masses. Old school riders will remember the Burton video 'Board with the World' where the riders were seen shredding everything. The two mountains that make up the 1100 acres of terrain are Grante Mountain and Red Mountain. Both offer a variety of runs that will mainly suit riders who can already board, first timers are going to have their work cut out. The trail map lists many of it's runs with a star meaning extreme which is what the runs live up to. Grante is the biggest of the two areas which is easily accessed from the base lodge via a chair lift. Once at the top you can head off in a variety of directions, but a point to note is that most of the runs at the top are for advanced riders although the Ridge Road will take novices off to some easy stuff. Freeriders should check out the Buffalo Ridge which takes you down one side of Grante into bowls, natural hits and lots of trees. Sara's Chute a double black takes you down steeps and through tight trees which eventually brings you out onto 'Long Squaw' a simple green that leads back to the base lodge. On the Paradise side of the mountain the terrain will suit those wanting some tamer stuff and where carvers can lay out some big ones on runs like 'Southern Comfort' On Red Mountain freeriders will find 'Hole in the Wall' is worth a visit before dropping down into 'Lower War Eagle', 'Old Bastards Trees' is also worth a look if only to see if the name fits. Carvers on Red will find 'Face of Red' the place to pose while novices should try the Upper and Lower Back Trails. The half pipe and fun park are easily reached however freestylers will also find heaps of natural hits and stuff all over the place.

Although there is some accommodation at the base lodge area most beds are found in the town of Rossland just 3km from the slopes which offers a variety of places to kip at, eat in or drink out of. Although Rossland is not exactly a happening place it's still cool and offers a number of night time options.

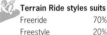

Winter snowboard periods between Dec and April.

No summer snowboarding

Top Elevation	2040m
Base	1187m
Vertical Drop	853m
Longest run	7km
Total ride area	11000 acres
Snowmaking acres	0

Terrain ability suits
● Beginner	70%
● Intermediate	20%
● Advanced	10%

Terrain Ride styles suits
Freeride	70%
Freestyle	20%
Alpine/Carve	10%

Halfpipe and Fun Park

Shuttle bus runs daily between Rossland and the slopes by request.

Photo: Dudley. Red Mountain

1996/97 Lift Pass price guide (C$

	Student (13-18)	Adult
½ Day	$23	$28
1 Day	$32	$38
3 Day	$99	$85

Lifts open at 9.30am - to 3pm daily and 8.30 to 3.30pm in spring
Night riding possible
Chair lifts	1
Drag lifts	5
Foot free on drag lifts
Snowboard leashes required
No rear foot binding rules.

SNOWBOARD INSTRUCTION
1 lesson lift and rental beginner pack:
Adult $49, Youth (7-12) $43
3 day beginner pack includes hire.
Adult $120, Youth (7-12) $105
3 day improvement 3 x 2hr lessons
Adult $69, Youth (7-12) $62
Private lesson 1 hour $43 per person.

Snowboarde Guides
Check out the local secrets and best ungroomed
etc. with a guide, $25 for 2 1/2 hours session.
Only good riders taken

SNOWBOARD & BOOT HIRE
ADULT 1/2 day $23 - Full day $31.
CHILD (-15) 1/2 day $17 - Full day $24.
*Wrist guards and kids helmets also available

SNOWBOARD SHOP/S
LEROI'S SPORT SHOP
sales-hire-repair
(sport snowboard shop)

Heli boarding with Highland Helicopters

Olympic size swimming pool at the Aquatic centre in
Trail (6 miles from Rossland)

Life style

Eat at:
Rafter Lounge and cafeteria at the base lodge
The Powder Keg Pub for decent nosh.
Sunshine Cafe for cheap food morning, noon & night

Photo: Stuart Davidson.

Night time hangouts:
The Powder Keg Pub -
for booze and live music.

Photo: Burton/Red Mountain

Accommodation
Central reservations
+001 604 362 7700Σ

UPLANDER HOTEL
+1- 800 667 8741
ROSSLAND MOTEL
+1-604 362 7218
SCOTSMAN MOTEL
+1-604 362 7364
RAMS HEAD INN
+1-604 362 9577

Red Mountain Tourist Office
P.O Box 670
Rossland B.C V0G 1Y0
+001-604 362 7384
Snowphone: +1-604 362 5500.

Transfer;

By bus approximately 8-9 hours
journey to resort.

N/A

By car hire approximately 7 1/2
driving to resort.

Fly Vancouver International
Airport with connecting flights to
Castlegar domestic airport which
take about 1 hour 45 minutes.
From Castlegar bus or taxi to
the resort.

Driving use as a map
reference Red Mountain which is
125 miles north of Spokane on
highway 25 through Northport.
From Vancouver the distance is
about 400 miles.

SILVER STAR

Silver Star came about from the days of silver mining at the turn of the century. It's pure Canada and damn good as well. Any place that can boast an average snowfall of 570cm should be given a platform. Silver Star is a year round destination with a cool laid back appeal attracting families for summer activities when the snow has gone. However as soon as the snow returns the place becomes a riders paradise with stupidly large amounts of powder, lots of good off piste with big bowls and heaps of trees to shred through. The 1200 acres of terrain is largely suited to intermediate freeriders, with a number of good runs on which to progress. Advanced riders can see if they're up to their status with 11 double black diamond runs. The Putnam Creek area will sort out anyone, with steeps dropping down chutes and through trees - pure freeriding territory best for those in soft boots. A must is the Gowabunga down from the Paradise mid station. Carvers who can, will find this a good tester. Intermediate riders will find plenty of interesting terrain on the south face before going over to the north face. The Venace Creek express lift takes you to the summit where you will find open terrain and will give you the option of dropping back down on some wide open blacks or the more gentle stuff reached via the Sundance, a blue that takes you down through the tree lined runs and offers a number of early options to explore the Venice area. The Attridge access which is also a good intermediate area leads you down to a number of short blues that cut through the trees. On route the Christmas bowl is really cool and if you have the bottle, try the Attridge Face black run. Freestylers looking for air will be pleasantly surprised with the natural types, however the fun park and half pipe located of Big Dipper is the place to head for. Here grommets can play for hours. Although there isn't a sprawling mass of easy runs for beginners, what is available is sufficient, the Far Out is perfect for learning the early manoeuvres on. The local ski school will help you get going.

Off the slopes Silver Star's old fashioned Victorian theme offers cheap to steep places to kip in, with lodges available at the base of the slopes. Eating options are not only good but also cheap and as with night time hangouts all are within walking distance of the slopes. life style may not be major but its still cool, with a couple of drinking holes to check out.

Winter snowboard periods between Nov and April.

No summer snowboarding

Top Station	1915m
Base	1155m
Vertical Drop	760m
Longest run	8 Km
Ride area (acres)	1200

Terrain ability suits

● Beginner	20%
● Intermediate	50%
● Advanced	30%

Terrain Ride styles suits

Freeride	60%
Freestyle	20%
Alpine/Carve	20%

Half pipe and fun park located of Big Dipper

Photo: Don Weixl/ Sliver Star Resort

1996/97 Lift pass guide

Days	Child	Adult
1	$22	$42

Lifts open 8.30am to 3.30pm
Night riding 3.30pm to 9.30pm
*Tuesday to Saturdays

Chair lifts	5
Drag lifts	3

Lift policy is rear foot free on drag lifts and snowboard leashes are required.

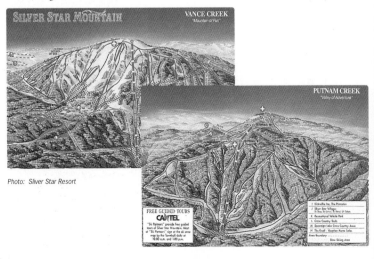

Photo: Silver Star Resort

Snowboard Instruction
1¹/₂ hr lesson $25
5 day lesson package $110

Snowboard and boot hire
1 day hire for standard board $32
5 day hire for standard board $150

Snowboard repair & service
Full base tune service $24

Snowboard Shop/s
Brian James Ski & Sport

Snowmobile rides
Silver Star Guided Tours
Tel +1-604 558 5575

Eat at
Sheriffs Cafe
Paradise Camp
Putnam Station
Vance Creek Saloon

Night Time hangouts
Vance Creek Saloon
for live music food and pool

Photo: Don Weixl / Sliver Star Resort

Accommodation
Central Reservations
+10800 663 4431
Vanace Creek Hotel
+1 604 549 5101
The Kickwillie Inn
+1 604 542 4548

Silver Star Tourist Office
PO BOx 2,
Silver Star Mountain
BC. Canada. V0E 1G0
http://www.silverstarmtn.com

+1 604 542 0224
Snowphone +1 604 542 1745

By bus approximately 4¹/₂ hours journey.

Fly Vancouver or Calgary international airport with domestic flights to Kelowina.

Transfer:

N/A

By car hire approximately 3¹/₂ to 4 hours to the resort.

Driving use as a map reference Vernon which is 20km from the resort. From Calgary use Highway 97 to Vernon. From Vancover use Highway 1 & 5 to Coquihalla.

67

MONT SAINTE-ANNE

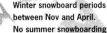

Mont Sainte-Anne is the largest resort on the east coast of Canada. The resort which plays hosts to ISF events, has some pretty good terrain to shred suiting all levels on an area spread over 3 faces. Being a French speaking resort the trails have French names which is basically a pain in the arse when trying to explain about 'La' this or 'Le' that spot. The runs are cut out of trees which offer the advanced riders the best stuff on the south face with double blacks like the 'La Saint Laurent' and 'Les Sept-Chutes' to test you. See I told you so. The 'L'Espoir' is a cool run to lay out some carves, which eventually brings you out at base. Those just getting to grips with a board will find a number of easy wide blue runs to tackle like the 'L'Anore' on the north face. Here you can cut your first carves before trying out the 'La Surprenante' and beginners are also given free access to a couple of easy slopes. Mont Sainte-Anne has a 5,400 square meter fun park and a decent halfpipe for all those wannabe big air dudes. Off the slopes is a bit of a no no.

Accommodation is available locally but Quebec city 25 miles away is where the bigger and best choice for eating and drinking can be had. Snowboard shop - Vertical Snowboard (Quebec City)

Winter snowboard periods between Nov and April.
No summer snowboarding

Summit	800m
Resort height	175m
Vertical Drop	625m
Longest run	5.7 km
Ride area	400 acres
Snowmaking acres	340 acres

Terrain ability suits

● Beginner	22%
● Intermediate	48%
● Advanced	30%

11,000 sq-m, Fun Park.
175m halfpipe

Number of lifts 7
Rear foot free and Leashes compulsory

Mont Sainte Anne Tourist Office
C.P.400 Beaupre-Quebec
Canada G0A 1E0
+ 1 418 827 4561
Reservations: + 1 418 827 5281
Snowphone: + 1 418 827 4579
http://www.mont-sainte-anne.com

Nearest international airport:
Quebec Transfer time 30 minutes

KIMBERLEY

Kimberley is a small unusual town with a mixture of Austrian, Swiss and English styles, set in British Columbia. The resort has been operating as a winter playground since the 50's having developed into a happy go lucky place. Kimberley's 425 acres is fully open to snowboarders of all levels suiting intermediate riders in the main. Carvers will find the easy open flats perfect for leaving a signature. Freeriders will find tree boarding is available and accessible from the Easter Triple Chair. 'The Vortex' is a favourite among local snowboarders as the run is a natural halfpipe, in addition Kimberley has two snowboard parks (designed by local riders). One of the parks is on 'Rosa' and the second on the 'Main' which also has night riding on what is said to be the largest illuminated run in North America.

Kimberley offers a decent selection of places to stay from dollar hungry hotels to an El'cheapo camp site. The local snowboard hangout is the Snow Drift, and for nosh try out Mary's Kitchen for take outs.

Winter snowboard periods between Dec and Apr.
No summer snowboarding

Top Station	1982m
Base	1280m
Vertical Drop	702m
Longest run	4 miles
Ride area	425 acres
Snowmaking	15%

Terrain ability suits

● Beginner	20%
● Intermediate	60%
● Advanced	20%

2 Fun Parks

Number of lifts 6
No Rear foot rules but are Leashes compulsory

1 day adult pass $35 - 5 days $147
1 day Student pass $30 - 5 days $1

Kimberley Tourist Office
Po Box 40, Kimberley
British Columbia V1A 2Y5
+ 1 604 427 4881
http://www.kimberleyski.info-pages.com
Reservations: + 1 604 427 4887
Snowphone: +1 604 427 7332

Nearest international airport Calgary
Transfer time 5 hours

Snowboard instruction

	Adult	Child
Group 1½ hour lesson	$24	$19
Private 2 hour lesson	$65	$35

Rentals – 1day hire board and boots
$30.00

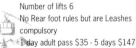

Snowboard shops
Bavarian Sports and Athletic Edge

TREMBLANT

Mont Tremblant an ex Indian hangout is located in the Laurentian Mountains. The resort has been sending mountain goers up and down it's two mountain slopes since the second world war and over the years Tremblent has splashed out millions of dollars on investment making this one of the best in Canada. It's two faces the South side and North side offer 500 acres or mainly advanced terrain best suited to the no nonsense freerider who wants trees and good piste. The North side offers the harder stuff, and riders wanting to give it all out on a long cruising run will find the Geant a decent trail, while the Glades on the Emotion will sort the wimps out. Both sides have a fun park based at the lower sections and easily reached by all levels. The best beginner runs are on the south side, the Nansen a 3.75 mile stretch will give novices something to tackling, while the McCloch will keep intermediates on their toes (or heels).

The cobbled village offers the usual array of hotels, condos and motels from on slope to within a six mile area of the runs. There are also loads of eating and watering holes.

Winter snowboard periods between Nov and May.
No summer snowboarding

Top Station	915m
Resort height	265m
Vertical Drop	650m
Longest run	3.75miles
Ride area	500 acres
Snowmaking acres	375 acres

Terrain ability suits

● Beginner	50%
● Intermediate	30%
● Advanced	20%

1 day hire $25- 2 day hire $50
+ 1 970 925 8272

2 Funparks

Number of lifts 9

Mont Tremblant Tourist office
3005, Chemin Principal.
Mont Tremblant, Quebec J0T 1Z0
+ 1 819 681 2000

Nearest international airport Montreal
Transfer time 1½ hours

PANORAMA

A small purpose built place that in the past has been a bit of a hit and miss resort hailing form the mining days. However Panorama has quite a lot going for it and is recognised as one of the tops in the west. A notable point is the fact that it offers some of the most convenient heli-boarding around. RK heli-skiing are within easy reach of all accommodation and offer hourly, daily or weekly trips that include excursions into the Purcell Mountains. Panorama offers the second highest vert in North America at 4300ft, the terrain is largely suited to intermediate snowboarders with some challenging double blacks for riders who can cut it. Freeriders with some savvy will want to try out Panoramas new 200 acre 'Extreme Dream Zone', which is a double black with steeps, deeps, trees and cliff jumps. Hit this stuff wrong and its stretcher time; be warned. Freestylers will be happy getting air out the park and pipe which has a cool selection of gaps, quarter pipes and rail slides to session.

A good thing about the place is that everything is in walking distance of the slopes. Lodging is slope side and offers dozens of options with condos, lodges and decent priced inns. There are a number of haunts to get grub, from silly priced restaurants to pub fare and fast food. Being a lazy low key place means it doesn't hit off big time but is still OK and good for a laugh – the locals are really friendly.

Winter snowboard periods between Nov and April.
No summer snowboarding

Top Station	2286m
Vertical Drop	1212m
Ride area	1280 acres

Terrain ability suits

● Beginner	20%
● Intermediate	55%
● Advanced	25%

200 acre Extreme Dream Zone, 1 half-pipe and fun park.

Number of lifts 8
Rear foot free and leashes required.

Panorama Tourist Office
Box 7000
Invermere BC V0A 1K0
+ 1 604 342 6941
Reservations: + 1 604 342 6941
http://www.panoramaresort.com

Nearest international airport Calgary
Transfer time 2½ hours

CANADA – 4 RESORTS

BANFF/SUNSHINE

Second largest of the three areas in the Banff National Park its long been open to snowboarding. Sunshine's 82 runs will suit all especially intermediates. Freestylers have a massive full on funpark to ride.

Lodging and main facilities at Banff
1 day pass $42, 5 day $233, 1 day hire $29
Fly to Calgary - Transfer 2 hours
Full resort details: + 1 403 762 6500

Vertical Drop	1071m
Longest run	5 miles
Ride area	2200 acres

Terrain ability suits:
● Beginner	20%
● Intermediate	55%
● Advanced	25%

1 half pipe   1 fun park   13 lifts

MONT HABITANT

Small tree lined resort 40 miles north of Montreal, fully open to snowboarders with runs that are best suited to intermediates who want to carve. Night snowboarding, half pipe and fun park all serviced by 3 lifts Lodging and facilities to eat and drink in.

1 day snowboard hire $18.00
Fly to Montreal - Transfer 1 hour
Full resort details: + 001 514 393 1821

| Vertical Drop | 170 meters |
| Longest run | 300m |

Terrain ability suits:
● Beginner	34%
● Intermediate	33%
● Advanced	33%

1 half pipe   1 fun park   3 lifts

SUN PEAK

Friendly locals place with good terrain for beginners as well as advanced riders wanting steep stuff. The fun park is one of the longest in North America. Resort offers all levels of snowboard tuition and operates a number of camps and race programmes.

1 day snowboard hire $18.00
Fly to Vancouver - Transfer 4 hours
Full resort details: + 001 ,604 578 7842.

Vertical Drop	867m
Longest run	8km
Ride area	1000acres

Terrain ability suits
● Beginner	24%
● Intermediate	54%
● Advanced	22%

1 half pipe, 1 900m fun park   96lift

STONEHAM

A low Key tree line area with 300 acres spread over 4 mountains, ideal for novices and advanced riders. Runs are wide and will appeal to carvers, with good options for freeriders. Lots of night riding on all ability terrain.
Lodging and main facilities at Quebec City

Fly to Quebec - Transfer 20 min
Full resort details : + 1 418 848 2411

Vertical Drop	420m
Longest run	3.2km
Ride area	300 acres

Terrain ability suits:
● Beginner	26%
● Intermediate	36%
● Advanced	38%

JASPER – MARMOT BASIN

Quite, no nonsense place with big bowls and tree lined trails for every level of rider. Really good for beginners, while offering advanced freeriders some cool off piste powder and excellent glade riding. Lodging and main facilities at Jasper

Fly to Edmonton - Transfer 4 ¹/₂ hours
Full resort details +1-403 852 3816

Vertical Drop	701m
Longest run	miles
Ride area	1000 acres

Terrain ability suits:
● Beginner	35%
● Intermediate	35%
● Advanced	30%

7 lifts

ANDORRA

A self governing principality under the joint sovereignty of France and Spain, Andorra is a tiny alpine state located in the heart of the Pyrenees, covering roughly about 470 square kilometres. You are not going to get major big stuff here. However, it's a friendly laid back country and Andorra does try hard to provide good resort services including halfpipes and parks. It's 5 main resorts, which have fairly good snow records also make extensive use of snow cannons to help when the real stuff is in short supply. In truth Andorra really has two distinctions, - one, a tax free giant electrical supermarket, and two a beginners only interest. Andorra's history goes back 700 years but it's snowboarding doesn't. Although snowboarding has been well accepted in Andorra for quite a few years, there's nothing of great note in its snowboard history. The first British Championships held overseas were in Pas de la Casa in 1992, but that wasn't exactly ground breaking stuff. You've probably read in countless ski guides how this country is good value for this and good value for that, but in reality although you can have a weeks riding in this small country, staying in one resort for seven days will soon bore the tits off you, unless you're a complete beginner where it offers loads of flat easy terrain. Although the 5 resorts are close to each other, getting around by local transport is a joke. The biggest of the resorts is Soldeu and the smallest Arinsal, whichever area you go to they all can be reached from either France or Spain, how ever don't rely on public transport, take your own car or travel with a tour operator. Andoras shouts its mouth of about being cheap and tax free, which is true if you want to buy cameras, radios or calculators by the dozen, food and booze is cheap in supermarkets, but you may be surprised with some bar prices. Visa requirements are relaxed and working in Andorra is no big drama.

Rider: Simon Smith

Status	Principality
Capital	Andorra-la-Vella
Area	465 sq km
Population	52,000
Density	112 people per sq km
Language	Catalan
Currency	French Franc / Spanish Peseta
Winter snowboard periods	December to April
Summer snowboarding	Zero
Country Snowboard styles	Freeride/Freestyle -35% Alpine/Caring -65% Soft boots 40% Hard boots 60%

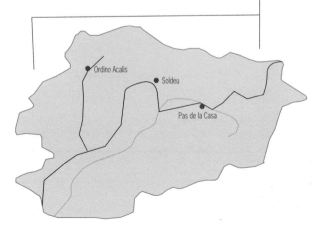

Ordino Acalis

Soldeu

Pas de la Casa

ARINSAL

Small area with plenty of open flats for beginners to start out on. totally lacking in anything for advanced riders. Intermediate riders wanting to find out what carving is like can practice with easy on a couple of red and black runs. Nothing for freestylers but possibilities of Heli Boarding. Village a 1km away is simple with nothing of interest, night times boozy.

Lodging and main facilities at Arinsal 1 km
Fly to Toulouse - Transfer to= 3¹/₂ hours
Full resort details + 00 376 835 822

Summit	2560m
Longest run	6km
Ride area	330 acres

Terrain ability suits:
● Beginner	43%
● Intermediate	33%
● Advanced	24%

 14 lifts

PAL

Small treelined resort that shares a lift ticket with Arinsal , offers a selection of red runs for intermediate freeriders to cut up, but naff all for riders who want some- thing to get their teeth into. The only black is short and boring. Nothing of note for freestylers but some playing to be had of hits along treelines. Village has nothing to offer, more available near by in La Massana.

Lodging and main facilities at Pal 1 km
Fly to Toulouse - Transfer to= 3¹/₂ hours
Full resort details + 00 376 836 320

Summit	2358m
Longest run	1.5km
Ride area	363 acres

Terrain ability suits:
● Beginner	35%
● Intermediate	60%
● Advanced	5%

 15 lifts

ORDINO-ARCALIS

Only opened in 19984 this purpose built resort offers a limited amount of off piste and a few trees to drop through suiting new boy freeriders. First time freestylers will be able to practice some ground tricks but there not much else and no great big air opportunities. Carvers just making the grade will find a few useful areas. No village of facilities, nearest 6kms.

Basic facilities at base area
Fly to Toulouse - Transfer to= 3¹/₂ hours
Full resort details +00 376 836 320

Summit	2600
Longest run	2.5km
Ride area	378 acres

Terrain ability suits:
● Beginner	55%
● Intermediate	36%
● Advanced	9%

 12 lifts

PAS DE LA CASA

Second largest of Andorra's resorts but nothing much for hard core freeriders, though a few possibilities for some powder. If there's plenty of snow in the resort area freeriders will find a few rails of apartment blocks and a half pipe on the slopes to play in (not massive though). Some night riding on flood lit slopes. Village cheap and lively with a few bars.

Lodging and main facilities at Pas / Casa
Fly to Toulouse - Transfer to= 3¹/₂ hours
Full resort details 376 855 692+

Summit	2600m
Longest run	2.5km
Ride area	300 acres

Terrain ability suits:
● Beginner	47%
● Intermediate	38%
● Advanced	15%

1 pipe 1 park.
 9 lifts

SOLDEU

The biggest resort its still not much to brag about. Theres a mixture of flat open runs as well as tree line stuff for beginners, with a few opportunities for carvers on some open reds. Once again nothing for riders with ability. Intermediate freeriders get a chance to cut it on a few of piste trails and through some while new school grommets will find a few hits.

Lodging and main facilities Soldeu
Fly to Barcelona- Transfer to= 4 hours
Full resort details + 00 376 85 1151

Summit	2560m
Longest run	8 km
Ride area	850 acres

Terrain ability suits:
● Beginner	59%
● Intermediate	24%
● Advanced	17%

21 lifts

Rider: Philippe in Solden · Photo: Jonny Barr

AUSTRIA

Austria; the little land locked blob situated between seven other countries, has two thirds of it's area lying in its own Alps, providing thousands of miles of full-on snowboard territory in over 760 resorts to suit every taste. Yep, the unofficial home of European snowboarding, Austria has lead the way in Europe having encouraged the sport at it's resorts for years. As far back as 1986 an Innsbruck based independent club called, Burton Snowboard Division set the scene with the youngsters and helped to produce a lot of top riders like Max Plotzeneder amongst others. Burton snowboards also set up it's first non-American headquarters in Innsbruck in 1992. Innsbruck is also the world-wide headquarters of the International Snowboard Federation (I.S.F). Snowboard Klinik, the boys who make your inserts, also hail from Austria and now Palmer, Nitro and others are made in Austria as is Red Bull that buzz drink that keeps you riding for days.

Austria's 7$^{1}/_{2}$ million people are best described as mega efficient, hard grafting and friendly. The snowboard population are a cool group of laid back riders split into a mix of freeride/freestyle and carving, all blended with an Austrian – US flavour. Austria also has a cool skate scene and some resorts even have ramps and pipes. Mayrhofen has had a midi ramp for years.

In the early days most riders were into freeriding and freestyle in softboots, however today it's very much a mixture of hard boot carvers and freeriding softs. This is reflected in the world rankings of top Austrian pro riders who rule in the gates. Carvers like Martin Fredinaindeinametz, Dieter Happ and that little honey Christine Rauter rip in hards, while Max Plotzeneder and Tommy Marsh rip in softs, in and out of the pipe. The Austrian Alps can't be said to be as extreme as some of the areas found in the French Alps, although there are plenty of places to scare the best of the best, St Anton has some great stuff for instance, but the majority of the resorts are best suited to intermediate freeriders and carvers, the often wide open flats will have hard booters wetting themselves.

Lots of resorts now provide parks and pipes for freestylers to play in, with Axamer Lizum near Innsbruck being a natural fun park.

Austria may list loads of resorts but most are tin pot nothings, a field with one short lift pulling you up. Many resorts are mid range in height and can be a bit doggie on the snow sure factor, so the best options are the glacier areas or resorts at around 1300 meters like Kaprun, Solden, St Anton or Princess Diana's favourite the Lech. Where ever you go in Austria, what is common is the high standard of facilities you get, and the overall sense of neat-ness and scary levels of nice-ness, buildings and accommodation are nice, bars nice, cafes nice, restaurants nice, streets nice, no cigarette ends lingering in gutters. Super markets nice, shops nice though a lot of what they sell isn't, and even the bogs are nice with electric infrared slash & dump disposers. Yep nice, though where the Austrians loose it is when it comes to its own music, or lack of fast food outlets and cheap bunk house or hostels to kip in. Beer on the other hand is the dogs bollocks and most night time haunts play UK/US music. A good thing to remember about Austria is that credit cards are not as widely accepted as in other countries, cash and travellers cheques are the excepted norm.

Photo: Galtur Resort

If you can speak the lingo, that is German then great, although the accents are localised and fluent speakers may well find themselves lost, however most Austrians speak good English and actually want to speak it. Mind you if you upset a liftie you will hear some choice German.

Travelling to and from Austria is a doddle with loads of options. If you're flying in, then Salzburg and Innsbruck are your main gateway international city airports for the Tryolean areas, while in Switzerland's Zurich airport serves the Arlberg parts of Austria and Germany's Munich is also a handy gateway airport for the Tryolean resorts.

Driving to resorts is no big drama, most resorts lie in long valleys with good road connections. Austrian accommodation is made up of Hotels, Guest Houses, Chalets, and Pensions (B&B's). Standards and price's vary from resort to resort. Hotels are usually very Schilling hungry and often frequented by happy family ski pundits from Germany. While Guest house's are in the mid price range they too often have nauseating bore's staying. The cheapest options are either a Pension or a group or people renting a chalet and like any country the normal rules of scamming rooms and doubling up on floors exist, but note Austrian inn keepers of small places are very wise and aware of what's going on. It's easier to get extras into the big hotels. Now Austria is member of the EEC European nationals should be able to get work with out permits.

Austrian Snowboard Federation: (ASA)
Leopoldstrasse 4, 6020 Innsbruck, Austria
Tel +43 (0) 512 565676
Set up in 1995.

Austrian snowboard styles favour:
Freestyle 40% - Freeride 55% - Alpine 5%.
Soft boots 85$ - Hard boots 15%.

Austrian Youth Hostels:
Cost from 150 schillings a night
Tel +43 (0) 222 533 53 53

Innsbruck Tourist office:
Tel +43 (0) 5356 21 55

Austrian Drive Guide
Breakdown - tel OAMTC 120 (24 Hours).
Vehicles drive on the Right.

Speed on	Motorway	Dual carrage	Single	Urban
	110-130	90	100	50km/h
If Towing	100	80		50km/h

Seat belts - compulsory
Tolls - Payable on a few motorways, some tunnels and bridges.
Alcchol level = 0.08%
Driving age limit = 18
Documents to carry, Identifiaction, Driving licence, Vehicle Reg,
Hire docs.
First aid kit,Compulsory
Warning Triangle - Compulsory
Snowchains, Recommended.

Photo: Tourist Office Innsbruck

Status	Federal Republic
Capital	Vienna
Area	88855 sq km
Population	7.7 million
Density	92 people per sq km
Language	German
Currency	Schillings
Neighbouring Countries	Germany - Czech Republic-Slovakia
	Hungary-Slovena- Switzerland - Italy
Winter snowboard periods	October to May
Summer snowboarding	May to September October
Highest Mountain	Grossglockner 3797m
Country Snowboard styles	Freeride/Freestyle -60%
Alpine/Caring	40%
Soft boots	60%
Hard boots	40%
Drugs	Cannabis and dope are illegal
	if your caught with 300g or more you
	could face 5 years in prison. Smaller amounts
	for personal use is treated lightley.
Death penalty	None
Military Service	Compulsory for male nationals
Alcohol drinking age	Age 18.
Age of consent for sex	Male 16-Female 16
Prostitution	legal
Tipping	5 t0 10% in restaurants and 10% in Taxis

AUSTRIA – INTRO

77

AXAMER LIZUM

Built in 1964 for the winter Olympics, this resort is a full on freeride-freestyle natural fun park. Although small don't be fooled. This is the playground for the Innsbruck crowd which includes Max Plotzeneder and top racer Christine Rauter and it's easy to see why. Axams is a quite no dramas place, free of holiday skiing crowds that is big on air and short on queues. Having hosted the Olympics twice the runs are obviously of a decent standard, with something to suit all. Freeriders and freestylers are going to get the best out of the slopes, with loads of natural hits, big banks and gullies that form natural pipes to drop in and out of. Freestylers looking for the best hits should take the short funicular train ride to the top, then from here follow the number 1 blue run off to the left. This will bring you out on to some really cool terrain which is mixed with red runs, the best hits being found on the left by the red 2 run, although you will find loads all the way down. Intermediate freeriders wanting some off piste and trees will not be disappointed. Although limited there's some good stuff to be found if you go right at the exit point of the funicular train and follow the line of the red trails 4 and 3. Euro carvers will look and feel out of place here, as it's not Autobahn territory. Saying that there is room to crank some big carves, especially down trail 1 and 2. Riders already past the novice stage and with a few bruise's under their belt will be able to collect a few more down trails 5 and 5a, while experienced riders can go for it down the blacks on trail 10 reached via a chair lift from the base area. First time snowboarders can loosen up and get to grips with boarding on the easy trails at the bottom which have beginner snowboard friendly drag lifts.

Although there are a few accommodation options at the base area of Axams-Lizum, the main village of Axams has a much wider choice of beds and eating haunts. Alternatively Innsbruck is only 25 minutes away where you get a massive choice coupled with the best happenings. Innsbruck, which can be reached each day by a regular bus service, also has a Macdonalds and a damn fine pizza restaurant by the river. There's also a couple of hostels and a cool Pension called Pension Paula. For all your snowboard needs visit Sport Check one of the first main snowboard shops in Austria, or Holy Cow both in Innsbruck.

Winter snowboard periods between Dec and April.

No summer snowboarding

Top Station	2340m
Lifts rise from base	1583
Vertical Drop	700m
Longest run	7km
Pisted ride area	33km

Terrain ability suits:

● Beginner	46%
● Intermediate	39%
● Advanced	15%

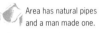

Terrain Ride styles suits:

Freeride	50%
Freestyle	40%
Alpine/Carve	10%

Area has natural pipes and a man made one.

Lifts open at 9.00-4.00pm week days,
Half-day tickets run from 9am to 1pm
or 12am to 4pm

Photo: Axamer-Lizum Resort

Photo:: Axamer-Lizum Resort

Photo: Axamer-Lizum Resort

SNOWBOARD SHOPS
Axams
SPORTHAUS OLYMPIA
Sales-Hire-Repair.
(Ski/snowboard shop)

Innsbruck
SPORT SPECIAL +43-5125 28 67 07
Sales-Hire-Repair.
(Sport/snowboard shop)
FREDS SPORT STORE
+43-512 563 890
Sales-Hire-Repair.
(Sports/snowboard shop)

ROUND AND ABOUT & LIFE STYLE

SKATEBOARDING
Happening in Innsbruck.
For decks etc check out Freds

Eat at:
Macdonalds in Innsbruck;
Pizza restaurant next to
the bridge by the river

Night time hangouts:
Cafe Central in Innsbruck for
booze & full on snowboard
Jimmys Bar for booze and a

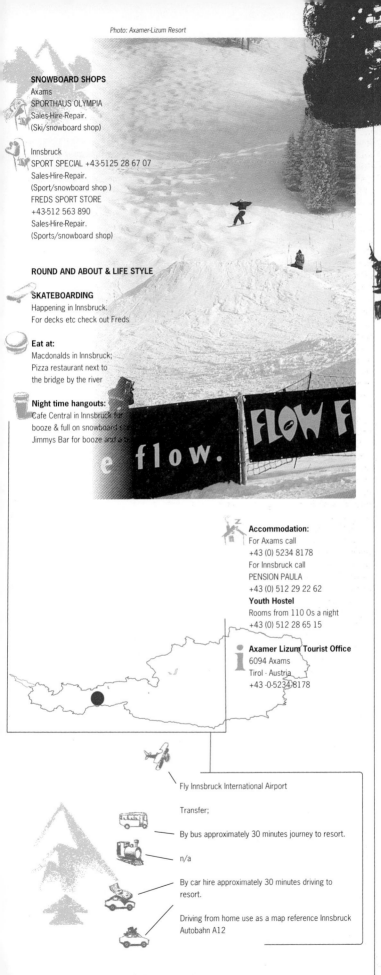

Accommodation:
For Axams call
+43 (0) 5234 8178
For Innsbruck call
PENSION PAULA
+43 (0) 512 29 22 62
Youth Hostel
Rooms from 110 Os a night
+43 (0) 512 28 65 15

Axamer Lizum Tourist Office
6094 Axams
Tirol - Austria
+43 -0-5234 8178

Fly Innsbruck International Airport

Transfer;

By bus approximately 30 minutes journey to resort.

n/a

By car hire approximately 30 minutes driving to
resort.

Driving from home use as a map reference Innsbruck
Autobahn A12

AUSTRIA – AXAMER LIZUM

79

FIEBERBRUNN

Here lies a small resort but one that is really cutting it with the snowboard world in Austria. Nestled between Zell am See and St Johann in an area that has quite a few easy to reach and better known resorts, Fieberbrunn has fast become the place to check out.

Although small it's really cool and very snowboard friendly. The International Snowboard Federation loved it so much that it's now regularly hosting big events attracting the worlds top riders.

Fieberbrunn's terrain is not the most testing with only a couple of black runs. It will appeal to intermediate and novice hard booters wanting easy flats in order to master carving. There's nothing much for advanced freeriders or the hard core freestyler to tackle, although some interesting stuff can be found to test the not so sure rider. The main runs on the Streuboden which can get a bit crowded at weekends are reached via a short journey on an unusual gondola system which goes to two levels. The first level will bring you out to easy terrain around some trees, while the second takes you to some open reds and a black run. Freeriders should try the stuff over on the Reekmoos area where there is some off piste but don't be expecting much. Freestylers wanting air will find the pipe the best option. The longest thing on offer for carvers is the Number 1 run which brings you out at the base of the mountain. Beginners have a number of good areas to start out on, and if you want to avoid the drag lifts to begin with then head for the runs down off the first gondola station. The local ski school handles snowboard instruction with pro instructors on the staff.

If you're the sort of sad git that is bothered by the way the village looks then Fieberbrunn will appeal to you, it's one of those picture post card joints that ski press get so excited about and write so much bull. The small village is spread along a section of road with the possibilities of some walking to the lifts. The village centre, set back of the road has a selection of shops and supermarkets as well as eating haunts but no fast food. Accommodation comes as standard grade 1 Austrian from hotels to the pensions. Night time is not hard core and takes the sad form of Apré ski. The main haunts are the Londoner Bar, The River House and Plauscherl.

**Winter snowboard periods between December and April.
No summer snowboarding**

Top Station	1870m
Resort height	800m
Vertical Drop	792m
Longest run	4km
Ride area	50km
of marked piste	
Snowmaking	7km of piste

Terrain ability suits

● Beginner	34%
● Intermediate	50%
● Advanced	16%

Terrain Ride styles suits:

Freeride	40%
Freestyle	5%
Alpine/Carve	55%

Big pipe and park located at the Wintersport area "Streuboden". Flood lights allow for night time pipe riding until 10pm daily

Lift pass rates for 1996/97

	High season		Low season	
	Adult	Child	Adult	Child
1 day	320-	170-	320-	
6 day	1580-	875-	1270-	
14 day	2800-	1540	2240	

Lifts open at 8.15am to 6.30pm.

Gondolas	2
Chair lifs	2
Drag lifts	19

Rear foot free on drag lifts and leashes compulsory

Photo: Tourist Office Fieberbrunn

Photo: Burton

SNOWBOARD INSTRUCTION
1 day lesson OS500-
3 1/2 days OS900-
6 1/2 days OS1380-

SNOWBOARD & BOOT HIRE
3 day hire OS1115 -
6 day OS2125 -

Snowboard shop/s
Boarders Syndicate
+43 (0) 5354 6345
Sales-hire-repair.
(Ski/Snowboard Shop)

Sport Kogel
+43 (0) 5354 2266
Sales-hire-repair.
(Ski/Snowboard Shop).

Nigh time hangouts
The Londoner Pub
(for a beer at steep prices).
The River House
(for a beer although not a happening place).

Photos: Tourist Office Fieberbrunn

Fieberbrunn Tourist Office
Spiebergstrasse 21
Postfach 2. A-6391 Fieberbrunn
Tirol Austria.
+43 -0-5354 6304

Fly Salzburg international airport

Transfer;

By bus approxametely 2 hours to the resort

By train direct into Fieberbrun

By car hire approxametely 1 hour to the resort.

Driving via Munich use as a map reference autobahn
A93/A2 exit Kufstein via St Johann to Fieberbrunn.
Via Innsbruck autobahn A12 exit Wogl via St Johann
to Fieberbrunn.

ISCHGL

This is Austria at its best. It may not be the most testing place but it offers something for everyone with decent slopes and an OK village, all helping to make it one of the top allround snowboard haunts in the country. Ischgl has been attracting snowboarders to it's wide open and long runs for years. It's a place where the I.S.F stage slalom and half pipe events on a regular basis culminating in the World Championships in 1995 which means its has to have something to offer. Ischgl butts up with the Swiss duty free resort of Samnaun which can be reached by connecting lifts. The Silvretta lift pass covers four other nearby resorts, (Samnaun, Galtur, Kappl and See).

Being a high resort, Ischgl is a snow-sure place that will please intermediate riders most, especially the hard boot carvers with wide motorway piste where you can put in big arcs and easily make those 360° snow turns. Some of the best interest is on the Idjoch with a mixture of blue and red runs to check out. Advanced riders will find plenty of stuff to keep them busy though not bowled over. The Pardatschgrat, a black run leading back into the village with the lower section cutting through some trees is worth a look, you'll also find some good off piste opportunities and some sound freeriding down the runs of the Palinkopf.

Ischgl's permanent halfpipe located on Idalp has been giving air heads the opportunities to pull tricks since 1993. The pipe is full-on and used for I.S.F events. There's a pipe in Samnaun as well. Freestylers will find plenty of natural hits with bowls, banks and gullies to pull air off, there are also a few of drop off's but in the main, new school grommets will have fun practising there flatland tricks on the main runs.

The village of Ischgl is all Austrian with a fair bit going on and mainly inhabited by visiting German and Scandinavian skiers. This is not the cheapest of places and skint or budget conscious riders will need to do some serious scamming or cutting back to see a 7 day trip through. There are loads of options for lodging, with dozens of hotels guest house and pensions. Eating in Ischgl is easily described as bland although good, and once again lacks a fast food or burger joint. Night time is OK but nothing major, the main happening haunts are your usual Austrian après ski bore and stupid Tee dances which skiers flock to wearing silly coloured lip sticks and face paints.

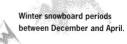

Winter snowboard periods between December and April.

No summer snowboarding

Top Station	2864m
Resort height	1400m
Vertical Drop	997m
Longest run	14km
Ride area	200km of
marked piste linked with 4 resorts.	
Snowmaking	7km of Piste

Terrain ability suits:
- Beginner 27%
- Intermediate 63%
- Advanced 10%

Terrain ride style suits:

Freeride	40%
Freestyle	20%
Alpine/Carve	40%

2 halfpipes, 1 in Ischgl and 1 in Samnaun. Boarders Paradise is a big park with hits, rails a freeriding mogel area and a new schools area.

Lift pass rates 1996/97

	High season		Low season	
	Adult	Child	Adult	Child
2 day				
	725-	475-	655-	475-
6 day				
	1890-	1165-	1720-	1165-
10 day				
	2760-	1630-	2540-	1630-

Lift open at 8.30am to 5pm

Gondolas	3
Cable cars	2
Chair lifts	10
Drag lifts	22

No rear foot rules leashes not required.

SILVRETTA SKIARENA 1400 - 2900 m

Samnaun

ISCHGL

Photo: Tourist Office Ischgl

82

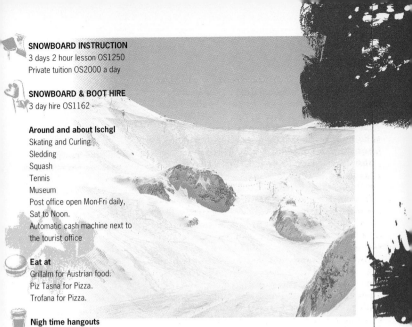

SNOWBOARD INSTRUCTION
3 days 2 hour lesson OS1250
Private tuition OS2000 a day

SNOWBOARD & BOOT HIRE
3 day hire OS1162

Around and about Ischgl
Skating and Curling
Sledding
Squash
Tennis
Museum
Post office open Mon-Fri daily,
Sat to Noon.
Automatic cash machine next to
the tourist office

Eat at
Grillalm for Austrian food.
Piz Tasna for Pizza.
Trofana for Pizza.

Nigh time hangouts
Kuhstall
Nikis Stadl

Photos: Tourist Office Ischgl

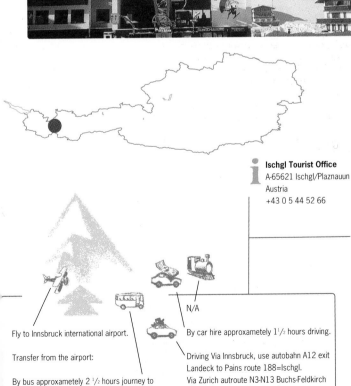

Ischgl Tourist Office
A-65621 Ischgl/Plaznauun
Austria
+43 0 5 44 52 66

Fly to Innsbruck international airport.

Transfer from the airport:

By bus approxametely 2 ½ hours journey to
resort.

N/A

By car hire approxametely 1 ½ hours driving.

Driving Via Innsbruck, use autobahn A12 exit
Landeck to Pains route 188=Ischgl.
Via Zurich autroute N3-N13 Buchs-Feldkirch
-Bludenz route 188 via Galtur.

AUSTRIA – ISCHGL

KAPRUN

Winter or summer Kaprun cuts it big style. The resort is set beneath the Kitzsteinhorn glacier which extends to a height of 3203 meters, making it a perfect place to ride in winter with a good snow record, and long into the summer on the Glacier. A number of snowboard manufacturers often use Kaprun in the summer to host team training sessions and board testing programs. In the winter riders of all levels will find something to shred, though it has to be said that much of what is on offer here, or at the nearby neighbouring resort of Zell am See is best suited to intermediate freeriders and carvers. The main runs are on the Kitzsteinhorn via a journey on the cable car or funicular train to the Alpincentre and then further on up where freeriders can reach some good off piste powder. From the Alpincentre you can access wide open areas perfect for those carving dudes who have made the grade and those just starting out.

Beginners can get going on a number of easy runs on the Maiskogel mountain reached by a drag lift from the centre of the village or if you cant handle a drag take the cable car at the north end of the village. Beginners are spoilt when it comes to snowboard instruction, Kaprun was the first Austrian resort to have an independent snowboard school. If you get bored with Kaprun then Zell am See is only a ten minute bus ride away, which gives you access to an extra 80 km of piste covered by the same pass. Like Kaprun, Zell will suite novices and intermediate riders with a few good blacks to take on. Freestylers are well sorted with a pipe at Kaprun all year round and a pipe during the winter at Zell am See. One off point about Zell is that snowboarders are not allowed to ride outside marked runs. This is a tree friendly area, which is fair enough so long as skiers are restricted as well.

Kaprun the town is a fairly big place and as one expects provides a lot of good Austrian style sleeping options at mixed pocket prices. Lodging includes a Youth Hostel and the normal array of chalets and pensions. Night time is laid back and has a good feel with some snowboard life style to be had at a few good bars. Check out Austrian pub or the Bauber or the 'Fountain bar'. For Skaters there used to be a bit of a skate scene in Schutdorf about 6km away.

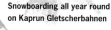

Snowboarding all year round on Kaprun Gletscherbahnen

Top Station	3029m
Resort height	800m
Vertical Drop	1132m
Longest run	8km
Ride area	130km of marked piste linked with Zell am (See resorts)
Snowcannon	25km of piste

Terrain ability suits: (all areas)

● Beginner	53%
● Intermediate	32%
● Advanced	15%

Terrain Ride styles suits:

Freeride	40%
Freestyle	20%
Alpine/Carve	40%

2 Halfpipes, one in Kaprun and 1 in Zell an See.

Lifts open at 8.30 - 4.30pm
Half-day tickets run from 12.30pm

Lifts:
Gondolas 1
Cable cars 2
Funicular Trains 2
Chairlifts 3
Drag lifts 8

SNOWBOARD INSTRUCTION
3 ½ days tuition OS1300

SNOWBOARD & BOOT HIRE
3 day hire OS1000

SNOWBOARD SHOPS
FUNKY MOUSE
Tel: +43 (0) 6547 87 15 16
Sales-Hire-Repair.
(Ski/snowboard shop.)

Skateboarding:
some street in Kaprun
Ramp at Schutidori.
(6 miles away).

Nigh time hangout
The Fountain Bar.

Photo: Sang Tan

Photo: Tourist Office Kaprun

Accomodation.
Youth Hostel:
Kaprun. Rooms from Os20 per night.
Tel: +43 (0) 5 6547 8507

Kaprun Tourist Office
Salzburger platz 601
A-5710 Kaprun. Austria.
+43 -0- 6547 8643.

By train to Zell am See then take a
15 minute bus ride to Kaprun

Fly to Salzburg international airport.

By car hire approxametely 11/2
hours driving.

Transfer from the airport:

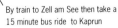

Driving Via Salzburg West autohbahn
A10 exit Bischofshofe to Zell am See
168 to reach the resort.

By bus approxametely 2 1/2 hours
journey to resort.

SOLDEN

One and a half hours from Innsbruck along the Otz Valley lies the high altitude resort of Solden and Hochsolden, a well established haunt for snowboarders that has been allowing radical dudes on its slopes for years.

This easy to reach resort has all year round snowboarding with the available slopes on two glacier areas of which part of the glacier area remains closed during the winter to preserve the runs for the summer months. Winter riding takes place on the slopes of Solden and the sub village of Hochsolden, a small resort perched above Solden allowing for some long riding back into town.

Solden is more or less a euro carvers-come-freeriders place with a lot of good piste and off piste to shred. There are a number of long, wide, open runs to pump down and cut up skiers on, which on the lower areas thread through the tree line. Freeriders wanting to go for it should try out some of the stuff on the Hochsolden area, there a cool black runs all the way back into the Solden and brings you out at the gondola to take you straight back up again. For a bit of a heart pumper the off piste stuff under the top section of the Gaislachkogl cable car is well worth a look, but not for wimps. The run is steep at the top and mellows out on to some reds and blacks which descend back down to the village offering a few hits along route. Although this is not the most major freestyle resort its better than most and there are loads of natural hits and gullies to get air from. Alternatively Solden now has a half pipe where grommets in the baggiest of trouser can perform to the on lookers.

Beginners can cut it with ease on the lower slopes which are reached by foot from Solden, or head up the main runs via a gondola which cuts out the drag lift beginner problems, once up there's plenty of space to fall around on and at the end of the day there's a long blue back down into Solden.

Lodging and lifestyle in Solden can be pricey, and reflects the normal Austrian styles. There are a lot of places to kip and most are walking distance from the slopes or can be reached by a short free shuttle bus ride. Food and booze is pricey so check out the supermarkets to save on the schillings. Night time is mixed. However, there are a few OK places to get messy without the numpties in green lipstick around. Das Stampel bar is worth a check and is OK.

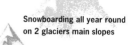

Snowboarding all year round on 2 glaciers main slopes

Top Station	3235m
Resort height	1377m
Vertical Drop	1771m
Longest run	12km
Ride area	180km
(of marked piste linked with Hochsolden)	
Snowcannons	10km of piste

Terrain ability suits: (all areas)
- Beginner — 42%
- Intermediate — 44%
- Advanced — 14%

Terrain ride style suits:

Freeride	40%
Freestyle	20%
Alpine/Carve	40%

Lift rates (Schillings):

	Adult	Child
1 day	440	270
2 days	1150	680
5 days	1790	1020
10 days	2820	1490

Lifts open at 8.30am-4.30pm
Half-day tickets run from 12.30pm

Lifts:

Gondolas	2
Cable cars	1
Funicular Trains	0
Chairlifts	18
Drag lifts	12

Rear foot free on drag lifts.
Snowboard leashes required.

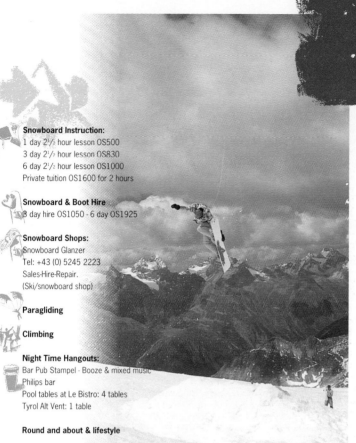

Snowboard Instruction:
1 day 2½ hour lesson OS500
3 day 2½ hour lesson OS830
6 day 2½ hour lesson OS1000
Private tuition OS1600 for 2 hours

Snowboard & Boot Hire
3 day hire OS1050 - 6 day OS1925

Snowboard Shops:
Snowboard Glanzer
Tel: +43 (0) 5245 2223
Sales-Hire-Repair.
(Ski/snowboard shop)

Paragliding

Climbing

Night Time Hangouts:
Bar Pub Stampel - Booze & mixed music
Philips bar
Pool tables at Le Bistro: 4 tables
Tyrol Alt Vent: 1 table

Round and about & lifestyle

Sports centre:
Bowling at the leisure centre
Curling
Mountain Bikes
Ice rink
Post office Mon. - Fri. daily,
Sat till 11.00am

Eat at:
Cafe Carola
Bierhimmel
Nanu

Rider : Philippe - Photo: Jonny Barr

Accommodation
Pension Glanzer
single B+B from OS120 per night
slopes 5 mins
Tel: +43 (0) 5254 2223

Solden Tourist Office
Otzal Arena
A-6450 Solden Tirol, Austria
Tel +43 (0) 5254 22120
http://www.tis.co.@//oetzal.arena
Snowphone: +43 (0) 5332 2666

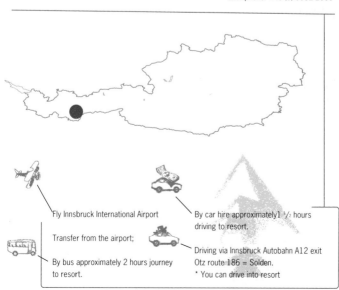

Fly Innsbruck International Airport

Transfer from the airport;

By bus approximately 2 hours journey
to resort.

By car hire approximately 1 ½ hours
driving to resort.

Driving via Innsbruck Autobahn A12 exit
Otz route 186 = Solden.
* You can drive into resort

ST ANTON

Each to their own, but many who know their snowboard terrain would agree that St Anton is about the best you can get in Austria. Now really behind snowboarding which hasn't always been the case, St Anton has loads of really good snowboarding to offer all levels, be you a freestyle freak, a piste carving poseur, a freeride speed king or simply a nappy wearing new boy. St Anton has the reputation for being expensive and attracting the fur clad Ferrari owning skiers, and while they drip over their chalet balcony's sipping pink gins, snowboarders can roam freely over miles of excellent terrain, with steeps, deeps, air and trees on both side of the mountain slopes that rise up from the resort.

The Arlberg ski pass allows you to ride the linked areas of St Anton, St Christopher and Stuben. If you're an advanced rider, worm you way up to the Kapall area where you'll find loads of good freeriding terrain with decent natural hits. Alternatively head to the summit of Vallugagrat via the Galzig cable car to reach some major off piste stuff with long runs back down to St Anton and St Christopher, but be warned it's not for the weak knead. Intermediate riders just getting it together will find loads to help especially on the Gampen and Kapall areas. While the easier runs on the Galzig is easier it tends to get busy with numptie skiers. Riders who try out the Renl area which is on the opposite side of St Anton to the Gampen runs, will find full on freeriding terrain which is generally crowd free.

First time skiers won't handle this resort, but beginners on a snowboard will if they have some balls about them. If you're a wimp who wants flat, no incline blues then give this place a miss. Freestylers not content with the natural hits will be able to satisfy themselves in the park and pipe.

St. Anton doesn't come cheap, with much of the accommodation in chalet form, although B&B's are available. Chalets allow you to cram as many in as possible but keep an eye out for the landlord or squealing Brit skiers. Food and booze is pricey though you can feed well at least once every third day with out breaking the bank, filling in with a trip to the supermarket. Night time; although St Anton is pretty good and offers good places to check out, to get the latest low down on St Anton check out the Underground Snowboard Shop it's cool and offers a lot.

Winter snowboard periods between November and April

No summer snowboarding

Top Station	2811m
Resort height	1303m
Vertical Drop	1502m
Longest run	8.km
Ride area	200km
of marked piste linked with	
St Christopher	
Snowcannons	10

Terrain ability suits:

● Beginner	30%
● Intermediate	40%
● Advanced	30%

Terrain Ride styles suits:

Freeride	60%
Freestyle	30%
Alpine/Carve	10%

Halfpipe and fun park
located on the Rendl area.

Lift tickets (Schillings)

	Adult	Chlid
½ day	345-	205-
1 day	480-	274-
5 days	1940-	1160-
10 days	3280-	1970-
Season	8100-	4640-

Lifts open at 8.15-4.30pm
Half-day tickets run from 12.30pm

Lifts:

Gondolas 1
Cable cars 10
Funicular Trains 1
Chairlifts 33
Drag lifts 44

Rear foot must be free on drag lifts.
Leashes required but not compolsory

Photo: Tourist Office St Anton

Snowboard instruction
1/2 day lesson OS 450
3 day lesson OS 1200

Snowboard & boot hire:
1 day hire Os340 - 5 day OS1300
Demo boards 1 day OS370.

Snowboard repair/service:
Hot wax & edge service OS450

Snowboard shops:
UNDERGROUND.
Tel: + 43 (0) 5446 3858
Sales-Hire-Repair-Instruction.
(snowboard shop)

Photos: Tourist Office St Anton

Paragliding

Climbing

Around and about
Sports centre
Skating
Bowling

Night time hangouts
Amadeus
Piccadilly
Underground

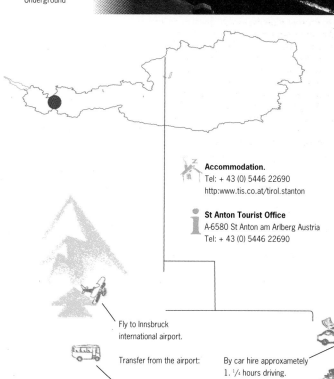

Accommodation.
Tel: + 43 (0) 5446 22690
http:www.tis.co.at/tirol.stanton

St Anton Tourist Office
A-6580 St Anton am Arlberg Austria
Tel: + 43 (0) 5446 22690

Fly to Innsbruck
international airport.

Transfer from the airport:

By bus approxametely 1 1/2
hours journey to resort.

By Train directly into the
centre of ST Anton

By car hire approxametely
1. 1/4 hours driving.

Driving Via Innsbruck, use
autobahn A12 exit
Landeck route 197/E60 -
St Anton.

INNSBRUCK

Innsbruck. A city, a host to the Olympics, an all year round tourist attraction and for those who care, the birthplace of Beethoven the geezer who made dodgy singles that lasted for hours.

Unlike normal Austrian resorts, Innsbruck is a big place and doesn't resemble a resort at all, it's really a working city. Not only does it have a number of resort within a few miles, one of which stretches up out of the city, it is also the gateway to loads more resorts with only a little daily driving. If you are going to stay in Innsbruck and travel to different resorts you'd be advised to have a car. Although there are bus services to most areas, you'll be tied to certain times, and really it won't be practical.

Most of the areas that surround Innsbruck aren't up to much for snowboarding in terms of size or degree of difficulty. Seegruber which is reached by lifts leading out of the City is tiny but can be cool for a bit of slipping and sliding around for an hour or two. Igls is also small but as it has hosted Olympic ski events, there is more on offer and will keep beginners happy for a day or so. Mütters, again small, links with Axams which is mega for snowboarders, while Tulfes has the biggest vert. All the Innsbruck area resorts along with Axams, are covered by a single lift pass; the Innsbruck Stubai Glacier Pass and reached by a free shuttle bus. If the snow is not happening at any of the resort you can swap round and if there is no snow at all then the bus will take you up to the Stubai Glacier, about 90 minutes from Innsbruck which is also a summer snowboard destination.

Innsbruck as a city may not be New York or London but it still has a good scene and is home to a big snowboard culture going back to day one. There are dozens of bars, loads of places to eat including a Macdonald's and plenty of places to boogie or see live music. What's great about Innsbruck is that it doesn't have the horrible apré ski crowds especially the idiots from Britain. With Innsbruck having an international Airport, though slightly intermittent, it's really easy to reach by air from most countries, or alternatively trains from all over the place arrive in the centre of Innsbruck on a daily basis.

Top station	3200m
Bottom Station	575m
Pisted runs	112km
Vertical drop	1460m
Longest run	9.6km

Terrain ability suits:

● Beginner	20%
● Intermediate	50%
● Advanced	30%

Lifts	52

Stay at:
Pension Paula:
Tel: +43 (0) 5122 922 62

Eat at:
Macdonalds
The Pizza place beside the river and the bridge.

Drink at:
Cafe Weiner
Jimmy's

Snowboard Shop at
Sport Check
Freds Snowboard shop

International Snowboard Federation
A-6020 Innsbruck
Pradlerstrasse 21
Austria
Tel: +43 (0) 512 342834
Fax: +43 (0) 512 342834-29

Burton Snowboards
Hottinger Au 85,
A-6020 Innsbruck
Austria
Tel +43 (0) 512 22820
Fax +43 (0) 512 286811

Innsbruck Tourist Office
Burggraben 3
A-6021 Innsbruck
Tel +43 (0) 512 59 8 50
fax +43 (0) 512 59 8 50-7

Photo: Tourist Office Innsbruck

GALTUR

Like a lot of things size doesn't always matter, which is true in the case of Galtur. Small it is but that doesn't detract from the fact that is still OK. Located at the head of the Paznaun valley a short distance from Ischgl, unlike its more popular and more extensive neighbour, Galtur is a more laid back affair and a lot more quieter without all the hype. Although the immediate terrain doesn't measure to mega status with its fairly ordinary runs, the 40kms of piste that are on offer, do nicely for some cool riding, What's more Galtur share's a lift pass for the Silvretta area which takes in Ischgl amongst others giving a combined possible 250 km to cut and flatten, so if Galtur proves to be a bit boring after a few days then move around.

Freeriders in softs looking for some off piste areas will find a few good runs to tackle. These won't test the advanced rider too much, but should keep you intermediate's happy. The red and black runs on the Saggrat will please carvers of all levels especially hard booters, however hardcore freestylers won't completely love this place. Air heads can always visit the pipe at Ischgl or on the Swiss side at Sannan. Novice riders should have no real problems unless you are crap at using drag lifts which serve the easy runs, but as the lift lines are generally quite, you'll be able to keep trying without too much hassle from irate skiers.

Galtur is a simple Austrian village, with the normal stuff on offer from hotels to pensions but at rather high prices, as is eating and drinking which is the usual Austrian offerings of OK but a little repetitive. Still it will appeal to some.

Winter snowboard periods between December and April.

No summer snowboarding

Top Station	2299m
Resort height	1767m
Vertical Drop	662m
Longest run	3.5km
Ride area	40 km of piste
Snowmaking	6km of piste

Terrain ability suits:

● Beginner	10%
● Intermediate	60%
● Advanced	30%

Terrain Ride styles suits

Freeride	35%
Freestyle	5%
Alpine/Carve	60%

Fun park and halfpipe

3 ¹/₂ day snowboard lesson OS 990

Lifts open at 9am to 4.30pm daily
3 day adult pass OS 840-

12 lifts, where back foot must be free on drags, though leashes are not compolsory

ℹ **Galtur Tourist Office**
A-6563 Galtur
Austria
Tel: + 43 (0) 5443 521
Reservations: + 43 (0) 5443 521

AUSTRIA – INNSBRUCK, GALTUR

Photo: Tourist Office Galtur

Fly to Innsbruck international airport.

Transfer from the airport:

By bus approxametely 2 ¹/² hours journey to resort.

 N/A

By car hire approxametely 2 hours driving.

Driving via Innsbruck autobahn A12 exit Landeck to Pains route 188 via Ischgl = Galtur.

Via Zurich autoroute N3-N13 Buchs-Feldkirch-Bludenz route 188 via Schruns = Galtur.

KITZBUHEL

Chances are if you know Austria you would have heard of Kitzbuhel in the Tyrol. This is one of the big Austrian areas that link up to form a safari of cool terrain mainly for beginners and intermediates, though advanced riders will find plenty of steep. Ski journals go on about this place as the bees knees. While good it may be the fact that it's way over crowded with skiers, especially Brits and can be dodgy on the snow sure factor are points to note.

Still, when the snow has dumped no rider should get bored. There's enough room to shred with out constantly bumping into dayglo wearing two plankers. The steeps, trees and powder should suit the freerider wanting to cut it with ease, while euro carvers in hard boots will find enough motorway piste to lay out some big arcs. The half pipe on the Kitzbuhler Horn is good enough to keep the freestylers happy and there's plenty of terrain for ground trick grommet's to perform off. This is a good place for beginners with loads of good and easy progressing terrain serviced by chairs and drags offering the nervous T-bar virgin good options.

Lodging in a town like Kitzbuhel is no big problem, with heaps of beds at OK prices in pensions and apartments. Mercifully Kitzbuhel has a Macdonalds which some skier's feel lowers the tone of the place (idiots). Boozing: It goes off in a few places that are worth checking out, but beware skiers are apré-ing all over the place.

**Winter snowboard periods betwee
November and April.**
No summer snowboarding

Top Station	2000 m
Resort height	800m
Vertical Drop	1200m
Longest run	6.8km
Ride area	160km of pist
Snowmaking	13km

Terrain ability suits:

● Beginner	50%
● Intermediate	42%
● Advanced	8%

1 halfpipe on the Kitzbuhler Horn

Number of lifts 64
*Rear foot free and Leashes
compulsory.

Kitzbuheler Tourist Office
A-6370 Kitzbuhel. Hinterstadt 18
Austria.
Tel: +43 (0) 5356 2155

Nearest international airport: Salzbu
Transfer time = 1 1/2 hours

SAALBACH-HINTERGLEM

Saalbach-Hinterglem are two villages that become one large snowboard area covering 200km of piste with 60 lifts forming a snowboard circus. It can get busy here, but with the way the place is laid out things aren't to scary and lifts queues are not the worst in Austria.

A resort that has hosted world cup ski events needs good terrain too so that is exactly what you get here with trees, steep bits, powder and natural hits, not to mention 13 km of snowboard only runs for freeriders and carvers, along with two halfpipes and a fun park to suit all levels and style of freestyler. If you get bored or can't handle it, take up brass rubbing or train spotting as it will suit you better.

Advanced riders wanting off piste powder will find some good stuff to be had on the north side of the valley. Freeriders may find the Zwolferkogel black run a bit of a tester especially if you're only just coming to terms with your riding level. Intermediate riders will get the most out of the slopes, with plenty of reds to edge down and polish up on before giving the blacks a look in. Beginners will soon see big improvements in their riding with ample slopes that are easy to reach and negotiate. There are a number of ski schools which offer snowboard instruction at every level.

Village services are in walking distance of the slopes as are a lot of Schilling hungry hotels; however there are a good selection of youth style hotels to kip at cheap rates. Hanging is not bad with some cool joints to get drunk in, disco's are pricy so tank up before hand.

**Winter snowboard periods betwee
December and April.**
No summer snowboarding

Top Station	2100m
Resort height	1003m
Vertical Drop	1000m
Longest run	7.5km
Ride area	200km of pis
Snowmaking	20%

Terrain ability suits:

● Beginner	54%
● Intermediate	37%
● Advanced	18%

**2 Half pipes 1 fun park
Boardercross circuit
13 km snowboard area.**

60 lifts no ride rules
1 day adult pass OS 400-

Saalbach Tourist Office,
A-5753 Saalbach 550,
Austria
Tel: +43 (0) 6541 7272
Reservations: +43 (0) 6541 7272

International airport: Salzburg
Transfer time: 1 hour

ALPBACH

Alpbach is a small easy going out-back that is full-on for hard boot carvers who like their piste wide and void of any trouble spots. New boys just learning what an edge is and how to carve it, should soon become competent and able to leave nice tracks behind them as they descend the mostly red runs. Advanced riders will find that the couple of blacks runs are not to be treated with arrogance, otherwise it will end in tears. Freeriders in softs should try out the runs around the Wiedersberger Horn which offer powder on a good day. For those wanting trees you will find some tight Firs around the lower slopes which are worth dropping through, while freestylers fed up with looking for natural hits will be able to take their frustrations out in Alpbach's halfpipe and funpark, which aren't mega but OK for most streetstyle grommets. The easy runs here are good enough to help most of those still in nappies to soon progress into trousers and take on the red runs higher up.

Alpbach's accommodation and hangouts are a short shuttle bus from the slopes, which is no big drama but you won't find much to shout about unless you like your nights quite and boring, though there are a few joints to get messy and boogie.

Winter snowboard periods between December and April. No summer snowboarding

Top Station	2050m
Resort height	1100m
Vertical Drop	973m
Longest run	4.2km
Ride area	40km of piste
Snowmaking	20km

Terrain ability suits:

● Beginner	14%
● Intermediate	68%
● Advanced	18%

**1 Half pipe
1 funpark**

Number of lifts 21
*Rear foot free and Leashes compulsory

Alpbach Tourist Office,
Moeben 604, Postfach 31,
A6236, Alpbach
Austria
Tel: +43 (0) 5336 5211

Nearest international airport: Innsbruck
Transfer time =1 hour

BRANDENTAL BLUDENZ

This neat little resort is stretched along the Brand valley close to the Swiss border. Thankfully this place is crowd free, which is pretty important when you see how much of the terrain is suited to beginners. The runs are wide with nothing here that will worry the level headed advanced rider much, although there is stuff to do on the only black that will make sure you treat the mountain with respect. Freeriders looking for trees will find a good selection of tight stuff to weave through which should set a bit of a challenge for the intermediate rider. The red run that descends out through the Lorenzital valley is a decent long run that will certainly appeal to soft boot freeriders, while carvers in hard boots will find the blues and reds on the top section of the Paludalpe the place to arc some big turns.

Beginners should excel here as the easy runs are easy allowing for quick progression. For those who need it Brands "Surfing University" caters for all levels and all styles of tuition with clinics for freestyle, freeriding, powder, mogels and race training.

Village wise Brand is a spread out affair of 3500 beds mixed between Hotels and Pensions, with the usual style of Austrian eating spots. Night time, forget it. Buy a carry out at the supermarket and listen to your walkman.

Winter snowboard periods between December and April. No summer snowboarding

Top Station	1920m
Resort height	1050
Vertical Drop	870m
Longest run	6km
Ride area	50km of piste

Terrain ability suits:

● Beginner	57%
● Intermediate	43%
● Advanced	0%

1 pipe

Number of lifts 8
*Rear foot free and Leashes compulsory

Brand Tourist Office
TVB Brandnertal,
A-6708 Brand, Austria
Tel: +43 (0) 5559 555-0
Reservations: +43 (0) 6541 7272
Snowphone: +43 (0) 5559 555-0

International airport: Innsbruck
Transfer time = 1 ½ hours

PITZTAL

A major area with high altitude riding on big open slopes with deep powder, suiting every style and level of rider. The pipe and park are excellent, freestylers won't be disappointed. Summer riding too. Services good and varied in a number of villages.

Lodging and main facilities in St Leonhard
Fly to Innsbruck - Transfer to = 50 mins
Full resort details + 43 (0) 5413 8216

Top Station	3440m
Longest run	15km
Ride area	40km of piste

Terrain ability suits:
- Beginner   33%
- Intermediate   52%
- Advanced   15%

1 half pipe, 1 fun park and a new fun park for kids.
12 lifts, no ride rules.

BAD KLEINKIRCHEIM

Low key area with heaps of full-on freeride terrain to suit advanced and intermediate riders. Loads of tight and open trees to check out as well as a good pipe for air heads. Decent flats for carving and the beginner terrain is perfect. Village Austrian!

Lodging/facilities - Beds & bars near slopes
Fly to Klagenfurt - Transfer to = 1 hour
Full resort details + 43 (0)4240 8212-0
http://www.BKKallincl.co.at/

Vertical Drop	973m
Longest run	4.2km
Ride area	85km of piste

Terrain ability suits:
- Beginner   15%
- Intermediate   77%
- Advanced   8%

1 half pipe with sounds
32 lifts no ride rules
7 day adult pass os 1835-

SCHRUNS

A beginners paradise, with long wide open easy runs. OK for intermediate riders but lacking for advanced riders. The 12km blue and red runs will give carvers to chance to lay out some big ones. OK for new schoolers doing ground tricks, with trees to play in.

Lodging/facilities - Beds & bars near slopes
Fly to Zurich - Transfer to = 2 hours
Full resort details +43 (0) 5556 73940

Vertical Drop	2303m
Longest run	12km
Ride area	35km of piste

Terrain ability suits:
- Beginner   67%
- Intermediate   33%
- Advanced   0%

Fun park and half pipe
13 lifts no ride rules
2 day adult pass OS 780-

BADGASTEIN

A large old fashioned resort free of the package tours, offering steeps, deeps and trees for advanced and intermediate riders.

Plenty of beginner stuff but beware of drag lifts. Freestylers have two pipes and good natural hits. Check out Sportgastein.

Lodging/facilities - Beds & bars spread out
Fly to Salzburg - Transfer to = 1½ hours
Full resort details +43 (0) 6434 25310

Vertical Drop	2790m
Longest run	11km
Ride area	250km of piste

Terrain ability suits:
- Beginner   20%
- Intermediate   40%
- Advanced   40%

2 half pipe
53 lifts, no ride rules
7 day adult pass 2210-

LECH

A top Austrian resort that attracts the rich, famous and Royal is also a full on snowboarders place for all levels with major freeride terrain and excellent powder. The 300m long fun park area has a 1/2 pipe, a 1/4 pipe and obstacles.

Lodging/facilities - Beds & bars near slopes
Fly to Zurich - Transfer to = 2½ hours
Full resort details +43 (0) 5583 2161-0

Vertical Drop	2444m
Longest run	5km
Ride area:	260km of piste

Terrain ability suits:
- Beginner   40%
- Intermediate   40%
- Advanced   20%

1 half pipe , 300m fun park
86 lifts, no ride rules
7 day adult lift pass OS 2520

MAYRHOFEN

Long established snowboard haunt offering great opportunities for beginners; good stuff for advanced freeriders with steeps and trees, and easy reds for piste carvers. Hintertux further up the valley is open all year for snowboarding on the glacier.

Lodging/facilities, 7500 beds & Skate ramp
Fly to Innsbruck - Transfer to = 1 hour
Full resort details +43 (0) 5285 411633
http://.nettours.co.at/ibat/t/mayhofen.

Top Station	2220m
Longest run	4.5km
Ride area:	90km of piste

Terrain ability suits:
- Beginner   23%
- Intermediate   61%
- Advanced   16%

Half pipe and fun park
30 lifts, no ride rules
3 day adult pass OS 885-

A QUICK RIDE AROUND TWELVE OTHER AUSTRIAN SNOWBOARD RESORTS

Resort	Mountain Information and Travel.

	Summit	Resort	Vert. Drop	Ride Acres
ELLMAU	1827m	800m	500m	Riderable piste 250km
Tyrol	●Beg 37%	●Int 53%	●Adv 10%	Half Pipe **?** Park **?**

Convenient place with good terrain for carvers. longest run 5km. 20 lifts
Information Tel +43 (0) 5358 2301. Fly to Innsbruck 1½ hour transfer.

	Summit	Resort	Vert. Drop	Ride Acres
KIRCHBERG	1963m	860m	1250m	Ridable piste 160km
Tyrol	●Beg 39%	●Int 46%	●Adv 15%	Half Pipe Park

Linked to Kitzbuhel but smaller. Good for novices. longest run 8km. 64 lifts
Information Tel +43 (0) 5357 2309. Fly to Salzburg 1½ hours transfer.

	Summit	Resort	Vert. Drop	Ride Acres
HINTERTUX	3208m	1476m	1730m	Ridable piste 86km
Zillertal	●Beg 35%	●Int 55%	●Adv 10%	Half Pipe ✔ Park ✔

Glacier open all year with excellent freeriding. longest run 12km. 20 lifts
Information Tel +43 (0) 5287 6060. Fly to Innsbruck 2 hours transfer.

	Summit	Resort	Vert. Drop	Ride Acres
NIEDERAU	1900m	830m	800m	Ridable piste 42km
Tyrol	●Beg 62%	●Int 32%	●Adv 6%	Half Pipe ✔ Park ✔

Loads of easy flats for hard boot beginners. longest run 7.5km. 37 lifts
Information Tel +43 (0) 5339 8255. Fly to Innsbruck 1½ hours transfer.

	Summit	Resort	Vert. Drop	Ride Acres
OBERGURGL	3080m	1930m	1299m	Ridable piste 110km
Otztal	●Beg 35%	●Int 55%	●Adv 20%	Half Pipe ✔ Park ✔

Great place for all levels just beyond Solden. longest run 8.5km. 22 lifts
Information Tel +43 (0) 5256 258. Fly to Innsbruck 1½ hours transfer.

	Summit	Resort	Vert. Drop	Ride Acres
OBERTAUREN	2312m	1740m	1000m	Riderable piste 120km
Salzburger	●Beg 30%	●Int 40%	●Adv 30%	Half Pipe ✔ Park ✔

Deep snow and trees to suite advanced freeriders. longest run 2.5km. 26 lifts
Information Tel +43 (0) 6456 252. Fly to Salzburg 1½ hours transfer.

	Summit	Resort	Vert. Drop	Ride Acres
SCHALDMING	2700m	750m		Ridable piste 152km
Styria	●Beg 29%	●Int 61%	●Adv 10%	Half Pipe ✔ Park ✔

Good carvers place with night riding till 22.00pm. longest run 8km
The resort has a top snowboard school for kids.
86 lifts, ride rear foot free and leashes are required. 5 day pass os1605-
Information Tel +43-3687 22268 . Fly to Innsbruck 1½ hours transfer.

	Summit	Resort	Vert. Drop	Ride Acres
SERFUS	2699m	1430m	950m	Ridable piste 80km
Tyrol	●Beg 38%	●Int 49%	●Adv 13%	Half Pipe ✔ Park ✔

Loads of easy flats for hard boot beginners. longest run 7km. 37 lifts
Information Tel +43 (0) 5476 6239. Fly to Innsbruck 1 hours transfer.

	Summit	Resort	Vert. Drop	Ride Acres
SOLL	1827m	700m	1135m	Ridable piste 250km
Tyrol	●Beg 43%	●Int 49%	●Adv 8%	Half Pipe ✔ Park ✔

Cool place and good park and pipe for freestylers. longest run 7.5km. 90 lifts
Information Tel +43 (0) 5333 5216. Fly to Innsbruck 50mins transfer.

	Summit	Resort	Vert. Drop	Ride Acres
WESTENDORF	1830m	800m	1070m	Ridable piste 40km
Tyrol	●Beg 36%	●Int 64%	●Adv 0%	Half Pipe ✔ Park ✘

First timers will have a good time. Nothing testing to try. Longest run 8km
14 lifts no leash or rear foot rules. 1 day adult pass Os 320-,7 day Os1670-
Information Tel +43-0 5334 6230. Fly to Salzburg 2 hours transfer.

	Summit	Resort	Vert. Drop	Ride Acres
ZELL AM ZILLER	2264m	580m	1635m	Ridable piste 47km
Zillertal	●Beg 35%	●Int 60%	●Adv 5%.	

Good for hard boot intermediate piste lovers. longest run 7km. 25 lifts
Information Tel +43 (0) 5282 2281. Fly to Innsbruck 1 hour transfer.

	Summit	Resort	Vert. Drop	Ride Acres
ZELL AM SEE	1965m	758m	1220m	Ridable piste 80km
Zillertal	●Beg 38%	●Int 50%	●Adv 12%	Boarder cross circuit

Easy flats, good all round place close to kaprun. Longest run 6km. 27 lifts
Information Tel +43 (0) 6542 2600. Fly to Salzburg 1½ hour transfer.

RIDER'S OWN NOTES ON AUSTRIA

AUSTRIA – RIDER'S NOTES

FINLAND

Finland is a country which most outsiders will be aware is a snow covered country during most of the winter months, due to its close position to the North pole and Arctic regions. Some will also know that Finland has some of the shortest periods of daylight in Europe. There will be those who have read that Finland can be majorly cold, bloody freezing in fact with temperatures often plummeting below -50c. What many people outside this home of that idiot Santa Claus, (mind you great working hours he has - one day a year), will not be aware of is that like its Scandinavian neighbours Norway and Sweden, Finland helps to produce some of the best young freestylers in the world. 19 year old female world champ Satu Jarvela and 22 year old male world champ pro freestyler Sebu Kuhlberg, along with mates 23 year old Mika Enroth and 23 year Aleksi Vanninen, head a country that is freestyle through and through. Some would ask how can such a small country with a small population produce so many good freestylers? The answer surely lies in the fact that the resorts in Finland are tiny and offer so little in terms of riding long and extreme runs that the main thing to get into is riding a pipe; this country has almost as many pipes as country folk, and this isn't a new thing. The Finns realised early on that they may not be able to put on super Gs but half pipes were no trouble.

Resorts in Finland are small with nothing high or adventurous, many need long journey times to reach. One thing for sure is that Finland's not cheap, and what ever resort you go to there aren't major resort facilities to choose from, although what you do find is of a high standard. The main form of accommodation is Chalets, which for a group of riders chipping in and sharing the beer and food money, a few days trip is worth the effort. The locals are really cool and despite small hills you could do worse in other countries.

Rider Satu Jarvela. Photo : Finnish Snowboard Association

Status	Republic
Capital	Helsinki
Area	337,030 sq km
Population	5 million
Density	15 people per sq km
Language	Finnish & Swedish
Currency	Markka
Neighbouring Countries	Norway-Russia-Sweden
Winter snowboard periods	December to April
Summer snowboarding	Late riding in July
Highest point	Haltia 1328 m
Country Snowboard styles	Freeride/Freestyle -85%
Alpine/Caring -	15%
Soft boots	85%
Hard boots	15%
Drugs	All drugs are illegal
Death penalty	No capital punishment
Military Service	Nationals join the army by choice
Alcohol drinking age	18
Age of consent for sex	Male 16-Female 16
Prostitution	Illegal

Finnish Tourist Board
PO box 249 Etelaesplanadi 4
FIN-00131 Helsinki
Tel +358 -0-403 011

Finnish Snowboard Association

FACT FILE

Finnish Snowboard Population   40,000
Finnish Snowboard Federation (FA)
Radiokatu 20,00240 Helsinki, Finland
Tel +358 - 400 -414 587
E-Mail: ari.mentu@amen.pp.fi
Set up in 1988 now has 45 members
Independent of the French skiing associations
To Join cost 200 FIM a year and is open only
open to Finnish nationals

Finnish snowboard styles favour
Freestyle 65% - Freeride 20% - Alpine 15%.
Soft boots 85% - Hard boots 15%.

Number of boards sold in Finland 1995/96
Freeride 3000- Freestyle 6000 - Alpine 1000
Most favoured Finnish resort: Tahko
Most popular Finnish snowboarder; Sebu Kuhlberg
Finland has one snowboard manufacturing company
Finland 1996/97 events calendar include a series of 12
races, the Helsinki City Jump Event and the Junior World
Championships at Ruka (12th to 17th march 1997.)

StFINNISH DRIVE GUIDE
Break down - Tel - Autoliitto +359-90 694 0022
Vehicles drive on the Right

Speed On	Motorway	Dualcariageway	Single Urban
	100-120	80-100	50km/h
Towing	80	80	50km/h

Seat belts - Compulsory for drivers and passengers
Tolls - Payable on motor ways and some tunnels
Alcohol level = 0.05%
Driving age limit - 18
Document to carry-International Driving permit,
Vehicle Registration, Green Card,
Country Identification, Number Plates, Hire Docs
Fuel - Sold in Litres
First Aid Kit - Recommended
Warning Triangle - Compulsory
Snow chains - Recommended
Head lights must be on at all times
outside built up areas

Tahko

Himos

✈Helsinki

Rider: Sebu Kulberg. Phot: Finnish Snowboard Association

99

FINLAND

Resort	Number of runs	Maximum vertical	Longest run	Half pipe	Number of lifts	Accommodation bed spaces	Information
Northern Finland							
Heinapaa	2	25m	120m	✔	1	0	+358-981 370 050
Isosyote	21	192m	1200m	✔	11	5000	+358-988 838 150
Kalli	1	50m	350m	✔	1	0	+358-9698 227 482
Levi	43	325m	2500m	✔	15	7000	+358-9694641 246
Luosto	7	230m	1500m	✔	4	3500	+358-9693 624 400
Olos	10	210	1400	✔	4	2000	+358-9696 532 001
Ounasvaara	5	140m	600m	✔	4	120	+358-960 369 037
Paljakka	15	190m	1340m	✔	9	1000	+358-986 755 120
Pyha	8	280m	1600m	✔	8	2500	+358-9692 812 081
Ruka	28	201m	1300m	✔	22	12000	+358-989 8681231
Saariselka	12	180m	1500m	✔	6	8000	+358-9697 668 882
Salla	11	230m	1300m	✔	6	2500	+358-9692 879 711
Suomu	10	240m	1500m	✔	4	2000	+358-9692 12 951
Taivalvaara	8	100m	1000m	✔	3	120	+358-988 841 661
Ukkohalla	11	170m	1400m	✔	5	1500	+358-986 748 500
Voukatti	11	170m	1100m	✔	10	3000	+358-986 664 0411
Yllas	33	463m	3000m	✔	18	10000	+358-9695 565 511
Central Finland							
Hakarinteet	4	103m	850m	✔	3	100	+358-941 846 123
Bomba	7	125m	1300m	✔	3	400	+358-976 431 062
Kasurila	8	102m	700m	✔	5	0	+338-971 416 100
Kaustinen	5	60m	500m	✔	4	130	+358-968 8611 810
Laajavuori	4	100m	800m	✔	4	470	+358-941 311 1087
Lakis	3	90m	700m	✔	3	100	+358-966 565 1575
Rinteet	7	145m	104m	✔	5	600	+358-973 673 141
Mustavaara	7	90m	720m	✔	3	0	+359-973 719 890
Para	4	72m	580m	✔	3	0	+359-962 2672 960
Pukkivuori	2	55m	350m	✔	3	0	+359-934 475 5600
Purnuvuori	4	100m	700m	✔	2	25	+359-918 160 904
Riihivuori	7	120m	800m	✔	4	300	+359-941 3731 911
Vatuski	8	55m	450m	✔	2	0	+359-972 555 3353
Southern Finland							
Alhovuori	9	80m	650m	✔	6	0	+359-90-226 2553
Ellivuori	5	86m	800m	✔	5	0	+359-932 525 4111
Kalpalinna	18	92m	450m	✔	18	30	+359-917 688 1484
Kulomaki	4	80m	440m	✔	3	0	+359-914 488 283
Meri-Teijo	8	80m	600m	✔	3	300	+359-924 363 880
Messila	9	111m	800m	✔	9	120	+359-918 86 011
Myllymaki	5	70m	400m	✔	4	0	+359-953 413 3733
Peuramaa	9	55m	440m	✔	10	0	+359-90 296 2055
Ruosniemi	3	30m	180m	✔	3	0	+359-939 639 3200
Salomonkallio	2	32m	250	✔	3	0	+359-939 537 4999
Sappe	6	120m	750m	✔	4	200	+359-936 538 2160
Talma	7	55m	450m	✔	6	0	+359-90 236 036
Tiirismaa	4	104m	700m	✔	4	0	+359-918 788 1331
Vihti Ski	6	82m	480m	✔	5	0	+359-90 227 1751

HIMOS

By no means the smallest resort in Finland, Himos is still a small place compared to southern Europe. Located in the mid-southern areas of Finland about 3 hours from the capital Helsinki, Himos is very popular with Lapland's snowboarders - especially freestylers. To make up for the boring terrain the resort provides two halfpipes and a fun park which they call 'The Street', with hits and rails. Covering two slope areas, the North and West, the 15 evenly matched runs are nothing to get excited about, they are extremely short, the longest only just manages about 1000m. Freestylers sessioning the park and pipe will stay content and novice freeriders will find a bit of terrain to stay happy on, with a couple of runs to progress on and a few trees to check out, Beginners have loads of easy flats to start on, but advanced riders will soon tire of the repetitiveness of covering the same runs. Full hire and instruction is available and as this is a soft boot country services are geared that way.

Lodging is available in a number chalets or hotels but nothing is cheap, and don't be expecting a happening night time scene. Overall, the place is not totally crap, it just doesn't offer much to do on or of the slopes.

Winter snowboard periods between Nov and April. No summer snowboarding

Vertical Drop	140m
Longest run	950km
Ride area	15 runs
Snowmaking covering 5 runs	

Terrain ability suits

● Beginner	40%
● Intermediate	33%
● Advanced	27%

2 Pipes and a Park

Number of lifts	10
1 Day adult pass	120,- Fim
1 Day board hire	110,- Fim

Himos Tourist Office
Himosvuori, 42100 Jamsa, Finland
(+358 -9 42 86 105
Reservations(+358 -9 42 86 105
Snowphone(+358 -9 42 86 105

Fly to Helsinki
Transfer time = 3 hours
by car bus or train.

TAHKO

Regarded by Finland's snowboarders as their number one resort, which when compared with much that is on offer in the country it's easy to see why. The I.S.F like it enough to hold events here. The terrain here is not bad, with runs that cut through trees, offering slopes to suit intermediate and novice riders. For the few who dare to be seen in hards you can cut a some big wide turns, however you won't be putting in too many before you hit the bottom. This is a soft boot place and offers freeriders the opportunity to progress on a number red runs, with some trees to check out including a small off piste section through the spruce. Advanced riders, are the ones who will find Tahko a pain; there is nothing here to test you or keep you interested for more than it takes to do all the 12 or so runs once. If all you want is to flop about for a few hours then fine, the reds will stimulate for a period. Freestylers have a good pipe and new school ground grommets have plenty of easy flats to spin over or fakie along. Beginners; this another easy to cope with resort but note: most lifts are drags.

There is a choice of accommodation near to the slopes but be aware, it's pricey here, as is partying - not that there is any of note. The best options are for groups staying in one of the chalet, and boozing on the duty frees.

Winter snowboard periods between Nov and April. No summer snowboarding

Vertical Drop	200m
Longest run	1200m
Ride area	12 runs
Snowmaking covering 12 runs	

Terrain ability suits

● Beginner	50%
● Intermediate	50%
● Advanced	0%

Half Pipes and Park

Number of lifts 9	
1 Day adult pass 120,- Fim	
1 Day board hire 120,- Fim	

Tahko Tourist Office
Tahko, Finland
+358 -9 71 464 8200
Reservations(+358 -9 71 464 8222
Snowphone(+358 -9 71 464 8200

Fly to Helsinki distance -450km
Domestic flight to Kuopio -55km
Siilinjarvi is the nearest train -40km
by car bus or train.

FRANCE

Fifty six and a half million French people are the lucky owners of some of the best snowboard resorts in the world and, without doubt, the most extreme and biggest areas in Europe. For all of France's faults; like their love of garlic or the blowing up of other peoples' countries for target practice, to the unacceptable constraints that the French ski authorities impose on snowboarding - their refusal to allow it to go it alone and be it's true self - the French have got it when it comes to mountains. Chamonix should be on the calling card of all snowboarders at some stage in their life, while Serre Chevalier has got to be the largest natural freestyle fun park in the whole world. Resorts vary from the old to the new, offering anything you may want to do on a snowboard, at any level. Like the Austrians, the French have also played an important role in shaping the way for European snowboarding, with a long time healthy attitude towards the sport despite the politics. However, unlike the Austrians or other European countries, the French have added a very distinctive style of their own in terms of the way they ride, and their image. The term Euro carving is as French as the Eiffel Tower. In the early days French riders only seemed interested in ski boots and plate bindings fixed to stiff boards, with no nose profile, clad in revolting flowerier Jumpers or all in one pink ski suites, wearing day-glo headbands; mention soft boots and you were thought of as suffering a bad foot complaint. Although there were freestylers around France in the mid eighties, they were very few and far between. One early French rider, known for his carving, is the Burton ace Jean Nerva, who wore softs early on. However, thankfully things have moved on and Freeride and Freestyle are as common as the carvers including Guillaume Chastagnol, a notable French freestyler who can ride the pipe as well as many a Scandy or Yank. The French dominate Slalom titles, Nicolas Conte, Philippe Conte, Eric Rey, Alexis Parmentier and Isabelle Blanc to name but a few. One of the reason why there are so many top French carvers may come from the fact that to teach snowboarding in France you must first be a skier, and take a ski instructors test that includes race training, this gives rise to the high levels of quality carvers.

Rider: Regis Roland- Photo: A Snowboards - Les Arcs

Resort Page finder

FRANCE

What makes French resorts stand out from the rest of Europe is the actual difference in the resorts themselves, some are simply ugly with great terrain but dodgy lifts while others are modern in all aspects, but there's no uniformity as in Austria. Of note is Flaine; it looks like a nuclear power station perched up a mountain, while Serre Chevalier has a mixture of the old and new that somehow won't mix. Avoriaz defies true description and Val Thorens is simple and basic.

Good facilities are commonplace though. In the villages or in some case towns, most that goes on will suit snowboarders. You can find cheap accommodation with the French favouring apartments which are easy to get extra bodies in. Fast food, good bars, places to hang with pool all go towards creatinga good snowboard scene. However, France is the favourite destination for British skiers who flock here in their thousands brining their sad apres ski with them.

Getting to French resorts is no drama, you could suffer the stigma and go with a Ski tour operator who will be able to offer some really cheap deals, or alternatively there are now a number of good snowboard holiday companies to go with. Most resorts are reached by road and when you travel through France on route, avoid the motorway toll roads they will sting you dearly in the pocket, travel at night and use the quiet A roads. Flying to France there's a number of routes with the principle airports for connection to resorts being Grenoble, Lyon, Chambery and Geneva in Switzerland. Some resorts can be reached by train direct or by train and then bus. Whichever, train services in France are excellent. On the money side, France is not cheap, but you can get by if you eat fast food or buy from supermarkets (where booze is really cheap) and leave out the over-priced restaurants. That goes for discos too; late night bars are just as good. Working in France is possible in bars, restaurants or shops but without a ski nstructors' certificate, teaching snowboarding is not allowed, ski schools keep a close eye on what is going on the slopes, however you can do snowboard guiding.

Finally beer in France is good, food's OK and music dodgy if its French.

French Snowboard Population 45,000
Federation de Snowboard
Le Solaris
Z.A de Pre
Tel +33 76 52 37 74
Set up in 1987 now has 4000 members
Independent of the french skiing associations
To Join cost from 170 ff, a year and is open to foreign riders to join.

Overall French snowboard Champion for 1996/7
Male – Romain Retsin
Female – Marie Classu
Austrian snowboard styles favour
Freestyle 10% – Freeride 30% - Alpine 60%.
Soft boots 50% – Hard boots 50%.

Most favoured French resort:
Avoriaz / Tignes / Isola 2000
Most popular French snowboard personalities
Jean Nerva and David Vincent
Most famous French snowboard personalities
J. Claude Killy and Alain Prost
French snowboard magazines:
Snowsurf – Surf Neige – Snowbeat

Snowboard Manufactures (40 in all)
Hot   +33-0-8460 00 80
A Boards   +33-0-8460 00 80
Oxbow   +33-0-8460 00 80

Travel.
Fly – Air France Central reservations
0181 742 6600

Rider : Ian Felton · Photo: Stig

FACT FILE

Map labels: Strasbourg, Lille, Calais, Dunkerque, Boulogne-sur-mer, Dieppe, Le Havre, Paris, Reims, Dijon, Nantes, Clermont-Ferrand, Bordeaux, Bayonne, Toulouse, Marseille, Nice, Monaco, Geneva, Avoriaz, Flaine, Chamonix, Bourg-saint-maurice, La Plagne, Courcheval, Alberville, Serre Chevalier, Aix-les-bains, Chambéry, Grenoble, Lyon, Les Deux Alpes

Photo credits: Rider Edo Brass, Les Deux Alpes. Photo A. Green

Status	Republic
Capital	Paris
Area	543,965 sq km
Population	56,500,000
Density	104 people per sq km
Language	French
Currency	Franc
Neighbouring Countries	Belgium - Luxembourg - Germany- Switzerland - Italy - Spain
Winter snowboard periods	October to May
Summer snowboarding	May to September
Highest Mountain	Mont Blanc 4808 m
Country Snowboard styles	Freeride/Freestyle -40%
Alpine/Caring	60%
Soft boots	50%
Hard boots	50%
Drugs	Cannabis and dope are illegal through out France
Death penalty	None in France
Military Service	Until recently compulsory now though voluntary
Alcohol drinking age	Age 18.
Age of consent for sex	Male 16-Female 16
Prostitution	Illegal

105

AVORIAZ

Avoriaz is easily one of the top French snowboard resorts and is seen by many as the snowboard resort capital of Europe. The management here have been very positive in the promotion of the sport for instance Avoriaz was one of the first areas to have a snowboard only section with a pipe, park and ride area with its only lift not open to skiers. Further more the resort has been producing a snowboarders passport covering all aspects about Avoriaz for a number years. The 150 km of piste in Avoriaz link up with a number of areas in both France and Switzerland creating one of the largest in Europe with some major of piste to shred. However what's on offer in Avoriaz is more than enough to begin with, providing terrain to suite every level and style of rider whether its trees, big cliff drops, powder bowls or easy wide flats its all here. Freestylers flock here for the natural hits and big air opportunities, some of the best is found around the Linderets area, as well as the that available in the fun park with loads of obstacles and the pipe which is deep and long and has sounds blasting out. The resort is as much suited to carvers as well as freeriders, with plenty of wide open slopes for Euros to lay out big turns, the reds down the Chavanette and the Arare are the dogs for edging the board over while freeriders with bottle will find the steep blacks on Hauts Forts worth a go. Beginners should find Avoriaz no problem with plenty of easy flats around the base area to try out the first falls, before progressing up to higher blues and reds which can be reached by chair lifts which will help those who cant get to grip with T-bars and Pomma button lifts. Riders really wanting some major off piste can try heli-boarding across the Alps with prices from 250F a person for a trip and its worth it.

Every one gets the odd off day and will fancy doing something other than riding, in Avoriaz they put on services normal found in US resorts, Quad riding and Snowmobiles are a buzz but don't bail the machines it could hurt.

As for Avoriaz's village the first thing to point is if your in to burning things then leave your matches at home because the buildings here are made of wood, tons of it, however it caters well for snowboarders not being fancy, there are plenty of cheap food places and night time hang outs are cool with a number of good options. For snowboard needs call in on Street Trash a well established snowboard shop with a long reputation and good attitude.

Winter snowboard periods between Dec and April.

No summer snowboarding

Top Station	2350m
Resort height	1800m
Vertical Drop	1093m
Longest run	5km
Ride area	150km of piste
Snowcannons	18

Terrain ability suits

● Beginner	54%
● Intermediate	33%
● Advanced	13%

Terrain Ride styles suits

Freeride	40%
Freestyle	30%
Alpine/Carve	30%

Half pipe and park with sounds.
Snowboard only area with pass - 100F a day

1996/97 Lift Pass price guide
Covers Portes Du Soleil
*French Franc

	Low season		High season	
	Child	Adult	Child	Youth
½ day	92	139	92	139
1 day	131	199	131	199
5 days	531	804	531	804
7 days	677	1026	677	1026
Season	2269	3435	2269	3435

Lifts open 8.45am to 4pm week

Cable Cars	1
Bubble Cars	2
Chair lifts	20
Drag lifts	19

Photo: Avoriaz Resort

SNOWBOARD INSTRUCTION
1 day lesson   220F
5 days lesson   1000F
(+30-0-50 74 12 64)

SNOWBOARD & BOOT HIRE
1 day hire for standard B&B 150f
5 day hire for standard B&B 680f
Junior boards 110-130cm 1 day B&B 135f

SNOWBOARD REPAIR/SERVICE
Full base Tune service

SNOWBOARD SHOP/S
STREET TRASH +39-0-50 74 18 01
Sales-Hire-Repair
(independent snowboard shop J)
EMERY PRO SHOP (+39-0-50 74 12 64)
Sales-Hire-Repair & Instruction
(Ski/Snowboard shop)

Heli-boarding 1 trip from 250F per person
Info +39-0-50 74 11 13

Snowmobile rides 150F to 300F.

Quad bikes from 40F to 90F

Hangliding for beginners 300F
Paragliding 30 minutes 300F

Climbing School and Wall

Skateboard ramps in village

LIFE STYLE
Eat at - MARIE BRIOCHE (24hr)

NIGHT TIME HANGOUTS
Le Choucas
The Place

Photo: Jacquot Bertrand

Accommodation
Reservations +39-50 74 72 72

CHALET SNOWBOARD
For a week's snowboard trip
which includes guiding
Tel-(UK) 01235 767 182

Avoriaz Tourist Office
Place Centrale
74110 Avoriaz
39 - 50 74 02 11

Fly Geneva International Airport

Transfer from the airport;

By bus approximately 3 hours journey to resort.

By train to Thorn les Bains 30 minutes from the
resort transfer by bus.

By car hire approximately 2 hours driving to resort.

Driving from home Avoriaz is 650 km from Paris,
motorway via Macon, Bourg en Bresse, Bellegrade
and Clues.,- Roads via Taninges, Les Gets,
Moraine = Avoriaz.

CHAMONIX

If you get the opportunity to visit Chamonix do whatever your age or ability, because this place has to be seen to be believed. The first ski trails were here over a hundred years ago and have grown into 11 separate snowboardable areas. A regular bus service runs to each area making life stress-free at no charge if you have a lift pass. The lift system in each area is easy to use and well linked together, giving you access to so much off-piste riding you'll never get to see it all. Although Chamonix is recognised worldwide for its extreme terrain it also has very varied terrain to suit everyone and contrary to popular belief beginners can ride Chamonix, the easy slopes at Les Planards and Les Chosalis are perfect for trying the early manoeuvres before progressing up to the runs at Le Tour and Le Brevent. Freeriders wanting to cut it here should take the cable car to the top of the Brevent which offer you a couple of testing runs back to the mid point. However Freeriders wanting to experience the real Chamonix will buckle up with glee when they see what's on offer up at Argentiere, any rider who is easily intimidated forget it this is the DOGS balls, the powder and off piste Utopia of Europe. Be warned though the off piste here can be extremely dangerous and you should not venture too far without a guide and certainly not without studying a piste map, bail this place and its bye bye. That said the experience you will get from the terrain is orgasmic and is only really suited to those in softs. Hard boot carvers stick to the piste. Freestylers don't really need a fun park or pipe as there's so much natural stuff with major cliffs to drop off and trees to cut through. However, the locals aided by the Dope lads have built a cool fun park area in Le Tour, which has quarter pipes and half pipes to play on if the real stuff is to much.

Chamonix is not a resort as such, but a town with loads of character and home to local pro rider Babs who now rides his own signature board for Nidecker. The town which has loads going on is not in easy reach of the slopes, you will need to bus around which doesn't run at night, though taxis do. There are plenty of inexpensive places to kip with a number of Bunk house to lay out in. Night time is full on snowboard lifestyle with loads of cool hangouts, check out ET, a bar run by snowboarders where you can also get your hair cut. Guinness and cheap food is best served at the Jeckyll and Hyde. Be aware that Chamonix may not look an expensive place but it can be.

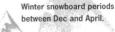

Winter snowboard periods between Dec and April.

No summer snowboarding

Top Station	3806m
Resort height	1035m
Vertical Drop	2773m
Longest run	21km
Ride area	171km of piste.
Snowmaking	75+ cannons

Terrain ability suites

● Beginner	35%
● Intermediate	45%
● Advanced	20%

Terrain Ride styles suites

Freeride	60%
Freestyle	35%
Alpine/Carve	5%

Half pipe and park at Le Tour

Page rider, Viv Jenkins from
Liverpool England
Sponsored by Liquid Snowboards

Lift Pass price guide
(for all Chamonix lifts except the Logan cable car (French Franc)

	Adult	Child
1 day	350	250
3 days	510	360
4 day	660	460
5 days	790	550
7 days	1050	740
Adult season pass from 4100F		

Lifts open 8.30am to 4pm daily

Cable Cars	4
Mountain Trains	1
Gondolas	4
Chair lifts	17
Drag lifts	30

Photo: Chamonix Resort

Rider : Ben Graham, photo Alex Badley

SNOWBOARD INSTRUCTION
3 ½ day lessons 670ff

SNOWBOARD & BOOT HIRE
1 day hire for standard B&B 148f
5 day hire for standard B&B 670f
Junior boards 110-130cm 1 day B&B 128f

SNOWBOARD SHOP/S
CHAMONIX MOUNTAIN BIKES
+33-50 53 54 76
Sales-Hire-Repair
(Bike snowboard shop)
SPORT EXTREME +33-50 55 98 50
Sales-Hire-Repair
(Ski/Snowboard shop)

Hangliding
Paragliding

Climbing School and Wall

Skate boarding
Ramps in Silences half an hour away.
Plenty of rails and street action in Chamonix

Accommodation
Reservations +33-50 53 23 33

LIFE STYLE
Eat at -
THE JECKYL AND HYDE
ICE ROCK CAFE
LE BREVENT
THE OFFICE

A Chamonix hamburger costs from 15f

Le Belvedere bunk House
ARGENTIERE
+33 -50 54 02 59

Chamonix Tourist Office
BP25-45 Place du Triangle de l'Amite,
74400 Chamonix , Mont Blanc
France.
+33 - 50 53 00 24

NIGHT TIME HANGOUTS
Et - snowboarders hangout
chilled beer 10f
Mill Street- loud tunes
a beer costs from 15f
La Cantina - Hip-hop, Jazz and Jungle
a beer costs

Fly to Geneva
International Airport

Transfer from the airport;

By bus approximately 2 1/2
hours journey to resort.
Fare from 290F

By train stop in the centre
of Chamonix.

By car hire approximately
1Ω hours driving to resort.

Drive via A 40 or Autoroute
Blanche 205 to Chamonix
16 km from Switzerland at

Cole des Montets and 11km
from Italy via the Mont
Blanc tunnel.

109

COURCHEVEL

Courchevel; over priced, over hyped and frequented by fur clad Channel No 5 smelling, high spending Frenchies from the cities, mixed with the large package tour groups from the UK. However with all that Courchevel is actually a good place to ride and forms part of the three valleys area, a massive grouping of resorts and snowboard terrain. Like big areas offering kilometre after kilometre of slopes, there is certainly something here to allow all riders to perform, with steeps, wide runs, good off piste and easy flats for novices. This is an area that you are not going to do, all in the space of a weeks trip and remember it. The runs are set out on three levels, 1550, 1650 and 1850, and all provide separate services. 1850 and 1650 link very closely and have most of the main runs. What you find on 1650 isn't that different although it tends to be a little less crowded with some good terrain for beginners such as The Pyramide a long blue which is ideal for trying out those first linked turns. 1650 offers freeriders some good off piste opportunities although there is just as much to search out up on 1850 which can be accessed easily from the village. The cluster of blacks with steeps and couloirs up at La Saulire area will set the old heart pumping. The reds here are also going to suit freeriders as much as you Euro carvers - the wide runs allow the chance to pose in front of other piste visitors as you edge from heel to toe extending the arm and laying out the hand in the snow. Freeriders and new school grommets will find plenty of stuff to leave many a ski school group shaking as you fakie past at 90km an hour doing 180 ground spins next to the last in the group before wiping out the instructor at the lead, (collect points on Brit skiers). The snowboard area on 1850 where you can get some cool air is thankfully free of two plankers. If you're looking for serious air Courchevel has a big ski jump.

Lodging is spread out in the three numbered areas, with chalets and apartments the norm, and being a Franc hungry resort be warned food and night time don't come cheap, so make good use of the supermarkets and scam skiers beers in the pubs. Avoid discos like the plague unless you find some ones gold credit card or fat wallet then you can unload it and have a ball at someone else's expense.

Winter snowboard periods between Dec and May.

No summer snowboarding

Top Station	3199m
Resort height	15/16/1850m
Vertical Drop	1402m
Longest run	5km
Ride area	180km of piste
(linked with other resorts)	650km
Snowmaking	11km

Terrain ability suits

● Beginner	49%
● Intermediate	37%
● Advanced	14%

Terrain Ride styles suits

Freeride	45%
Freestyle	5%
Alpine/Carve	50%

Snowboard areas with pipe on 1850.
For competent riders Plantrey slope
For beginners Verdons slope

Courchevel lift Pass price
1550-1650-1850

French Franc

	Adult	Child (-16 years)
1 day	180	125
2 days	348	244
6 days	863	604
7 days	950	665
Season	3930	2750

Lifts open 8.30am to 4pm week

Cable Cars	1
Gondolas	9
Chair lifts	16
Drag lifts	41
Bucket lifts	1

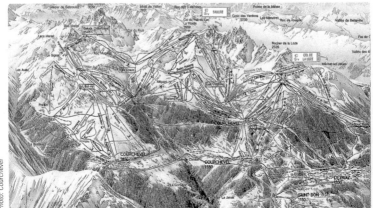

SNOWBOARD INSTRUCTION
3 days x 2 hours 400F
5 days x 2 hours 650F

SNOWBOARD & BOOT HIRE
1 day hire from 95-130F

SNOWBOARD SHOP/S
HOOKIPA SURF -at 1850
Sales-Hire-Repair +33 79 08 12 61
(independent snowboard shop)

SNOW COCO -at 1850
Sales-Hire-Repair +33 - 79 08 37 61
(Independent snowboard shop)

Heli-boarding +33 - 79 08 00 91

Snowmobiles +33 -79 08 15 43

Rafting on snow +33 -79 08 39 60

Ice Climbing +33-79 08 39 60
Climbing Wall at 1850. +33 -79 08 19 50

Hangliding /Paragliding +33 79 08 39 60

LIFE STYLE

Laundries at 1550,1650,1850.

Night Time
L'Equipe
The Refuge Club
Kalico bar
L'Albatross

Courchevel Tourist Office
Mintel 3615 Courchevel
+33-36 68 73 03
http://www.courchevel.com

Fly to Lyon
International Airport

By train to Moutiers then
transfer by bus.

Transfer from the airport;

By car hire approximately 2
hours driving to resort.

By bus approximately 3 1/2
hours journey to resort. Fare
from 290F *******

Driving from home use as a
map reference Paris- Moutiers
Autoroute A43/RN90 to
Moutiers = Courchevel.

FLAINE

Flaine is a purpose built 60's mess that architects must have designed in the space of 5 minutes and built with 5 million tons of waste concrete. Ugly? The ski world, who this place was designed for, keep moaning about it. You can't open a journal without the place being slagged off in some respect. So what if it is an eyesore? As far as snowboarding is concerned, it offers some good and varied terrain for any rider at any stage of their ability. Flaine sits in a big bowl which forms part of the Grand Massif area which includes the linked resorts of Samoens, Morillon, and Les Carroz collectively offering 260km or so of piste to slide over. Like most of France, Flaine has loads of good areas for Alpine carvers to show off on. The area seems to attract a lot of Euros in hards who can be seen cranking down the long reds and steep blacks. Freeriders in softs are in a minority here even though the terrain offers some great opptunities for off piste riding with some long intresting runs to tackle, the area above the Samoens lift is pretty good while the trees into Les Carroz will give you a good lesson on how to treat wood at speed. Advanced riders should check out the Combe de Gers which is a steep back bowl that drops away with 700 meters of vert, (dont bail this one). To get the best off piste riding its worth going with a guide at the beginning of a trip so you find the best spots inorder to try out later on, a guide will cost about 360F for 2 hours and is worth it. Heli boarding also offers a good way to explore the out of reach stuff, a single trip will set you back about 1500F which is a few beer chits. Even though this is a bit of a Euro carvers hangout Freestyler are going to find plenty of hits and theres a pipe if the natural stuff is not your cup of tee. L-plate riders have a number of easy flat runs close to the village area reached by foot which are serviced by a free lift, how ever to progess you will need to buy a pass a head up to the more intreasting runs, theres a coupe of long blues leading away form the top of the Les Grandes Platieres cable car that will allow novices to find out what linking tuns are like.

Flaine is not a massive or happening village, nor is it the most expensive. Lodging is basic and apartments are the main bed spots. Night time is noisy and you can have a good time even with the mixture of apre ski and Brits around. To really find out about Flaine call in at Backside snowboard shop these guys have been here for years and no there stuff.

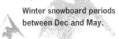

Winter snowboard periods between Dec and May.

No summer snowboarding

Top Station	2500m
Resort height	1600 m
Vertical Drop	900m
Longest run	14km
Ride area	150km of piste
(linked with other resorts)	260km
Snowmaking	80 cannons

Terrain ability suits

● Beginner	10%
● Intermediate	6525
● Advanced	14%

Terrain Ride styles suits

Freeride	50%
Freestyle	20%
Alpine/Carve	30%

Half Pipe	Yes
Fun park	Yes

Flaine lift Pass price guide
1550-1650-1850
* French Franc

	Adult	Child. (-16 years)
½ day	135	107
1 day	153	117
2 days	330	250
5 days	770	550
7 days	945	665
Season	3200	2400

Lifts open 9am to 4.30pm week

Cable Cars	1
Gondolas	1
Chair lifts	6
Drag lifts	15
Rope Tows	1

Photo: Flaine photo 2000

SNOWBOARD INSTRUCTION
6 day lessons with 3 hours a day 695F

SNOWBOARD & BOOT HIRE
1 day hire for standard B&B 115F
6 day hire for standard B&B 600F

SNOWBOARD SHOP/S
BACK SIDE (+33 - 50 90 85 16
Sales-Hire-Repair-Instruction
(independent snowboard shop J)

Heli boarding +33 - 50 90 80 01

Snowmobiles +33 -50 90 83 06

Ice Driving School +33-50 90 82 59

Climbing Wall +33 -50 90 80 74

Hangliding /Paragliding +33 79 08 39 60

LIFE STYLE

Eat at
L'Eloge for fast food.
Chez Daniel for pizza, delivery service
+33-50 90 80 06

Night Time hangouts
White Grouse Pub, for Booze
Cimes Rock Cafe, Live music
Le Diamant Noir, Booze and Pool

Accommodation
Reservations +33-50 90 80 01

HOME INTERNATIONAL
APARTMENTS AND STUDIOS
+33-50 90 82 93

Flaine Tourist Office
74300 Cluses
+33-50 90 80 01

By train to Clues then
transfer by bus.

Fly to Geneva International
Airport

By car hire approximately
1Ω hours driving to resort.

Transfer from the airport;

Geneva - Chamonix autoroute
to Cluses. Via the N205
towards Sallanches-route
D6 to Flaine.

By bus approximately 2 hours
journey to resort. Single fare
from 220F

FRANCE – FLAINE

LA PLAGNE

La Plagne; another sixties throw back that is now a nineties carvers paradise. This high up snow-sure, purpose built resort is a strange affair of 11 villages nestled above below and amidst the trees. Collectively the villages link up to form an area of some 210 kilometers of terrain that is full on for carvers of all levels, OK for the intermediate freeriders who like the piste and don't like being intimidated by scary black runs. It is boring for hard core freestylers but perfect for L-plate riders with loads of easy terrain to get going on. This a very popular resort and is visited by the mass ski crowds, however snowboarders are just as welcome and can roam freely over the whole mountain. Ease and convenience is the key factor here; all the slopes are reached easily and boarding to and from your beds is a dream.

The hundred and eleven lifts travel in every direction linking all the runs in one way or another. Carvers who want to go fast and simply pose on the wide open runs will find this place hard to beat it really is hard boot 360 snow carving territory. The red run Roche de Mio which takes you down to Les Bauches is a piste worth a visit for intermediate riders. The less accomplished hard booters will find the easy wide blues in the main La Plagne bowl the area for learning how to hold an edge, while advanced riders who know how to hold an edge can prove it by cutting some snow on the long steep black runs down from Bellecote. Freeriders fancying some off piste hard core extreme, this is not your place. However, the runs on the glacier down to Les Bauches do offer some hope as does the Col du Nant which will test you out. Freestylers are left cold here. There's no park or pipe and no plans for one, and the terrain is not the greatest for natural stuff, all said though, there are hits to be found and new school grommets with twin tips will find the wide piste excellent for doing ground tricks in and out of ski groups. The number of ski schools here make it easy to get tuition at every level though its all geared to teaching carving rather than freeriding and freestyle.

As far staying at La Plagne; with a choice of some 45,000 beds there's a big selection which is largely apartment blocks and chalets that vary is size and cost. Overall this isn't a scary money place but there again there's not much to spend your money on. Nightlife is naff with few options or good choices. Still you could try out the Olympic Bob Run or the Bob Raft which should set the old ticker racing.

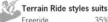

Winter snowboard periods between Dec and April.

No summer snowboarding

Top Station	3250m
Resort height	2100m
Vertical Drop	2000m
Longest run	15km
Ride area	210km of piste
Snowmaking	50 cannons

Terrain ability suite

Beginner	12%
Intermediate	55%
Advanced	33%

Terrain Ride styles suits

Freeride	35%
Freestyle	5%
Alpine/Carve	60%

No Half Pipe
No Fun park

La Plagne lift Pass price guide
* French Franc

	Low season		High season	
	Adult	Child	Adult	Child
½ day	117	88	156	117
1 day	160	120	213	160
5 days	630	475	840	630
7 days	840	630	1120	840
Season	4800	3600	4800	3600

Lifts open 9am to 5.pm

Cable Cars	1
Gondolas	8
Chair lifts	32
Drag lifts	70

Photo: La Plagne resort

SNOWBOARD INSTRUCTION
$\frac{1}{2}$ day lesson 160F
3 $\frac{1}{2}$ day lessons 395F
5 $\frac{1}{2}$ day lessons 430F

SNOWBOARD REPAIR SERVICE
Hot Wax & edge service 170F

1 day hire for standard B&B 120F
6 day hire for standard B&B 765F

SNOWBOARD SHOP/S
Hire and sales are available in
any one of 35 ski shops.

Snowmobiles 1 hour ride cost 340F

Bob Sleigh a ride cost 460F
Bob Rafts a ride cost 170F

3 Climbing Walls

Hangliding/Paragliding
cost from 400F a flight

LIFE STYLE

Laundrette = yes

Eat at
Loads of places to eat, with cheap to dodgy
priced restaurants. Lots of Pizza joints.

Night Time hangouts
Loads of bars and Discos spread out between
all the villages, King Cafe is popular live
music hangout.

Accommodation
Reservations
+33-79 09 79 79

La Plagne Tourist Office
Le Chalet BP 62-F73211
Aime Cedex. France
+33-79 09 79 79

Fly to Geneva
International Airport

Transfer from the airport;

By bus approximately 3 hours
journey to resort. Return fare
from 360F

By train to Aime 15 minutes
to the resort transfer by bus.

By car hire approximately
2 hours driving to resort.

Motorway to Albertville
(A43 & A430) to
Moutiers = :La Plagne

FRANCE – LA PLAGNE

115

LES DEUX ALPES

After winding your way up a long steep road you eventually arrive at Les Deux Alpes often written with a 2. However whichever way you write it, this is one of those high altitude all year round purpose built resorts that doesn't resemble a nuclear power station. As you drive through its quite an impressive place which isn't totally matched on the slopes, although what is on offer is good. It could become somewhat repetitive if you're staying a long time. This resort may not be in the major league of big area resorts but it still has a qualifying 200 kilometres of slopes that serve advanced and intermediate riders while giving grace to beginners. The resort has played host to one of the largest known gathering of snowboarders where everyone is involved. The Mondial snowboard exhibition (French distributors public board test) is an event that attracts thousands of riders from all over France and abroad. The event is held at the beginning of the season and the resort now closes the area to skiers to make it snowboard only. Back in 1993, so many unexpected snowboarders turned up a mini riot occured. There is also a series of races which attract the pro's; it is definitely worth going. The terrain, which is fairly featureless, will no doubt keep carvers happy with plenty of wide motorway runs, though they won't test the advanced rider too much. Most of the flats are blue grade with a few reds that run back into the village. Freeriders who can ride will find the 12 kilometre un-pisted run down to Le Grave the dogs bollocks especially if fresh snow has dumped. Novices should give this a miss, although the top section is gentle it doesn't stay that way. At La Grave you can take the Cable car back up and make your way back to the main area. There are a few flat areas at the base for beginners to get started on but the best novice runs are up at the top sections which allow for long rides back into the village. This is not a top freestyle place but is serves ok with a pipe when conditions are favourable. The local ski schools look after basic snowboard tuition up to advanced.

Les Deux Alpes offers loads of apartments as well as a number of good chalets and hotels. For budget seasoners there's even a Hostel, and plenty of cheap food joints. Night time is OK with bars frequented by Brits on ski packages. If the village area is free of snow, skaters will find some street action in the centre shopping complex.

Snowboarding all year round, Summer snowboarding best between May and August

Top Station	3568m
Resort height	1650m
Vertical Drop	1999m
Longest run	12km
Ride area	200km of piste
Snowmaking	4 km of piste

Terrain ability suits

● Beginner	62%
● Intermediate	28%
● Advanced	10%

Terrain Ride styles suits

Freeride	50%
Freestyle	15%
Alpine/Carve	35%

Half pipe in the winter is not always maintained, but is looked after in the summer.

Lifts open 9am to 5.pm

Cable Cars	1
Gondolas	4
Mountain trains	1
Chair lifts	25
Drag lifts	30

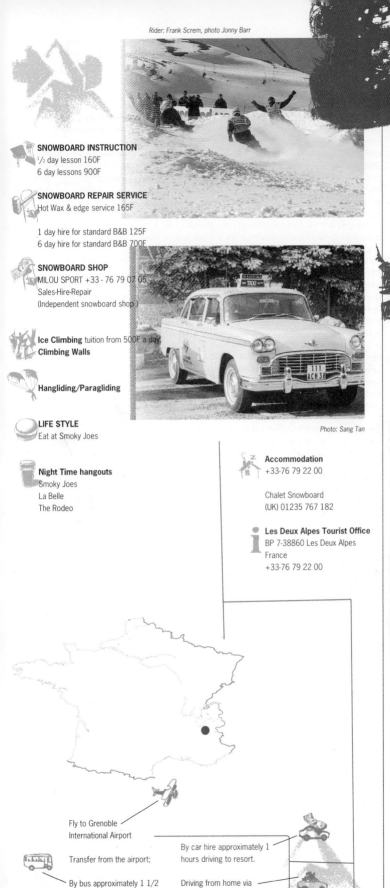

Rider: Frank Screm, photo Jonny Barr

SNOWBOARD INSTRUCTION
½ day lesson 160F
6 day lessons 900F

SNOWBOARD REPAIR SERVICE
Hot Wax & edge service 165F

1 day hire for standard B&B 125F
6 day hire for standard B&B 700F

SNOWBOARD SHOP
MILOU SPORT +33 - 76 79 07 05
Sales-Hire-Repair
(Independent snowboard shop.)

Ice Climbing tuition from 500F a day.
Climbing Walls

Hangliding/Paragliding

LIFE STYLE
Eat at Smoky Joes

Photo: Sang Tan

Night Time hangouts
Smoky Joes
La Belle
The Rodeo

Accommodation
+33-76 79 22 00

Chalet Snowboard
(UK) 01235 767 182

Les Deux Alpes Tourist Office
BP 7-38860 Les Deux Alpes
France
+33-76 79 22 00

Fly to Grenoble
International Airport

Transfer from the airport;

By bus approximately 1 1/2
hours journey to resort.
Return fare from 360F

N/A.

By car hire approximately 1
hours driving to resort.

Driving from home via
Grenoble route RN 91 to the
Lac du Chambon dam and
then the D213 to Les Deux
Alpes. Grenoble 70km.

SERRE CHEVALIER

Serre Chevalier is simply the dogs B's with heaps of major terrain, tight and open trees to weave through, extreme drop offs to get the adrenalin going, big bowls with silly amounts of good powder, countless banks and gullies, super fast flats to push the hair back, hits everywhere and a giant, natural fun park all located next to an unassuming old fashioned French village. This is a great place, as one local rider once put it "who needs fun parks when this place is a complete fun park at every level and distinction?" Serre Chevalier is for everyone with an area that links up with Briancon and Le Monetier to provide 230 kilometers of terrain, Serre Che's area is the biggest and is where the best happenings are, open and tight trees gullies and bowls, long steps and hits every where for freeriders and freestylers, advanced riders are simply going to wet themselves with this lot, its perfect soft boot territory, there are dozens of runs for intermediate riders to check out with carving areas for hardbooters. If you want wide expanses of powder without having to hike, check out the stuff of the Balme chairlift. For those who have the bottle, the Olympique, a black race run basing out at Chantemerle is certainly going to set the adrenalin off, you can get serious speed down this one, advanced riders as well competent intermediate boarders will manage it but novices should give it a miss. The runs around Frejus are more suited to first timers with a number of easy runs that bring you back down into the village via some tree trails, a point to watch is that some of the drag lifts can be a nightmare, often travelling at length in speeds suited to riding down not up. Watch out for the sharp turns that some pommas make through the trees. Master Serre Chevaliers drags and you will have no trouble anywhere else in the universe. Freestylers simply go and session the lot because hits, jumps and trails are everywhere. There is also a man-made fun park and pipe should you need it.

The convenient options for accommodation and slopes are either Chantemerle which has apartments along with a few lively bars. Villeneuve which is a couple of kilometers away also has apartments as well as chalets and some old style hotels, like Chantemerle there are a number of shops and watering holes but on the whole the villages are low key, good but not bright lights stuff, don't bother with any of the discos silly money for beer, stay in the bars where you'll find live music and beer till very late.

Photo Tourist Office Serre Chevalier

Snowboarding between December and April.

No summer snowboarding.

Top Station	2830m
Resort height	1400m
Vertical Drop	1450m
Longest run	15km
Ride area	250km of piste
Snowmaking	13 km of piste

Terrain ability suits

Beginner	42%
Intermediate	46%
Advanced	12%

Terrain Ride styles suits

Freeride	60%
Freestyle	30%
Alpine/Carve	10%

Fun park has hits and a half pipe

Page rider Euan Baxter
from Nethybridge Scotland

Area lift Pass price guide
French Franc

	Adult	Child
1/2 day	127	87
6 days	835	550
7 days	920	605
14 days	1480	960
Season	3255	2115

Lifts open 8.30am to 4pm

Cable Cars	3
Gondolas	6
Chair lifts	16
Drag lifts	47

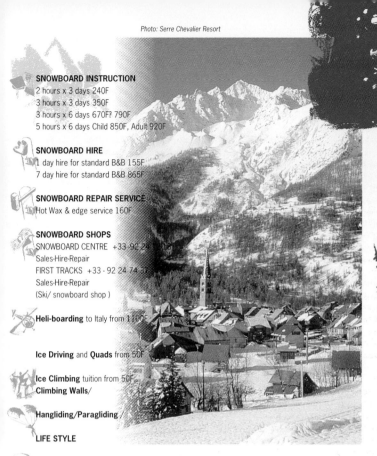

Photo: Serre Chevalier Resort

SNOWBOARD INSTRUCTION
2 hours x 3 days 240F
3 hours x 3 days 350F
3 hours x 6 days 670F? 790F
5 hours x 6 days Child 850F, Adult 920F

SNOWBOARD HIRE
1 day hire for standard B&B 155F
7 day hire for standard B&B 865F

SNOWBOARD REPAIR SERVICE
Hot Wax & edge service 160F

SNOWBOARD SHOPS
SNOWBOARD CENTRE +33-92 24 ?? ???
Sales-Hire-Repair
FIRST TRACKS +33 - 92 24 74 3?
Sales-Hire-Repair
(Ski/ snowboard shop)

Heli-boarding to Italy from 1100F

Ice Driving and **Quads** from 50F

Ice Climbing tuition from 50F
Climbing Walls/

Hangliding/Paragliding /

LIFE STYLE

Eat at
Le Frog
Le Refuge
Nocthambule

Laundrette = Yes

Night Time hangouts
White Hare Liever Blanc
Iceberg
La Grotte du Yeti

Photo: Lieve Blanch Hotel

FRANCE – SERRE CHEVALIER

Fly to Grenoble
International Airport

Transfer from the airport;

By bus approximately
2$^{1}/_{2}$ hours journey to resort.

By train to Briançon 10 minutes
to resort transfer by bus or taxi

By car hire approximately
2 hours driving to resort.

Via Grenoble route RN 91 to
Serre Chevalier= 108 Km

Accommodation
+33-92 24 71 88

Le Refuge
+33-92 24 78 08
Hotel Le Blanc
+33-92 24 74 05

Serre Chevalier Tourist Office
BP 20-05240 La Salle Les Alpes
France
+33-92 24 71 88
Snowphone +33-33-92 24 71 88

ST LARY

If you think that all French ski resorts are massive and purpose-built shams then think again because St Lary is neither massive or a collection of sad buildings aimed at cramming in skiers. This relatively small place has been operating as a ski resort since the 50's although the village which lies in the French Pyrenees goes back much longer. The main village of Saint Lary lies in the Aure Valley at 630 meters, above is located two small villages, Saint Lary La Cabane at 1600 meters and Saint Lary Pla D'Adret at 1700 meters, all three are connected by a series of lifts with the upper villages reached by road or from Saint Lary by a cable car which takes you up to the slopes. Today the resort has become a full on friendly snowboarders' area with 600 hectares of terrain that is best tackled by novices and riders with a few points on their score card. Advanced and hard core riders wanting major long steeps are going to find this place a bit to easy without that many challenges. The cluster of black graded runs of the Tortes Chair offer some opportunities for freeriders to excel on fairly featureless terrain, alternatively the area known as Bassia is pretty cool and will suite freeriders with some trees to check out lower down. The Arbizon, a new black run is also an interesting steep that will appeal to freeriders. Unfortunately freeriders looking for vast powder bowls are not going to get them here but alpine carvers looking for fast wide piste to lay the big turns will find the few reds OK and should provide those getting to grips with hard boots and asymmetric boards some early learning opportunities. However beginners will certainly find the easy blues spread out across the resort perfect for learning on, with a mixture of chair lifts and drags to ferry you around. The short, easy stuff reached from Saint Lary Pla D'Adret will sort you out before trying out the runs over on Vallon Du Portet. The Corniche is a long, easy blue that freeriding novices will soon be able to handle. New school freestylers will find most to interest them in the snowboard park on Vallon Du Portet which has a boarder cross circuit as well.

Accomodation and services here are limited but are nonetheless okay, with the majority of options in Saint Lary rather than up in the other two villages which do have beds and places to eat and drink in.

Winter snowboard periods between Dec and Apr
No summer snowboarding

Top Station	2450m
Resort height	830m
Vertical Drop	844m
Longest run	4km
Ride area	600 hectas.
Snowcannons	80

Terrain ability suits:

● Beginner	74%
● Intermediate	15%
● Advanced	10%

Terrain Ride styles suits:

Freeride	40%
Freestyle	10%
Alpine/Carve	50%

Fun park has hits and a half pipe

Lifts 32
No binding or leashes rules
6 day lift pass cost from 630F

Saint Larry Tourist Office
37 rue Principale -65170 Saint Lary
Soulan, France
(+33-62 39 50 81
Reservations(+33-62 39 40 29

Fly to Tarbes airport - 80 km to resort

Photo: St Lary resort

TIGNES

Tignes: the all year round snowboard favourite of many a snowboarder thanks to the Grande Motte Glacier. If you have been into the sport for a number of years you should already know of this place and its offerings. If you happen to be one of the many millions of newcomers to snowboarding then a little history:

Tignes is one of the major snowboard resorts of France and has long been hosting national and international events. Thoughout the year snowboard teams and manufacturers host training camps and events here. The most famous event to have taken place here was the Kebra Classic which soon became the event of the early season. Back in the late eighties, any rider who was anyone made it to the event, however sadly politics and money got in the way and the event soon became a no go situation.

Still Tignes is certainly not a no go place, the terrain on offer here is extensive. Tignes lies at 2100m and is reached after a drive over an impressive dam with a major piece of graffitti slap bang in the middle. Sufferers of vertigo should keep eyes closed going over as its a long way down. Tignes which links up with Val D'Isere on the mountain has some 300km of piste of all grades and having been an Olympic host the runs are certainly up to scratch. Advanced riders will be able to polish up on their skills on a number of decent blacks and loads of reds. Carvers of all abilities are provided with dozens of on piste options to lay out those carves, however if you have a decent freeriding board and want to put it to good use, then the off piste opportunities here are great, the best and sensible

option is to go with a guide. Situated at the Tomeuse chairlift is a place called Valtee Perdue where there is amazing off piste, but take it easy especially after fresh snow has dumped, as avalances in this area take little to trigger off. There are many lines you can choose to come down, one in particular is to the right on decent. In summer there's no chance of riding this but in the winter it's a 30m deep gorge, a bit like a giant Boardercross, at one point you have to take your board off and use a rope to drop through a hole to continue. Freestylers should be well satisfied with the terrain here with plenty of hits, cliffs, gullies and some trees to shred through, and if the natural stuff is not enough to excite you then check out the pipe and park off the Palafour chairlift .

Tignes for lodging and night life is split into two areas which are both in easy reach of the slopes and hangouts, the place is pricy but you can get by, there's quite a few bars and joints to eat in as well as the supermarket offerings. During the summer months, skaters are provided with a half pipe and some fun boxes in Le Lac. There are a number of good snowboard shops in Tignes that will be able to help you out, check out the famous Kebra Surfing or Sweet Snow for everything.

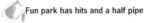

All year snowboard periods

Top Station	3500m
Resort height	2100m
Vertical Drop	1200m
Longest run	6km
Ride area	300 km of piste
(linked with Val D'Isere)	
Snowmaking	25km

Terrain ability suits

● Beginner	62%
● Intermediate	29%
● Advanced	9%

Terrain Ride styles suits

Freeride	50%
Freestyle	20%
Alpine/Carve	30%

Fun park has hits and a half pipe

Number of lifts	102

Rider;Siomon Smith - Photog San Tan

KEBRA SURFING
+33 92 243 74 37
Sales Hire instruction

SWEET SNOW
+33-79 06 39 92
Sales Hire instruction

Tignes Tourist Office
Centrale de reservation,
Access Minitel, France
(+33-79 06 15 55
Reservations(+33-79 06 15 55
Snowphone(+33-79 06 15 55

Fly- Lyon airport- 2 1/2 hours to resort

Page rider: Alban Thom from Scotland

VAL THORENS

Yet another purpose-built French resort with an overall holiday camp feel to it. Life began for Val Thorens back in the 70's and is said to be Europe's highest resort that has, since opening, had a good snow record throughout the winter months, while providing some summer snowboarding opportunities usually up to August. Don't be put off by the look as you approach because under the skin there's loads going on to make this place good. Part of the massive 3 Valleys area, Val sits up at 2300m at the end of a long road that passes through a couple of small resorts. The village which is totally car free sits in the middle of an array of slopes that rise from all angles out of the resort. One of the key factors about Val is its convenience; nothing is too far away from where you board, kip, eat or party. If you're on the lower levels of one of the many apartment blocks you may even be able to leap out of the nest, strap on the board, ollie over the balcony and land in a lift line ready to be dragged up to the wide open piste. The open expanse here provides some excellent terrain which suites intermediate and beginners most, with a large number of wide open pistes for carving in hards, to some cool soft boot freeriding territory. With a piste map check out some of the off piste terrain leading away to the right from the top of the Caron cable car, there's a decent black that runs under the cable car which is also worth a try, but novices stick to the runs of Moraine lift which is where you find some of the easy carving terrain. Freeriders wanting to play on some decent piste will do best to take the Funitel telecabine where your find a number of good reds to carve up and hits to leap off. Val doesn't have a park or pipe, so freestylers are going to have to make do with the natural stuff, which fortunately is in plentiful supply. There's cliffs to gain air off and new school grommets will find enough hits and rails to bonk over or grind on. A good freestyle area to check out for some serious air is off the Moutiere lift or the hits up and around the Funitel telecabine. Beginners can start out from the doorstep of their apartment on really easy basic flat pistes before going higher and harder.

Like France's other holiday camp style purpose built resorts, this place provides most accommodation in apartments, with all your services in easy reach of each other. Partying here is pretty full on but it may mean some mingling with the British apres ski lot who are very visible here.

Winter snowboard periods between Nov and May
Limited summer snowboarding periods

Top Station	3199m
Resort height	2300m
Vertical Drop	900m
Longest run	3km
Ride area	120 of piste
600 linked with Val D'Isere	
Snowmaking	60km

Terrain ability suits

● Beginner	49%
● Intermediate	37%
● Advanced	14%

Terrain Ride styles suits

Freeride	40%
Freestyle	20%
Alpine/Carve	40%

Lifts pass	5 days	680F
Number of lifts	27	

ABRAXAS SURF SHOP
+33 -79 00 0026
Sales, Hire, Instruction

3 V SPORTS
+33-79 00 01 72
Sales, Hire, Instruction

Snowboard tuition	5 days	610F
Snowboard hire	5 days	520F

Val Thorens Tourist Office
F-73440 Val Thorens,
Savoie-France
+33-79 00 08 08

Fly- Lyon airport- 2 ¹/₂ hours to resort

Resort   Mountain Information and Travel.

	Summit	Resort	Vert. Drop	Ride Acres
ALPE D'HEUZ	3330m	1860m	Vert 2009m	Rideable piste 220km
Dauphine	●Beg 46%	●Int 31%	●Adv 23%	

Olympic resort, good for all levels and styles of riding. Longest run 16km. 82 lifts
Information Tel +33- 76 80 35 41. Fly to Grenoble, 1 1/2 hour transfer.

	Summit	Resort	Vert. Drop	Ride Acres
LES ARCS	3226m	1600m	Vert 2400m	Rideable piste 150km
Savoie	●Beg 53%	●Int 31%	●Adv 16%	Half Pipe ✔ Park ✔

Long, steep blacks through trees to suit freeriders. longest run 7km. 79 lifts.
Information Tel +33- 79 07 12 57. Fly to Chambery, 2 1/2 hours transfer.

	Summit	Resort	Vert. Drop	Ride Acres
BAREGES/	2350m	1250m	Vert 1100m	Rideable piste 100m
LA MONGIE	●Beg 65%	●Int 29%	●Adv 6%	Half Pipe ✘ Park ✘

Largest area in the Pyrenees, good for carving. Longest run 7km. 53 lifts
Information Tel +33- 62 92 68 19. Fly to Tarbes, 1 hour transfer.

	Summit	Resort	Vert. Drop	Ride Acres
CHATEL	2067m	1200m	Vert 980m	Rideable piste 82km,
Savoie	●Beg 49%	●Int 39%	●Adv 12%	

Huge linked area of piste and off piste for all. Longest run 2km. 50 lifts
Information Tel +33- 50 73 22 44. Fly to Geneva, 2 hours transfer.

	Summit	Resort	Vert. Drop	Ride Acres
LA CLUSAZ	2362m	1100m	Vert 1299m	Rideable piste 130km,
Savoie	●Beg 70%	●Int 26%	●Adv 4%	Half Pipe ✘ Park ✘

Excellent for beginners learning to carve. Longest run 4km. 56 lifts
Information Tel +33- 50 32 65 00. Fly to Geneva, 2 hours transfer.

	Summit	Resort	Vert. Drop	Ride Acres
ISOLA	2610m	1800m	Vert 810m	Rideable piste 120km,
Savoie	●Beg 54%	●Int 35%	●Adv 11%	Half Pipe ✔ Park ✔

Full on French snowboard resort suit freestylers. Longest run 6km. 24 lifts
Information Tel +33-93 23 15 15. Fly to Geneva, 2 hours transfer.

	Summit	Resort	Vert. Drop	Ride Acres
LES MENUIRES	3200m	1450m	Vert 1100m	Rideable piste 120km
Savoie	●Beg 49%	●Int 37%	●Adv 14%	

Big linked area in the three Valleys all welcome. Longest run 3.5km. lifts 48
Information Tel +33-79 00 73 00. Fly to Chambery, 2 hours transfer.

	Summit	Resort	Vert. Drop	Ride Acres
MERIBEL	2952m	1450m	Vert 1200m	Rideable piste 105km
Savoie	●Beg 58%	●Int 28%	●Adv 14%	Half Pipe ✔ Park ✔

A bit of a British poncey ski hangout but ok to ride. Longest run 4km. lifts 57
Information Tel +33-79 08 60 01. Fly to Chambery, 2 hours transfer.

	Summit	Resort	Vert. Drop	Ride Acres
MONTGENEVRE	2460m	1850m	Vert 750m	Rideable piste 65km
Hautes Alpes	●Beg 48%	●Int 33%	●Adv 19%	Half Pipe ✔ Park ✔

On the Italian boarder, suit all, but not hardcore. Longest run 4km. lifts 23
Information Tel +33-92 21 90 22. Fly to Turin, 2 hours transfer.

	Summit	Resort	Vert. Drop	Ride Acres
RISOUL/VARS	2750m	1850m		Rideable piste 170km
Hautes Alpes	●Beg 56%	●Int 40%	●Adv 4%	Half Pipe ✔ Park ✔

Good freeriders soft boot resort, nothing testing. Longest run 3km. lifts 58
Information Tel +33-92 46 02 60. Fly to Grenoble 3 hours transfer.

	Summit	Resort	Vert. Drop	Ride Acres
VAL D'ISERE	3656m	1850m	Vert 1200m	Rideable piste 300km
Savoie	●Beg 59%	●Int 33%	●Adv 8%	Half Pipe ✔ Park ✔

Price but damn good resort, linked with Tignes for all levels of riding. Longest run 5km.
lifts 51, 1 day adult pass 213F. *Check out Surf Rider Snowboard Club
Information Tel +33-79 06 06 06. Fly to Geneva, 3 hours transfer.

	Summit	Resort	Vert. Drop	Ride Acres
VALMOREL	2356m	1400m	Vert 1192m	Rideable piste 163km
Savoie	●Beg 70%	●Int 20%	●Adv 10%	Half Pipe ✔ Park ✔

Suit both piste carvers and freestylers of all levels. Night riding from 6 to 9.30pm .
Longest run 4km. lifts 49 no ride rules. 1 day adult pass 32F
Information Tel +33-79 09 85 55. Fly to Geneva, 3 ¹/² hours transfer.

FRANCE – VAL THORENS, 12 RESORTS

RIDER'S OWN NOTES ON FRANCE

ANDY HETZEL

SHAUN PALMER

GERMANY

Forget Germany's past, because what it has to offer today is pretty cool and certainly a snowboard friendly country. Not many people associate Germany as a main snowboard destination, and although its no match for its close alpine neighbours, Austria, Switzerland or France, it can still boast loads of terrain. It's said that there are some 300 areas registered as having lifts etc. In truth the majority if they do even exist will simply be a small hill with a single rope tow stretching a few yards catering for geriatric langlaufers. The dozen or so of recognised downhill resorts are a mixture of OK, to a bit of a waste of time. Germany's winter playgrounds are all located in the southern most parts of the country, some of which cross over into Austria. They are usually a doddle to reach with good road access and efficient rail and bus networks from cities and international airports. The thing that seems to be consistent about German resorts is the efficient way things are run, set out and how you're looked after. Most places which, it should be said can be pricey, (but affordable none the less), are none to busy during the week but can be stupidly crowded at weekends when German townies load up their shiny BMW's and Merc's and shift south.

Germany has the biggest snowboard population in Europe - among them one of the worlds leading pros 'Peter Bauer', who hails from the mountain resort of Schliersee. Peter, a carving legend and long time sponsored rider by Burton, has helped put the sport on the map in Germany as well as elsewhere, and has paved the way for today's German hopefuls like male freestylers, Oliver Holzmann riding for Hooger and Nicholas Brichet riding Oxygen while 26 year old carver Hans Roesch riders for Nidecker and waving the bras for the females, Deuche babes Sandra Farmand (Nidecker), Sabine Wehr (Rad Air) and Nicole Fischer on Sims.

Germany riders seem to learn towards the hard boot carving style although there is a very healthy freestyle and freeride population, which has strong links with Germans big skateboard crowd. However you will notice a lot of sad set ups on the slopes, quite a few ski boot/plate binding numptys in day-glow all in ones. To be fair, on the whole the scene is cool and laid back and German riders know the score.

Hire and instruction facilities are as good as anywhere else in the world. You can hire soft boots, there's plenty of options on board styles and most places have demo set-ups. If your passing through a major town on route to a resort check out the snowboard shop, most are full-on and offer a better service than the ski/snowboard shops at the resorts. For instance in Frankfurt, 'Montimare' is a mega cool shop which has its own team and runs camps in the Alps. In Munich and Hamburg 'Sport Check', probably the largest snowboard shop in Europe is worth a visit, though the cool and full on snowboarders place to check out in Munich are 'Boarders' which is skate and snow, 'Heart Attack' which is surf and snow oriented. If your near Munster check out 'Titus' which is skate and snow.

Germans like to party and beer is about the best anywhere in the world, simply pure nectar. Clubs and discos are not bad although far to many bars allow euro pop. You can however find plenty of hard core to match the offerings from the UK or the US.

For those who are thinking about doing a whole season in Germany think again, the seasons are not that long and you are not going to be riding major amounts of different terrain each and every day. You will soon get bored shredding the same small areas week after week. However work is possible but you will need to speak the lingo or have a good grasp of it.

For the foreigners travelling to Germany its easy from any part of the world with major gate way airports linking up to one of the best road systems in the universe. Best advise is see a travel agent or tour operator.

Status	Federal Republic	Winter snowboard periods	December to April
Capital	Berlin	Summer snowboarding.	Nil
Area	356,755 sq km	Highest point	Zugspitze - 2963m
Population	79.5 million	Country snowboard styles	Freeride/Freestyle 50%
Density	222 people per sq km		Alpine/ Carve 50%
Language	German		Soft boots 40%
Currency	German Mark		Hard boots 60%
Neighbouring Countries	Denmark- Poland-	Drugs	Canabis as with all other
	Czech Republic-Austria-		drugs are illegal.
	Switzerland - France	Dealth penalty	No capital punishment
	Luxemborg - Belgium -	Military service	Male nationals have to do
	Netherlands.		a period in the Army.
		Alcohol drinking age	18
		Age of consent for sex	Male and Female is 16
		Prostitution	Legal in Germany.

FACT FILE

Snowboard shops

Boarders
Aberlestrasse 9, D-81371 Munchen
Germany
+49 0 897 2583 16

Montimare
Berger Strasse 28
60316 Frankfurt/ Main
Germany.
+49 0 69 405 9716

Sport Check +49 0 891 216 60

Titus
Von-Stuben Str 21
48143 Munster
Germany
+49 0 251 402 06.

Deutscher Snowboard Association (DSDV)
Postfach 120327
80031 Munchen
Germany
+49 89 7595 061

127

GARMISCH

Garmisch is Germany's most popular and best known resort located in the southern most part of Germany easily reached from Stuttgart, Munich or Innsbruck. This very German of German places is actually not too bad, indeed the ski world hosts all sorts of world ranking two plank events including ski jumping. What's more the place held the 1936 Winter Olympics though to be fair the world was a bit mucked up at that time so any one claiming such great historical roles should be viewed lightly. What may be seen as worthy then, is not always the case theses days. However, all said and done this is a resort where you can have a good time. Garmisch Partenkirchen is located beneath Germany's highest mountain, the Zugspitze where a cable car goes to the rocky 2964m summit but no ridable descent is possible. The five resort centres dotted around the village are all interconnected by buses and trains. On the mountain the slopes are divided into 4 areas and serviced by some 50 or so lifts. The Snowboarder's favourite is the Zugspitzplatt which is the only area not directly linked on snow with the other sections. It's also Germany's only glacier snowboarding area and offers 800m of vertical drop. In the main the piste here will appeal mostly to intermediate riders looking for easy descents to lay out some carves with a number of good options. Beginners are well catered for and a number of places are ideally suited to first timers, reached initially by cable car and then serviced by drag lifts. There are a couple of easy options for riding back down to the village which will please the novices, as well as some intermediate runs through trees to the car parks. Advanced riders will be able to do some hard stuff, but it's limited as is the off piste and powder. However, freestylers will be able to find a lot of good natural hits and if still not content then Garmisch has an OK halfpipe to pull air from all day. For instruction the Erwin Gruber Snowboard School is the place to contact, they offer a number of packages for all levels.

The two linked towns of Garmisch Partenkirchen offers a fairly large selection of accommodation, places to eat and loads of shops. If you're into spending, although there is no specific snowboard shop the ski shops will cater for your needs. For those feeling lucky there's a casino to try your hand in but to be honest it's a mugs game. Spend freely in the numerous bars instead where the scene is German through and through.

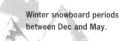

Winter snowboard periods between Dec and May.

No summer snowboarding

Top Station	2830m
Resort height	702m
Vertical Drop	1350m
Longest run	8km

Terrain ability suits:

● Beginner	13%
● Intermediate	76%
● Advanced	11%

Terrain Ride styles suits:

Freeride	45%
Freestyle	10%
Alpine/Carve	45%

2 Halfpipes at Zugspitzplatt

43 lifts no ride rules
1 day adult pass DM 59,-
Lifts times are 8.00am to 4.30pm

Snowboard instruction rates
1 day	Dm 59
2 days	Dm 99
3 days	Dm149
5 days	Dm 229

Photo: Garmisch resort

Garmisch Tourist Office
Schnitzschulstrasse 19
Post fach 1562. D-82455
Garmisch-Partenkirchen
Germany
(+49-088 21 1806
Snowphone +49 8821 797979.

Fly to Munich International airport
Transfer from the airport;
By bus approximately 1 hour 15 minutes journey to resort.
By train direct into Garmisch
By car hire approximately 50 minutes driving to resort.
Driving from home use as map reference Autobahn A95 Munich to Garmisch 140 km.
Via Innsbruck Autobahn A12 and route 177 distance 60km

MITTENWALD

Located in the Isar valley, this typical Bavarian town is a good freeriders place to check out, if only for the steep and famous Dammkar run said to be the longest in Germany. This is served by a cable car which climbs 1311 vertical metres with only one tower (suffers of vertigo keep your eyes shut). Some well challenging stuff for riders with brains. Beginners have plenty of easy trails while freestylers have a halfpipe on Kranzberg.
Fly to Munich, transfer 1¹/₂ hours.
Full resort details +49 0 8823 33981

Top lift exit	2244m
Resort height	912m
Ride area	22km of piste

Terrain ability suits:
● Beginner	47%
● Intermediate	41%
● Advanced	12%

1 half pipe

8 lifts

OBERAMMERGAU

Happy go luck place but not the most adventurous. The west side of the valley on the 1250m high Kolben is the place for novices and intermediate riders not looking for much but with some trees to ride. On the other side known as Laberjoch the runs offer more testing and challenging terrain. For freestylers wanting air check out the pipe and those wanting it you can do night riding at Steckenberglifts in neighbouring Unterammergau.
Fly to Munich, transfer 1¹/₂ hours.
Full resort details +49 0 8822 1021

Top lift exit	1684m
Resort height	850m
Ride area	24km of piste

Terrain ability suits:
● Beginner	60%
● Intermediate	30%
● Advanced	10%

1 half pipe
10 lifts

OBERSTDORF

Open runs, tree lines and steeps all form part of one of Germany's biggest and best resorts, as well as its most southerly. The I.S.F have found favour here and regularly stage top events. The ride areas dotted round the village include the Nebelhorn (reliable snow, halfpipe in the summit bowl and Germany's longest vertical), the Sollereck (new gondola for 1997) and the international Kanzelw area. Will suite all.
Fly to Munich , transfer 2¹/₂ hours.
Full resort details +49 0 8322 7000

Top lift exit	2224m
Resort height	815m
Ride area	44km of piste

Terrain ability suits:
● Beginner	31%
● Intermediate	45%
● Advanced	29%

1 half pipe
29 lifts

OBERSTAUFEN

Not the cheapest place. This is one of those very typical German village haunts with all that is needed to attract summer tourist by the thousand. Quite a few also make it for the winter in order to check out Oberstaufens seven small ridable areas located around it. Oberstaufen's main mountain is the Hochgrat which offers good off-piste and challenging runs. There is enough easy stuff for beginners to get going and some intermediate carving opportunities.
Fly to Munich, transfer 2 hours.
Full resort details +49 0 8386 9300

Top lift exit	1708m
Resort height	792m
Ride area	10km of piste

Terrain ability suits:
● Beginner	25%
● Intermediate	63%
● Advanced	12%

1 half pipe
2 lifts

SCHLIERSEE

The ski areas Taubenstein and St Ompfling at the Spitzingsee mountain lake (1085 m) above Schliersee are "the place to be" for Munich snowboarders at weekends. Often crowded but there's a great atmosphere. The access road is closed when parking lots are full (shuttle bus). The two mountains are interconnected by a free shuttle. Usually the steeper runs on west facing Taubenstein (serviced by a gondola) are less crowded.
Fly to Munich Transfer to 1 hour.
Full resort details +49 0 80 26 40 69

Vertical Drop	1600m
Longest run	800m
Ride area	36km

Terrain ability suits:
● Beginner	24%
● Intermediate	62%
● Advanced	14%

1 half pipe   1 fun park

18 lifts

Snowboard

uk magazine

SEXISM SELLS?
YOUR THOUGHTS PLEASE

This is our mate Michaela, isn't she smashing?

**Snowboard UK:
Seven Issues
a year.**

Gratuitous Snowboard Photograph

Snowboard UK: Unit 1a Franchise St,
Kidderminster, Worcs. DY11 6RE. England.

Tel +44 (0) 1562 827 744
Fax +44 (0) 1562 755 705

email: stig@sukmag.demon.co.uk
compuserve: 100333,3272

GREAT BRITAIN/ SCOTLAND

Rider :Steve Bailey - Photo: Stig

Great Britain the one time all powerful world wide empire, winners of the 1966 world cup and a nation foolish enough to allow itself to be governed for over ten years by a nasty arrogant women called Margaret Thatcher. Never mind. One thing the UK is not and that is an Alpine country. Apart from the offerings in Scotland there are no mountain ranges with high snow capped peaks. Despite this, Britain has a big snowboard population that has grown from the mid-eighties originating in Scotland. Indeed the UK once had a proper snowboard manufacturing company called Acid Snow, unfortunately the owners liked to party and alcohol got the best of them finishing the company off. The UK snowboard scene which has become very trendy with a host of pop stars and showbiz personalities getting involved is pretty hard core and reflects it's links with skateboarding, street action, fashion and music. Thankfully snowboarders are strongly in command of the sport in Britain although the windsurfing world have a big slice. However the ski authorities (the most pompous in the world) have been very slow to accept snowboarding, preferring to dismiss the sport out of hand, however since their idols, the Royal Family, were captured on snowboards last year the bowing yes men have begun to change tune.

Riding in the UK is possible on snow in Scotland, and in England at dozens of dry slopes. Scottish snowboarding is practically unheard of abroad and indeed there's a lot of people in England that are not too well acquainted with what's on offer north of the boarder. The five resorts stretched across northern Scotland serve the locals and punters from connecting towns and cites with snow that often lasts right through into the summer months of July. Mind you it should be said that we're talking about crap conditions for much of this time. The younger riders have now taken to building jumps on the last specks of snow and you can find mini fun parks on the Cairngorms even in August. All the resorts are similar in character but offer something different. Half pipes and fun parks are not always possible to build and maintain because of the inclement weather, however grommets are always building big hits all over the place. The scene is dominated by freeriding and soft boots, due to the fact the runs are very narrow often sandwiched between snow collecting fences with the terrain largely being uneven and rough. Very limited carving in hard boots is possible at one or two of the resorts but you won't be doing big Euro carves on motorway pistes. Scottish lifts can be a bit tricky for beginners at first but with a little practice most will cope. An encouraging note is that skiers are becoming more aware and comfortable travelling on T-Bars with a snowboarder alongside, which is good news since it will obviously cut down on the time spent in lift queues which can be lengthy in certain places. Snowboard instruction and hire is available throughout Scotland catering mainly for novices.

GREAT BRITAIN/ SCOTLAND

A couple of large points about snowboarding in Scotland is the cost. In general value for money is out the window, lift prices are stupidly way over the top for what is on offer and mountain restaurants are not hot either. A weeks trip to the 3 Valleys in France would be better value than a weekend on Cairngorm one of the main areas and one where they like to boast about having 17 or so lifts. Truth is had they planned the lifts correctly they could have got away with half that amount.

The biggest problem in Scotland is the weather which can be bloody harsh and unpredictable. The wind rolls over the mountains with ease and it's not unusual to actually have to force your way down the slope against a 70 mile an hour wind coming upwards. Your ability will be tested to the limits. On the plus side though, off the slopes the facilities are pretty good with cheap and cheerful services. Scots are amongst the friendliest people anywhere and will look after you well. Scottish riders are easily the most hard core and full on in the world, and they know how to party, there's no sick sad numpties doing apre ski in Scotland, it's pure hard-core snowboard life style. What Scotland lacks on the mountain it certainly makes up for off it. (If life style ever becomes an Olympic event Scotland would win constantly).

Getting to any one of Scotland's resorts should pose no real problems with good rail, air and bus links, with hitching a very good option. If you are planning to do a season at one of the resorts you'll be able to find work and accommodation with out too much bother. For those who want to teach snowboarding it's possible at all the resorts although one resort (Cairngorm) has been well out of order in trying to take over instruction and enforce a ski mentality. Don't be put off though, go and do your own thing, you can't be stopped.

British Snowboard Population	22,000

British Snowboard Association (BSA)
5 Cressex Road, High Wycombe
Bucks HP12 4PG + 44 01494 462225
Set up in 1990. Now has 700 members.
To join cost £15 a year.

Overall UK snowboard Champion 1996/7
Male: Neil McNab
Female: Becci Malthouse
Junior: Jamie Philp

Number of snowboards sold in Britain
during the 1995/6 season: 11,500
British snowboard styles favour
Freestyle 35% Freeride 60% - Alpine 5%
Soft boots 95$ - Hard boots 5%.

Number of snowboard Mags: 3.
Most favoured UK resort - Cairngorm
Most famous UK snowboarders - Prince Wills.
Britains first independent snowboard shop was
The Snowboard Academy est 1989 in Aviemore

Mags	
Snowboard UK	+44 01562 827744
White lines	+44 01235 536229
Ergo Sum	+44 0171 613 0718

Tour operators
Chalet Snowboards - for France
+44 01235 767182
Crystal Holidays - for Europe and US
+44 0181 399 5144
Rocky Mountain Tours - for US
+44 0151 733 7593
Virgin Travel - US   +44 01293 617181
Snowboard travel Insurance
Worldwide Travel +44 01732 773366

Fly
British Airways Central reservations
+44 0345 222111
Virgin Atlantic Central reservations
+44-01293 747747

UK airports to reach Scottish resorts	
Aberdeen	+44 01224 722331
Edinburgh	+44 031 333 1000
Glasgow	+44 0141 887 1111
Inverness	+44 01463 232471

Train	
British Railway	+44 0345 212282
Bus	
National Bus	+44 0990 808080
Car Hire	
Avis	+44-0645 123456
Budget	+44 0800 181181
Europcar	+44 0345 222525
Hertz	+44 0345 555888

Scottish snowboarder and master crafstman, Kieran Halliday

FACT FILE

BRITISH DRIVE GUIDE
Break down
AA: 0800 88 77 66 or RAC: 0800 828 282

Vehicles drive on the Left
Speed on: MOT 70, Dual 70, Single 60, Urban 30mph
When Towing   MOT 60, Dual 60, Single 50, Urban 30mph
Seat belts -Compulsory front and rear
Tolls: on a few big bridges
Alcohol level = 0.08%
Driving age limit: 17
Documents to carry: Driving Licence, Vehicle Reg, Green Card,
Country Identification, Number Plates, Hire papers.
Fuel: Sold in Litres
First Aid Kit: Recommended
Warning Triangle: Recommended
Snowchains: Recommended

Status	Constitutional Monarchy
Capital	London / Edinburgh / Cardiff
Area	244,046 sq. km
Population	57 million
Density	23 people per sq. km
Language	English/Gaelic/Welsh
Currency	Pounds
Neighbouring Countries	Republic of Ireland
Winter snowboard periods	December to April
Summer snowboarding	Zero
Highest Mountain	Ben Nevis 1347 m
Country Snowboard styles	Freeride/Freestyle 95%
	Alpine/Caring 5%
	Soft boots 95%
	Hard boots 5%
Drugs	Cannabis and dope are illegal
Death penalty	No capital punishment
Military Service	Nationals joint the army by choice
Alcohol drinking age	Age 18.
Age of consent for sex	Male 16, Female 16
Prostitution	Illegal

Rider: Darren (Firehead) Williamson

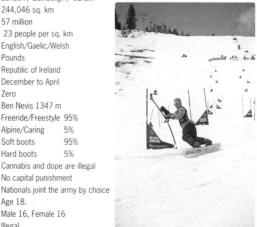

133

CAIRNGORM

The Cairngorms are said to be one of Europe's last great wildernesses with a climate, animal and plant life normally found in the Arctic.

Unfortunately the area that makes up the ski and snowboard parts are a joke. This is not the Alps, it's a range of low level treeless rolling hills, and will never be a match for the rest of Europe though it does provide some real snow to play on. The problem is that even with sun out, the wind down to zero and a fresh covering of snow, you are still confronted with the hard fact of ridiculous lift queues and way over priced bad value lift passes. You are shunted around on an antique chair lift system with notices warning about oil dripping on your clothes. This would not be allowed elsewhere. Pommas and T-bars infuriate beginners being so badly laid out that a lot of skating is called for. With all that said, once you do manage to get over the shock of pass prices and manage to battle your way on to the slopes you can actually do some good riding. Experienced riders used to long testing steeps will soon tire of Cairngorm with nothing much to tackle apart from the West Wall – the only black run. Bail this on an icy day and it could be your last.

'The White Lady' offers freeriders a good time as does the 'M1' race run for those who have the bottle, but forget about any off piste or trees. Carvers will find very little to arc about on, though the top section of the 'Coire Cas' and 'Coire na Ciste' can be OK when there's been a good dump of snow. Freestylers not out for much will be pleased to find there are some good natural hits and the jumps in the park are on occasion big, however because of the inclement weather there is no pipe. Beginners - this place is not really for you there are easy flats but they are limited and crowded with ski classes. The best stuff is up at the 'Ciste' but this is often unreachable because of winds closing down the chair lift.

Aviemore 8 miles away is an OK place, with loads of good options to sleep, eat and party at with prices to suit everyone. The town has loads of outlets to hire boards and boots which you are best doing in Aviemore if you want to avoid disappointment up at Cairngorm. Outside Chevvy's bar there's a half pipe for skaters and BMX'ers to session.

Winter snowboard periods between Dec and April.
No summer snowboarding

Top Station	1080m
Bottom lift	540m
Longest run	3.2km
Ride area	844 hectares
Snowmaking	0

Terrain ability suits:

● Beginner	35%
● Intermediate	60%
● Advanced	5%

Terrain Ride styles suits:

Freeride	60%
Freestyle	20%
Alpine/Carve	10%

Small Park with a few hits

Area Shuttle bus runs between the slopes and Aviemore daily: £4 return

A taxi cost from £9 one way.
Geordies Taxis: + (01479) 810118

Lift Pass price guide

	1 day	5 day
Adult	£17.00	£68.00
Junior	£8.50	£34.00

Lifts open 8.45am to 4pm

Chair lifts 4
Drag lifts 13

Rear foot out on drag lifts.
Leashes compulsory

Rider: Album Thom. Photo: Mark Lewes

SNOWBOARD INSTRUCTION
1/2 day lesson   £15
5 days lesson   £45

SNOWBOARD & BOOT HIRE
1 day hire for standard B & B £15
5 day hire for standard B & B £50
1 day hire for Demo B & B £20

SNOWBOARD REPAIR/SERVICE
Full base Tune service £25

SNOWBOARD SHOP/S
BOARDWISE +44 01479 810336
Sales-Hire-Repair & Instruction.
(Windsurf/Snowboard shop)

Photo: Ewan Kenny

ELLIS BRIGHAM - SNOWBOARD ASYLUM
+44 01479 810175
Sales-Hire-Repair & Instruction
(Ski/Snowboard shop)

Climbing School and Wall

Skateboard ramp in village
operated by Boardwise

Quads and off road driving

Go Kart track in Aviemore

Eat at:
Smithys Chip Shop, for fast food
The Ski-ing Doo, the riders restaurant
The Old Bridge Inn, the Pub restaurant
The Ossian, the full on restaurant.
The Tavern the Italian restaurant

Rider: Stewart Ratray. Photo: Mark Lewes

NIGHT TIME HANGOUTS
Chevvys Bar, the snowboarders scene
The Old Bridge Inn, the laid back Pub
Crofters Bar, the disco
The Kith & Kin, the out of town bar
The Illicit Still, the place for pool

 Accomodation
Ossian Hotel
+44 01540 651 242
Aviemore Chalets
+44 01479 810 624

Aviemore Tourist Office
Grampian Road, Aviemore,
Inverness-shire.
+44 01479363

The Snowboard Academys true team
Tony Brown - Steve Crampton - Darren Williams

Fly to Glasgow International
airport. Inverness operates
domestic flights.

Transfer from Glasgow airport;

By bus approximately 3 1/2
hour journey to Aviemore.

By train direct into Aviemore
with travel time about 3 1/2
hours.

By car approximately 2 1/2.
Driving: use as a map reference
the A9 north of Perth which is
80 miles.
Glasgow 140 miles.

GLENSHEE

The largest of Scotland's resorts and the only area that has snowcannons. It's much the same as the others, terrain to suit mainly intermediate freeriders, with some off piste, and drop-ins occasional found on Glas Maol. Coire Fionn area will suit Freestylers, but don't be expecting loads of big hits. Carvers can crank a few big turns down the Cairnwell, but its not very wide. Beginners have it easy with plenty of flat areas reached by foot from the car park. Full hire and instruction available at the resort.

Accommodation and local services are not very convenient here, you will need a car or it will be a real pain getting around. The main towns to stay at, with a choice of services, are Blairgowrie or Braemar.

Top Station	1051m
Longest run	3km
Ride area 40km of piste	

Terrain ability suits

● Beginner	61%
● Intermediate	34%
● Advanced	5%

No half pipe
No fun park

Adult 1 day pass from £16.00
Child 1 day pass from £10.00
26 lifts.
Resort Details Tel 013397 41320
Snowphone Tel- 0891 654 663

GLENCOE

The oldest resort in Scotland, Glencoe is a small, natural freestyle fun park with a number of hits and drop offs. Suiting all levels although not at all testing. Some of the best freestyle terrain is accessed from the Cliffhanger chair lift. Freeriders will find some OK terrain on the Main Basin top T-bar area, with the very limited amount of carving there found on the Etive Gladesrun reached by the top T-bar. Beginners will manage well here with a couple of no-drama easy runs to get back down.

The village of Glencoe is 6 miles away, it offers limited accommodation and local services. While Onich, 12 miles, and the town of Fort William, 30 miles, have a much bigger offering. For hire check out Mountain Madness in Onich.

Top Station	1081m
Longest run	1.6km
Ride area	7.2 sq miles

Terrain ability suits

● Beginner	60%
● Intermediate	33%
● Advanced	7%

Half pipe snow permitting
No fun park

Adult 1 day pass from £15.00
Child 1 day pass from £9.50
7 lifts.
Resort Details Tel 01855 811 303
Snowphone Tel- 0891 654 663

THE LECHT

The Lecht offers the best terrain in Scotland for total beginners with some well set out, easy to reach, runs. However, novices may like it but anyone with more than a few days under their belt will hate it - the runs are really small and won't offer you anything of a challenge. Riders with hard boots wanting to carve forget it, however new school freestylers will find a bit of terrain to pass a few hours on. As well as dry slope matting there is also floodlights for the occasional evening session. The nearest full on snowboard shop is ESP in Elgin.

The village of Tomintoul nearby, offers some lodging and local services, but the best option is to stay at Aviemore only 40 minutes drive away, with a bigger choice.

Top Station	810m
Longest run	800m
Ride area	600 hectares

Terrain ability suits:

● Beginner	65%
● Intermediate	29%
● Advanced	6%

Half pipe snow permitting
No fun park

Adult 1 day pass from £11.00
Child 1 day pass from £8.00
12 lifts.
Resort Details Tel 01975 651 440
Snowphone Tel- 0891 654 663

NEVIS RANGE

Nevis Range is Scotland's newest resort, with a modern lift system similar to European resorts, however this is not Europe and like the rest of Scotland it has its drawbacks. The terrain favours all levels but mainly intermediates, it's fairly uneventful although there's some cool riding to be had over in the Back Bowl with steeps for Freeriders. The Snowgoose Gully is the area for hard boots allowing a few sharp turns while beginners will be happy around the restaurant zone. Good hire and instruction is available at the resort or through The Snowboard Asylum in Fort William, which is the largest of the towns servicing Scotland's resorts and offers dozens of places to sleep, eat and drink. (There's even a McDonald's planned!).

Top Station	1150m
Longest run	1.6km
Ride area	720 hectares

Terrain ability suits:

● Beginner	65%
● Intermediate	25%
● Advanced	10%

No half pipe
Fun park yes

Adult 1 day pass from £17.00
Child 1 day pass from £9.50
12 lifts.
Resort Details Tel 01397 703 781
Snowphone Tel- 0891 654 663

MOUNTAIN MADNESS

Snowboard
Ski and
Bike hire
Tuition
Repairs
Free style
Boards
Soft
Bindings
Soft Boots
Close to
Glencoe
and Nevis
Range
Open 7
Days
From 7am in
Winter

Ali

find us at the Bike Shop
Cameron Court, ONICH, near Fort William
SCOTLAND. PH33 6RY. Tel/Fax: +44 (0) 1855 821500

GREECE

Get this, Greece the hot spot were bodies bare all on countless sun drenched beaches scattered around numerous islands, also has a winter sports industry. Yes although not well known and come to think of it not even thought of by most. Never the less you can snowboard at any one of 15 recognised ski centres, we say recognised, that's what the Greeks recognise them as, some are very dubious. However there are a number of mountain ranges where snow falls on a regular basis allowing the chance to shred it, and by the way we are not talking pox little hills here, these Greek mountains are serious, with the highest peak at Mt. Olympus rising to 2917m. Athens may be the historic home of the Olympics but just 2 and a half hours away is the resort of Parnassos, where you can ride some 20 runs. Although the Greeks allow snowboarders on the slopes they're not totally sure about the whole scene yet, and may at times seem a bit stand-offish but they're cool enough. What Greece is defiantly not is a freestylers playground, forget about half pipes or fun parks and you aren't going to be doing major euro carving on motor way runs, or going off piste to do some scary extreme terrain. But you certainly will find something to amuse you with, some of the areas may have stupidly short runs and be equipped with an antique single lift system located along side the resort's only building, and true the terrain is not that great, it's generally flat, not well groomed and not to adventurous but what the heck its snowboarding in Greece.

If you fancy giving Greek snowboarding a go remember to contact the resort prior to leaving to see if the place is actually open and check on the latest conditions. The resorts are unbelievable basic, many without any facilities. You won't find dozens of places to eat sleep or drink in and as for hard core partying at night 'Nope' basically this is Walkman or book reading accompanied by your duty free booze. Be well advised to take your own snowboard and boots because hiring options are almost zero and beginners don't go expecting to get intense expert snowboard tuition because your not going to (take a copy of self teach manual). Getting to resorts is best tackled by self driving forget any regular public transport service, though it does exist in certain places.

Greek short list

▲ Pangeo @ Kilada Orfea
▲ 1750m = 1 run 400m long, 1 lift
Overnight lodging and food services
Location 44km from Kaval
Info+30-0-51 835 952

Falakro @ Agio Pnevma
▲ 1720m = 3 runs longest 2000m, 2 lifts
Overnight lodging and food services
Location 43km from Drama
Info+30-0-521 33054/ 21893

Vrondou @ lailias
▲ 1600m = 1 run 1100m long, 2 lifts
Overnight lodging and food services
Location 27km from Seres
Info+30-0-321 23724

Vermio @ Seli
▲ 1500m = 8 runs longest 1800m, 3 lifts
Overnight lodging and food services
Location 22km from Veria
Info+30-0-332 71234

Vermio @ Tria Pende Pigadia
▲ 1420m = 4 runs longeŝt 2500m, 3 lifts
Overnight lodging and food services
Location 17km from Navoussa
Info+30-0-332 22208

Verno @ Vigla
▲ 1650m = 3 runs longest 2500m, 3 lifts
Overnight lodging and food services
Location 18km from Florina
Info+30-0-385-22354

Vassilitsa @ Diaselo Vassilitsas
▲ 1750m = 3 runs longest 1100m, 2 lifts
Limited hire and instruction available
Overnight lodging and food services
Location 45km from Grevena
Info+30-0-462 26100

Pindos @ Karakoli
▲ 1350m = 2 runs with 1 lift
Overnight lodging and food services
Location 2km from Metsovs
Info+30-0- 656 41211

Olympos @ Vrissopoules
▲ 1800m = 1 run 1140m long, 1 lift
Overnight lodging
Location 40km from Elassona
Info+30-0-493 23467, 23821

Pilion @ Agriolefkes
▲ 1500m = 3 runs longest 1045, 4 lifts
Overnight lodging and food services
Location 27km from Volos
Info+30-0-421 99136

Timfristos @ Diavolotopos
▲ 1800m = 4 lifts
Overnight lodging and food services
Location 12 km from Karpenissi
Info+30-0-237 22002, 23506

Parnassos @ Kellaria ,Fterolaka
▲ 1750m = 16 runs longgest 4km, 13 lifts
Overnight lodging and food services
Location 17km from Amfikleia
Info+30-0-234 22689, 22694

Parnassos @ Gerondovrachos
▲ 1800m = 4 runs longest 1800m, 3 lifts
Hire, Instruction and Shop.
Overnight lodging and food services
Location 195km from Athensl
Info+30-0-1 6433368

Helmos @ Vathia Lakka
▲ 1650m = 8 runs 4 lifts
Overnight lodging and food services
Location 214km from Athens
Info+30-0-692 22661, 22174

Menalon @ Oropedio Ostrakinas
▲ 1600m = 5 runs 3 lifts
Overnight lodging and food services
Location 30km from Tripoli
Info+30-0-796 22227

Burton Tean rider Nicole Angelrath at Zermatt CH - Photo: Trevor Graves

The ISF World Tour Preliminary Calendar

Month	Date	Resort	Country	Disciplines	Cat
November	27-1Dec	Laax	Switzerland	HP, GS, DU	WS
December	6-8	Wolf Mnt/UT	America	HP, GS	WS
	11-15	Ischgl	Austria	HP, GS, DU	WS
	19-22	Val d'Isere	France	HP, GS, DU	WS
January	9-12	Western Canada	Canada	HP, GS	WS
	9-12	Chamrousse	France	HP, GS, DU	WS
	15-19	Fieberbrunn	Austria	HP, GS, DU	MWC
	22-26	Oberstdorf	Germany	HP, GS, DU	WS
February	1-2	Innsbruck	Austria	HP, DU	NC
	5-9	Madonna di Campiglio	Italy	HP, GS, DU	WS
	5-9	Ozekotura	Japan	HP, DU	
	13-16	Leysin	Switzerland	HP, GS, DU	ISF EO
	25-2Mar	California	America	HP, GS, DU	ISF WC
March	6-9	Okemo	America	HP, GS, DU	MWC
	12-16	Ruka	Finland	HP, DU	ISF JWC
	14-16	North East Canada	Canada/USA	HP, GS, DU	ISF NA
	19-23	Stratton	America	HP, GS, DU	WS
	23-30	Les Arcs	France	HP, DU, GS, BX	BSA Champs

HP=Halfpipe, GS=Carving, DU=Duel, WS=World Series, MWC=Masters World Cup, NC=Nations Cup
ISF WC=World Championships, ISF NA=North American Championships,
ISF JWC=Junior World Championships.
For further details contact the ISF in Europe Tel + 43 512 34 28 34. http://www.acess.ch/isf/
ISF in North America Tel +1 303 949 5473

Rider : Chris Moran at Val D'Isere. Photo Sang Tan

October '96

Sun	Mon	Tue	Wed	Thu	Fri	Sat
		1	2	3	4	5
6	7	8	9	10	11	12
13	14	15	16	17	18	19
20	21	22	23	24	25	26
27	28	29	30	31		

Ride time calendar for October

95% of all resorts closed. Early snow at Glacier resorts that are open.

Some snowboard teams training on glaciers which will be crowd free.

Many hotels, bars and services in villages closed prior to Christmas.

Best possibilities of riding are in France, Austria, Switzerland.

Second winter edition of snowboard magazines out

Snowboard retail shows taking place in cities

Riders own monthly notes

Photo: John Beng - Aspen CO USA

November '96

Sun	Mon	Tue	Wed	Thu	Fri	Sat
					1	2
3	4	5	6	7	8	9
10	11	12	13	14	15	16
17	18	19	20	21	22	23
24	25	26	27	28	29	30

Ride time calendar for November

80% of all resorts still closed. First snow at open resorts.

Resorts that are open will be crowd free and have low tariffs.

Many Hotels, bars and services in villages closed prior to Christmas.

Best possibilities of riding are in US, France, Austria, Switzerland.

Third winter edition of snowboard magazines out .

Board X Snowboard show London at Royal Horticultural Halls 8-11th

Daily Mail Ski/Snowboard Show London at the Olympia 25th Oct - 3rd Nov 1996

Riders own monthly notes

Photo: Mathias Fennetux - Avoriaz

December '96

Sun	Mon	Tue	Wed	Thu	Fri	Sat
1	2	3	4	5	6	7
8	9	10	11	12	13	14
15	16	17	18	19	20	21
22	23	24	25	26	27	28
29	30	31				

Ride time calendar for December

100% of all resorts open by Christmas. Best snow at high resorts above 1500m. Low resorts may not have sufficient snow to run lifts.

The period spanning Christmas and New Year will be very busy with high resort tariffs. All resort services will be open.

Best possibilities of riding are in North America, Central Europe, poorest chances are Scotland, Greece and some of Spain.

Christmas editions of snowboard magazines out.

Riders own monthly notes

Rider Temple Cummins at Weigle - Photo: John Kelly

January '97

Sun	Mon	Tue	Wed	Thu	Fri	Sat
			1	2	3	4
5	6	7	8	9	10	11
12	13	14	15	16	17	18
19	20	21	22	23	24	25
26	27	28	29	30	31	

Ride time calendar for January

All resorts will be open though the low areas may still not have good snow. Best bet is stick to high or mid level areas to be snow sure.

The week after New Year resorts become quieter and lower tariffs exist.

Best possibilities of riding are in North America and all Europe.

Scotland may still have no snow.

Forth winter edition of snowboard magazines out.

Riders own monthly notes

Daniel Franck at Davos. Photo: Sang Tan

February '97

Sun	Mon	Tue	Wed	Thu	Fri	Sat
						1
2	3	4	5	6	7	8
9	10	11	12	13	14	15
16	17	18	19	20	21	22
23	24	25	26	27	28	

Ride time calendar for February

100% of all resorts open with good snow at levels.

Many resorts go to higher tariff rates the second week.

A lot of schools have their half terms in February so resorts can be very busy with families

Best possibilities to ride everywhere.

Snowboard magazines out some carrying first race results.

Riders own monthly notes

Photo: Oztal Arena Solden Austria.

March '97

Sun	Mon	Tue	Wed	Thu	Fri	Sat
						1
2	3	4	5	6	7	8
9	10	11	12	13	14	15
16	17	18	19	20	21	22
23	24	25	26	27	28	29
30	31					

Ride time calendar for March

Some of the best snow to be had at this period in all resorts. Towards the end of the month low level resorts may be struggling and snow could be thin on bottom runs.

Most resorts operate high tariffs. Some start to lower towards the end of the month depending on when Easter is. March is a busy month.

Final winter editions of snowboard magazines out loaded with early season results and happenings.

Riders own monthly notes

Rider: Gram (Grommit). Photo: Sang Tan

April '97

Sun	Mon	Tue	Wed	Thu	Fri	Sat
		1	2	3	4	5
6	7	8	9	10	11	12
13	14	15	16	17	18	19
20	21	22	23	24	25	26
27	28	29	30			

Ride time calendar for April

100% of all resorts open with spring snow which is fine to ride. Many low level resorts will have broken runs.

Pre Easter high tariffs large crowds. After Easter low tariffs few crowds.

Best chances to ride are countries with high level resorts and glaciers.

By the end of the month 80% of resorts switch off lifts.

Riders own monthly notes

Photo: Shaun Palmer at Tahoe. Photo by Chris Carnel

May '97

Sun	Mon	Tue	Wed	Thu	Fri	Sat
				1	2	3
4	5	6	7	8	9	10
11	12	13	14	15	16	17
18	19	20	21	22	23	24
25	26	27	28	29	30	31

Ride time calendar for May

Some of the high level resorts may still be operating but the best snow will be found at glacier resorts with good riding from 8 till mid day. Afternoons are still OK but conditions will be slushy. Powder still possible and a good month for tee shirt riding on crowd fee slopes at low tariffs. A lot of resort facilities will be closed for the pre summer tourist season.

Best place to go, Mt. Hood in the US, Blackcomb Canada and any of the glaciers in Austria, France, Italy or Switzerland. Also most anything in Norway.

Riders own monthly notes

Rider Matt Davis at Meribel - Photo: Sang Tan

June '97

Sun	Mon	Tue	Wed	Thu	Fri	Sat
1	2	3	4	5	6	7
8	9	10	11	12	13	14
15	16	17	18	19	20	21
22	23	24	25	26	27	28
29	30					

Ride time calendar for June

100% of all resorts closed apart from a few die hards using the last speaks of snow where lifts are not needed. Glaciers resorts are the place to head for. Lots of summer camps beginning. Snow conditions best in morning very wet in the afternoons. Summer board test happening. Many resort facilities closed up till middle of the month.

Best place to go, Mt. Hood in the US, Blackcomb Canada and any of the glaciers in Austria, France, Italy or Switzerland. Also Norway. Season kicks off, in the southern hemisphere countries; OK in Australia, good in New Zealand, OK in Argentina and OK in Chile.

Riders own monthly notes

Burton TeamRrider, Aleks Vanninen at Zermatt CH - Photo: Trevor Graves

July '97

Sun	Mon	Tue	Wed	Thu	Fri	Sat
		1	2	3	4	5
6	7	8	9	10	11	12
13	14	15	16	17	18	19
20	21	22	23	24	25	26
27	28	29	30	31		

Ride time calendar for July

Still good at Glacier resorts,though some getting thin and broken. Snowboard camps well underway on crowd free slopes at summer tariffs. A lot of top riders doing product testing for Manufacturers.

80% of resorts facilities back open for summer trade.

Best place to go, Blackcomb in Canada and any of the glaciers in Austria, France, Italy or Switzerland. Also Norway.

Height of season in the southern hemisphere countries, great stuff in New Zealand.

Riders own monthly notes

Rider Steve Bailey. Photo: Sang Tan

August '97

Sun	Mon	Tue	Wed	Thu	Fri	Sat
					1	2
3	4	5	6	7	8	9
10	11	12	13	14	15	16
17	18	19	20	21	22	23
24	25	26	27	28	29	30
31						

Ride time calendar for August

Snowboarding still possible at Glaciers but generally it's not that great.

All countries in the Southern Hemisphere are at the height of their season with the end of the month seeing a tailoring off and some resorts closing.

Riders own monthly notes

Rider: Simon (Snapper) Smith at Tignes. Photo: Sang Tan.

September '97

Sun	Mon	Tue	Wed	Thu	Fri	Sat
	1	2	3	4	5	6
7	8	9	10	11	12	13
14	15	16	17	18	19	20
21	22	23	24	25	26	27
28	29	30				

Ride time calendar for September

If you really want to snowboard you can, but even a lot of glacier resorts will be closed prior to the first new snow falls of the season.

The quietest month on the slopes but one of the busiest off them with new product arriving in the shops with all the new season gear.

Bumper issues of the first seasons magazines with supplements on boards and product reviews.

Riders own monthly notes

ITALY

Italy is somewhat different from the rest of Europe, a bit more temperamental it might be said. Rather sad mountain dress sense is quite obvious with a love for the all in one metallic and day-glow colour ski suits and the far too common option of only being able to hire crap boards with plate bindings and ski boots. That said Italy is a great place to snowboard, the food, drink and hospitality are pretty cool as long as you like pizza and pasta, and at the moment Italy is amongst the cheapest countries to go and visit with some good deals to be had on accommodation and holiday packages.

The Italians vary from the hard-core freerider, a minority it must be said who like to launch themselves off abundant cliffs and drops, to the soft core piste lovers in sad clothing and ski boots. The home of Martina Magenta - top female carver, Italy has produced a number of top pro's including the Dabbini's, Mario Dabbini's reign as overall world champion in 1989 riding for Sims was badly interrupted when he was called to arms in the Italian army. Today the country seems to be a carvers place but in fact some of the best freeriding in Europe can be found in the Aosta Valley where the resorts of Gressoney, Pila and Courmayeur are situated. These resorts offer heaps of terrain for every preference and style of riding though much of Italy has been a bit behind in providing fun parks and a big pipes. They are becoming a lot more common now. There is a growing healthy band of Italian freestylers and many resorts have snowboard clubs (over 600) with a good mixture of rider styles.

Italy has loads of small resorts tucked away that are well worth visiting but the often remoteness of many places mean that driving yourself is the best option. Many areas may have to be reached via high mountain passes. Some command tolls which can often be paid for with foreign currencies or credit cards. It's always a good idea to check with road authorities to see that passes are open, some stay closed all winter.

Most resorts are a mix and match of the old and new; night life is varied and depends on the time of year though Italians do like to party. They also have a tendency to simply hit the slopes - not to ski or ride but just to lay around on verandas and pose in their designer stuff. There's also an over indulgence in Apre ski and stupid face painting. Bars tend to be dark and smoky and sell thick coffee along with dodgy variations of that Italian favourite Grappa. Wherever you go in Italy the accommodation is likely to be basic cheap and OK. Scamming here is easy and you can usually get loads of extra bods in apartments. For those who want to work at a resort it shouldn't pose to many problems but if you want to teach snowboarding then you will need to learn the lingo. Visa and other legals are not rigorous, but don't get caught with any dodgy substances when you pass through customs because it's off to the calabush if you are.

Page finder

FACT FILE

Status	Republic
Capital	Rome
Area	301,245 sq km
Population	57,662,000
Density	191 people per sq km
Language	Italian
Currency	Lira
Neighbouring Countries	France, Switzerland, Austria, Slovenia
Winter snowboard periods	December to April
Summer snowboarding	Yes
Highest Mountain	Monte Blanc 4810 m
Country Snowboard styles	Freeride/Freestyle -35%
	Alpine/Caring -65%
	Soft boots -30%
	Hard boots -70%
Drugs	Canabis and dope are illegal
Death penalty	No capital punishment
Military Service	National service is in force
Alcohol drinking age	Age 18
Age of consent for sex	Male 16-Female 16
Prostitution	Illegal

Page & country rider: Lesley Mckenna

Photo: Tourist Office Val Gardena

Livigno
Bormio
Courmayeur Cervinia
Tirano
Aosta
Bergamo
Milan
Verona
Turin
Venezia
Genova
Bologna
Firenze
SAN MARINO

ITALY

Rome

Naples

Palermo

ITALIAN DRIVE GUIDE

Break down - tel - Automobile Club diItalia +1-06 49981

Vehicles drive on the Right

Speed On	Motorway	Dualcarage	Single	Urban
	130km	110km	90km	50km/h
Towing	80km	70km	70km	50km/h

Seat belts - Compolsory for front and back if fitted

Tolls - Payable on most motorways and some tunnels

Alchol level = 0. Heavy penalties for drinking and drivin

Driving age limit - 18

Document to carry-(translations in Italin a good idea) International

Driving permit , Vehicle Reg,Green Card,Country Identifaction,

Fuel -Sold in Litres

Firt Aid Kit - Recomended

Warning Triangle - Compolsory

Snowchains - Recomended

Federazione Italina Snowboard
Via Maldonado 8
37138 Verona Italy
+39 -45 834 1221

153

BORMIO

Bormio dates back hundreds and hundreds of years. It's quite possible that the Romans who put an ancient town near here could have actually been the first to shred the slopes in their tin hats. However Bormio as we know it today is not so old with its modern roots going back to the early sixties which is when it started dragging punters up its mainly intermediate all round terrain. This is a fairly busy place with an over kill of Italian skiers in some very sad all in one ski suits, however snowboarders have taken to this place and it has seen a steady increase of riders every year. The ski world do a lot of racing on the slopes here; indeed Bormio hosted the 1985 World Championships which suggests that there must be something on offer, which there is. The terrain is excellent for carvers of any level, the 14 km run from the top station down to the village provides plenty of time to get those big carves in. It's perfect for riders who want to see what its like linking turns. By the time you hit the bottom of this one you'll know. The off piste freeriding here is pretty good with powder bowls and trees to check out, the best stuff to head for is reached from the Cima Bianca where the runs start off steep and mellow out to test the best. Don't bother hitting this stuff in hards you'll regret it as this section is soft boot only terrain. Freestylers wanting to get big air will not find a great deal but there are plenty of natural hits. The resort doesn't have a pipe or park but don't be put off because 20km away is the resort of Passo Dello Stelvio linked by a regular shuttle bus where there is plenty of freestyle terrain including a pipe and park. The Stelvio glacier, the largest in Europe, offers the opportunity to snowboard during the summer, the specialised snowboard school Easy Rider runs a number of cool camps here. First time riders will find the slopes at both Bormio and Stelvo ideal for the basics and excellent for progression, what's more all the easy stuff can be reached without tackling a drag lift. All the ski schools at Bormio provide snowboard tuition.

Bormio is a laid back typical Italian place though it does suffer from having to many poncy shops. It also offers loads of places to kip down at reasonable prices. Food here is as you would expect - Pizza in the main. There are alternatives but pizza happens to be the cheapest which means more money for partying which is nothing to shout about but OK for a few beers at a number of bars and discos frequented by ski crowds.

Snowboarding possible all year round on the Stelvio Glacier and betwen Dec and April at Bormio

Top Station	3012m
Resort height	1225m
Vertical Drop	1686m
Longest run	14km
Ride area	25km
(linked with neighbouring resorts) 65km	
Snowmaking	8.5km

Terrain ability suits

● Beginner	30%
● Intermediate	50%
● Advanced	20%

Terrain Ride styles suits

Freeride	40%
Freestyle	20%
Alpine/Carve	40%

Half pipe and park
at Stelvio glacier where a one day adult pass cost 44000 lira.

1996/97 Lift Pass price guide Guide for Bormiol (Lira)

	Low season		High season	
	Child	Adult	Child	Adult
½ day	35000	35000	35000	35000
1 day	37000	44000	40000	47000
5 days	145000	210000	160000	235000
7 days	150000	220000	170000	250000
Season	530000	750000		

Lifts open 8.30am to 4pm daily

Cable Cars	2
Gondolas	1
Chair lifts	7
Drag lifts	6

Rear foot free on drag lifts

Easy Rider Snowboard Camps
4 day inclusive course
260000 lira + 190000 lift pass
(+39- 0-342 903 142

SNOWBOARD & BOOT HIRE
$^1/_2$ day hire for standard B&B 25.000lira
1 day hire for standard B&B 30.000lira
5 day hire for standard B&B 100.000lira

SNOWBOARD REPAIR/SERVICE
Full base Tune service 30/40.000lira

SNOWBOARD SHOP/S
ZETA SHOP +39-0-342 901 376
Sales-Hire-Repair
(Ski snowboard shop)

Motor sled hire
+39-0-342-921 050

Hangliding
Paragliding

Climbing School and Wall
+39-0-342-945510

Sports Centre
+39-0-342-901 482

LIFE STYLE
For Pizza eat at -
Cristall
Gramola
Jap
La Nuova Pastorella
La Stua

NIGHT TIME HANGOUTS
The Gorky
Vagabond
Kings Club

Accommodation

HOTEL FUNIVIA
+39-0-342 90 32 42
Hotel Olympia
+39-0-342 90 15 10

Bormio Tourist Office
Via Roma 131/B-23032
Bormio
+39 342 90 33 00
Reservations+39 342 90 33 00

Fly Milan International Airport

Transfer;

By bus approxametely 4 hours journey to resort.

By train to Tirano transfer by bus to resort 40km

By car hire approxametely 3Ω driving to resort.

Driving from home via Tirano A38 distance 40 km.

Via Innsbruck Autoroute A12 to Landeck then route 315/40/38 into Bormio.

COURMAYEUR

Courmayeur which is a stones throw away from the French resort of Chamonix, is a high level resort that sits in the shadow of Mont Blanc allowing for all year round snowboarding. On the snow its an OK place to shred; off the slopes its a typical Italian old style place that attracts millions of British skiers who copy their Italian counterparts by cladding themselves in expensive sad ski wear. The village is well spread out with no real chances of leaping out of the nest, Olling over a balcony and landing in a lift queue. You are going to have to do a bit of walking in order to take the cable car up to the slopes. The terrain which will please intermediate carvers but bore advanced freeriders insane. Be warned every man, jack and his dog hits the slopes at weekends and holidays. The thing you notice here is the amount of plate bindings and ski boots there are about, because this is a carvers pose place although many don't know what to pose in (ski boots are a NO NO people). Top Italian female carving pro Martina Magenta hails from here and can often be seen carving up the slopes. The runs off the Checrouit cable car offers some easy stuff for novices where you can try your first toe and heel turns in and out of the ski crowds taking out the stragglers. On piste carvers will find loads of runs to contend themselves with especially the areas under the Bertolini chair lift. The freeriding here is pretty damn good with some cool terrain to hit with the possibilities of some wood to cut at the lower section. If it's powder and off piste riding you want then Courmayeur is not the mega outlet like its close French neighbour, however there is some good stuff to be had with some steeps and trees down from the Cresta D'Arp. If you take the Mont Blanc cable car you can gain access to the Valle Blanche and ride into Chamonix though you will need to get the bus back. Freestylers here have to make do with the natural hits, as there is no park or pipe to ride but you can get big air and find enough to jib off, local ex junior freestyle champ Alain Vecchi sessions everything even the snow cannons.

Accommodation and all the other village bits like boozing and eating is OK and with loads of options at prices that don't always sting. Pizza, is high on the menu with a number of restaurants to pig out in. The failing here, is there are too many pointless poncy boutiques etc. and no dedicated snowboard shop but you can at least drink and party quite hard at a number of good bars where things go off loudly.

Snowboarding possible all year round with camps betwen May and Sept.

Top Station	2890m
Resort height	1224m
Vertical Drop	1000m
Longest run	4km
Ride area	100km of piste
Snowmaking	14km

Terrain ability suits

● Beginner	44%
● Intermediate	52%
● Advanced	4%

Terrain Ride styles suiteis

Freeride	40%
Freestyle	10%
Alpine/Carve	50%

1996/97 Lift Pass price guide
Guide for Courmayeur (Lira)

	Low season Adult	High season Adult
1 day	45,000	45,000
6 day	195.000	220,000

Lifts open 8.30am to 4pm daily

Cable Cars	7
Gondolas	3
Chair lifts	7
Drag lifts	15

Rider; Michel Vecchi

Eat at
La Boite

Drink at
Popps Pub
Bar Roma
American Bar

Courmayeur Tourist Office
Piazzale Monte Blanc
+39 165 84 20 60

Fly Geneva International Airport

Transfer;

By bus approxametely 3 hours journey to resort.

By train to Pre-St-Didier 8 minutes away or to Chamonix transfer by bus to resort 30km

By car hire approximately 2 driving to resort.

Driving from home via Geneve autohbah A40/N205 to Chamonix, to the Monte Blanc Tunnel = Courmayeur. Geneva to Courmayeur is 106km form Totino 150km.

LIVINGO

Something went a bit wrong when this place was given the go ahead by the local planning committee. It's basically a mess and badly laid out with old and new spread along the road side. Still it all adds to the character, but it's not totally crap and unlike so many other Italian resorts this place comes low on the poncy scale, although the sad gits in one piece ski suits shamefully riding in ski boots are still in evidence. As one of the cheaper resort in Italy the rich elite sun tanning numpties are not so common, however it has the other effect of attracting lots of first time skiers which does make the place busy on weekends and at holiday times. The height of Livingo helps ensure a good snow record that lasts quite late into the season. The slopes are spread across both sides of the valley and offer loads of no nonsense intermediate runs that will appeal to all rider styles. The way the area is set out means bussing around to certain areas with some notable bus queues. Once on the slopes the runs are reached by mainly drag lifts which will annoy some first timers but can be conquered. The marked pistes on your piste map will not always seem so on the ground with slopes criss crossing over each other. Those wanting some easy long carving will find the Vetta Blesaccia is the slope to check out; with it being a long descent you will have plenty of time to get the edge to edge carves sorted out. Riders with some history are not going to be too tested here, there's not that much to go for though the black down from the Della Neve is worth a go and should appeal to freeriders unless you're a wimp. There's not much to shout about as far as off piste is concerned. You can find some although it won't freak you out and some of the areas can be a pain in the arse for getting back to the resort. The trees here are also not the best but the easy beginner flats are. Novices should do all right on loads of easy runs although the drags will cheese some people off. Freestylers are going to get the best fun by riding fakie in and out of the ski schools. There are some cool hits to get air off but this is not a Freestylers paradise.

Off the slopes Livingo is cheap and cheerful with a lazy appeal. Accommodation is a mixture of hotels, B & B's and cheap apartments which are easy to overload. Night time is surprisingly OK and quite boozy. Plenty of throwing up in the streets here.

Winter snowboard periods between Nov and May

No summer snowboarding

Top Station	2755m
Resort height	1816m
Vertical Drop	1000m
Longest run	4km
Ride area	100km of piste
Snowmaking	12km

Terrain ability suits

● Beginner	44%
● Intermediate	45%
● Advanced	11%

Terrain Ride styles suits

Freeride	40%
Freestyle	10%
Alpine/Carve	50%

Lift Pass price guide Guide (Lira)

	High season	
	Adult	Child
6 days	240,000	160,000
	Low season	
	Adult	Child
6 days	210,000	145,000

Half day pass from 12.30pm 33,000lira

Lifts open 8.30am to 4pm daily

Gondolas	3
Chair lifts	10
Drag lifts	15

No lift rules for back foot
Leashes not compolsory

Snowboard Instruction
6 day course 2 hours a day 190,000lira
Tuition available at all 4 Ski Schools

SNOWBOARD & BOOT HIRE
¹/₂ dayhire for standard B&B 25.000lira
1 day hire for standard B&B 30.000lira
5 day hire for standard B&B 100.000lira

SNOWBOARD REPAIR/SERVICE
Full base Tune service 35.000lira

Snowmobiles
+39 342 996 077

Paragliding
+39 342 997 102

Mountaineering with guides

Fitness Centre

Pizza at
Bellavista
Lo Scoiattolo
Mariois

NIGHT TIME HANGOUTS
Galliis Pub
Marcos Video Bar
The Underground
Koleodis Disco

Photos: Tourist Office Livingo

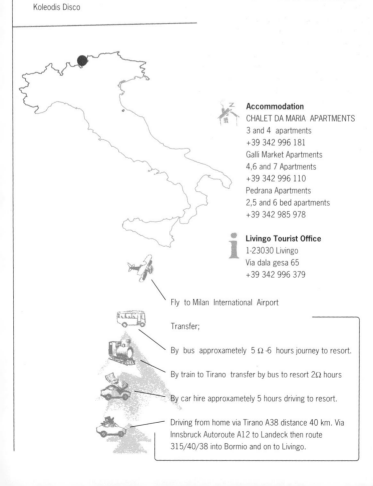

Accommodation
CHALET DA MARIA APARTMENTS
3 and 4 apartments
+39 342 996 181
Galli Market Apartments
4,6 and 7 Apartments
+39 342 996 110
Pedrana Apartments
2,5 and 6 bed apartments
+39 342 985 978

Livingo Tourist Office
1-23030 Livingo
Via dala gesa 65
+39 342 996 379

Fly to Milan International Airport

Transfer;

By bus approxametely 5 Ω -6 hours journey to resort.

By train to Tirano transfer by bus to resort 2Ω hours

By car hire approxametely 5 hours driving to resort.

Driving from home via Tirano A38 distance 40 km. Via
Innsbruck Autoroute A12 to Landeck then route
315/40/38 into Bormio and on to Livingo.

CERVINIA

Cervinia a something of a nothing and a place that you will love or simply hate. This is Italy through and through, bland no big deal, nothing major and full of stupidly kited out skiers. Yet for all that it's not a bad place to ride. Cervinia which links on the slopes with the big bucks Swiss resort of Zermatt, is a euro carvers paradise. The area has been attracting two plankers for years and in recent times more and more snowboarders have taken to the slopes and are very welcome though its fair to say that there's never been anything laid on for riders, no pipe, park or even a decent snowboard shop. Still the terrain is the main thing and its OK suiting all levels with most emphasis on intermediates runs as well as some testing stuff for riders with brains and a few carves under their belts. The runs rise up from the village at three main points and apart from a few areas the lower sections are not beginner friendly although there is a blue that leads down giving novices the chance to ride home. The main areas for beginners to get there first bruises are up at the Plan Maison which is fortunately reached by a cable car sparing the drag lift blues. Once on the runs then be prepared for some drag lift tackle in order to get to the amble of easy flats which also come with a heavy dose of ski schools. Carvers of the 'I can do brigade' can put it to the test here on a variety of reds and some steep blacks which can be tricky if you're not giving it your all. However the 22km red run Valtournenche is the place to carve long and hard while the blacks down into the village are cool and will appeal to freeriders a lot, as will some off piste opportunities at the link with Zermatt. Freestylers won't find that much though there are hits and any freestyler should be able to perform something even if just off the table tops around eating places (ask the Señor first if he minds Stalefish with his fresh pasta before going over it). If you buy the special pass you may find more on offer in Zermatt, or you could try some heli boarding. Off the slopes the place is a bundle of old, new and unsure, with heaps of places to kip. Hotel Fosson is a cool place with a bar that's owned by a rider. If you're scamming and on the cheap then cram into one of the many apartments. For booze and hanging out the Dragon is an option as is the Chimere disco if you want bop to euro pop. You can hire equipment here but the choices are not great with plate bindings and ski boots the main option.

Snowboarding possible all year round on the Swiss side of the Materhorn

Top Station	3478m
Resort height	2050
Vertical Drop	2000m
Longest run	22km
Ride area	230km
(linked with neighbouring Zermatt)	
Snowmaking	7.5km

Terrain ability suits

● Beginner	34%
● Intermediate	53%
● Advanced	13%

Terrain Ride styles suits

Freeride	35%
Freestyle	5%
Alpine/Carve	60%

Heli boarding possible

Photo: Tourist Office Cervina

Fly Geneva International Airport

Transfer;

By bus approxametely 3¹/₂ hours journey to resort.

By train to Chatillon transfer by bus to resort 30 minutes

By car hire approxametely 2¹/₂ driving to resort.

Driving via Geneva autobahn A40/N205- Chamonix-Monte Blanc Tummel-N26 Aosta Chatillon=Cervino.

1996/97 Lift Pass price guide (Lir

	Low season	
	Child	Adult
5 days	212000	212000
7 days	282000	282000

Lifts open 8.30am to 4pm daily

Cable Cars	2
Gondolas	6
Chair lifts	8
Drag lifts	9

No rear foot rules
No rules

Cervinia Tourist Office
Via Carrel 29
11021 Breuil -Cervinia
+39 166 94 9136

CORTINA

Cortina, big all round very Italian resort full of posers in fur hats. Not cheap, not great but OK to shred. This is Money Mountain with so many balcony posers laying around outside restaurants that the slopes are left quite. The terrain is OK for advanced riders, but will suit intermediates more. There are some decent long runs to crank a few serious carves, with ample areas to freeride and freestyle on. The 11 km run Sella Ronda is differently worth a visit with some of the most challenging located down from the Tofana which rises to 3243m and is accessed by cable car. From the summit you'll find plenty of stuff to check out offering some good powder riding especially if you're in softs. Cortina is particularly well suited to first timers with a number of easy slopes to start on and progress with. Check out the easy stuff around the mid section of the Tofana which can be reached by chair lift.

Hanging out in Cortina is no big deal, the place is large with a selection of apartments, silly priced hotels and loads of food joints offering the usual Italian fair. (Pasta). Life style is pretty boring here and the rich only go to make it very poncy.

Winter snowboard periods between Dec and April.

Top Station	3243m
Resort height	1220m
Vertical Drop	1800m
Longest run	11km
Ride area	140km of piste
Snowmaking	51km of piste

Terrain ability suits:

● Beginner	44%
● Intermediate	49%
● Advanced	7%

Number of lifts	53
1 day adult pass	49,00 lira
6 day adult pass	243,000 lira

No rear foot or leashes rules.
1 hour snowboard lesson 48,000 lira.

Cortina Tourist office
Pizzetta S. Francesco,
Cortina D'Ampezzo. Italy
+39 0 463 321 234
http://www.sunrise.it/dolomiti

Nearest international airport = Venice transfer 2½ hours.

LA THULE

La Thule, nestles a few kilometre's down the road from its more famous cousin Courmayeur. Unlike its neighbour this is a far more quieter resort, even though it has 135 km of piste to cut up. Bordering with France, La Thule links in the Aosta Valley with La Rosiere. This not just a hard boot carvers resort, the wide open pistes, steeps and trees are there for everyone. The terrain lies at a height that helps to insure good conditions prevail, backed up by snowmaking facilities. Freeriders have some good blacks to try out, the Diretta which runs through the trees is full on and will sort out those who think they know it all. There's also some cool freeriding to be had on the La Rosiere side, while those looking for off piste will find it off the San Bernardo chair. However the real off piste is best tackled by going heli boarding which is possible here. Apart from a couple of small nursery slopes at the base, the main easy runs are located above the Les Suches area which are served by chair lifts rather than all drags, however slow learners will not be riding back into the village.

The purpose built resort close to the slopes caters OK for your stay but there's nothing major, with just the basic offerings of cheap apartments and some over priced hotels, sleeping around 4000 people. There's no happening night life, although you can chill out with a few beers in a couple of bars.

Winter snowboard periods between Dec and April.

Top Station	2641m
Resort height	1441m
Vertical Drop	1230m
Longest run	10km
Ride area	135km of piste
Snowmaking	12km of piste

Terrain ability suits:

● Beginner	48%
● Intermediate	31%
● Advanced	21%

Number of lifts	15
1 day adult pass	44,00 lira
6 day adult pass	205,000 lira

No rear foot or leashes rules.
1 hour snowboard lesson 48,000 lira.

La Thule Tourist office
Via Collomb 11016 La Thule
Aosta Italy.
+39 0 165 884 179

Nearest international airport = Geneva transfer 2½ hours.

GRESSONY

Located in the Aosta Valley, Gressony is the neighbour to nearby Champoluc, with heaps of piste between the two. The good off piste offers lots of drops, gullies and cliffs. Perfect for the hard core freerider who likes something to get stuck into. For carvers there are ample of wide spaces and beginners have loads of easy flats to fall over on.

The small village has a few hotels and chalets to kip down in, some are very cheap as well. Night time is zero but the a few bars there are offer cheap drink and the locals are friendly and can party hard.

Top Station	3370m
Base	1640m
Ride area	70 km of piste
Terrain ability suits	
Beginner	31%
Intermediate	63%
Advanced	6%

Half pipe and fun park
12 lifts. No ride rules.
For full resort details
Tel +1- 39 125 355 185

MADONNA

Tries hard to satisfy snowboarders and does a fairly good job; this place is actually really good. The ISF now stage world ranking snowboard events on the largely tame intermediate slopes spread out over three areas. Hard boot carvers will be happy here as will freeriders with some cool tree runs around the Folgarida area. Total beginners have some decent easy runs to check out especially at Campo Carlo Magno though the bus ride is a pain. Although there are plenty of eating and sleeping options, it's not the cheapest and not the most convenient resort which is spread out all over the place. OK though.

Top station	2633m
Resort height	1550m
Ride area	150km of piste
Terrain ability suits	
Beginner	43%
Intermediate	40%
Advanced	17%

Half pipe and fun park
49 lifts no ride rules.
For full resort details
Tel +1 -39 465 442 000

PILA

Cool riding to be had on slopes that offer wide open carving territory and decent freeriding through trees. As an intermediates place who like to carve it up, there's not a great deal for competent riders to get stuck into, however freestylers and new school will find plenty of flats to fakie down. Beginners are going to find Pila OK, there's plenty of gentle flats reached easily and serviced by a well set out chair lift system. Off the slopes don't be expecting a great deal although it's not that bad, with accommodation and places to pig out and get drunk within in easy reach of the slopes.

Top station	2650m
Base lift	1750m
Ride area	60km of piste
Terrain ability suits:	
Beginner	34%
Intermediate	58%
Advanced	8%

Half pipe and fun park
13 lifts. no ride rules.
For full resort details
Tel +1 -39 0165/ 521 1000

SELA RONDA/VAL GARDENA

Forms part of what is said to be the largest ski/snowboard area in the world. It also has the sad claim to be the place where one of Britains best ever ski results was achieved by a particularly sad British skier. However this is not a sad place to snowboard. It is indeed very good with something for every one. The huge area of some 1000km and 460 lifts (not all linked) get you to terrain that has steeps and trees for freeriders and excellent piste for carvers and beginners. Accommodation and night time is very Italian with loads of good and sad options.

Top station	2400m
Base lift	1405m
Ride area	1100km of pis*
Terrain ability suits:	
Beginner	30%
Intermediate	60%
Advanced	10%

Half pipe. 465 lifts in the area.
For full area details
Tel +39 0471 792277

CARNO ALLE SCALLE

This is not really a resort that people have heard of but it is worth a visit if you fancy a road trip - especially if you fancy a night out in nearby Bologna. This resort has plenty of terrain to suit all standards and has some major gnarly off piste for freeriders to bury themselves in. The only draw back is that accommodation is 10km down the hill so you need your own transport. Night life is sad with only a cheesy disco bar and a number of smaller bars to visit, still things here are cheap.

ABEFORE

Like Carno, Abefore is not particularly well known yet this is a good allround resort with plenty of varied freeriding to be had; there's also a half pipe and fun park to be found providing enough snow has dumped. Off the slopes the place has a very young 'studenty' feel to it. Accommodation, food and booze is not just cheap but also pretty cool.

RIDER'S OWN NOTES ON ITALY

NORWAY

Norway has successfully staged the winter Olympics and now puts on regular ISF competitions though mainly with freestyle events, because Norway is the land of top freestylers and small resorts. Over the past few years Norway has become more and more popular despite the fact it's not a cheap place for foreigners to visit especially if you want to buy booze. However Norway is definitely well worth a road tip, any country that produces the skills of the likes of freestylers Terje Haakonsen and Daniel Franck must have something to offer. Norway's resorts may not be the biggest things in the world yet they are advanced and most have been building half pipes since day one, well before resorts in France had ever heard of snowboarding. The things that make this country so different from other European mountain areas is the resorts themselves which are generally low level with rolling hills and trees to the summits. That said Helmsedal is a match for many a resort in Austria or France and Lillehammer managed to put on the Olympics in 1994 which is no mean feat. The climate and daylight hours are also very different, with day time between December and January down to 7 hours. What you will notice is how damn cold Norway can become with temperatures plummeting to 50° and below not uncommon.

In a country that list over 160 resorts (much of theses are just cross country areas) the slopes are generally much quieter than other countries with lift queues almost un-heard off and pistes well looked after backed up by snowmaking. The terrain in most areas is best tackled by novices and intermediates. You won't get short of breath as the length of runs won't take long to do, so any hard boot piste lovers wanting to pump down mega length runs forget it and check out France instead. This country is a freestylers and freeriders place with lots of trees, but a lack of extreme and piste deep powder will find a full weeks riding a bit limiting unless all you want is a halfpipe. The season in many areas lasts quite long and riding on good snow in the months of May is quite common.

The resorts themselves are nothing to shout about, in the main they're simple and laid back with basic services on offer. Beer prices are so high that night time doesn't go off although you will find hangouts to party in. If you are flying in, then try and bring as much duty free as you can carry, however if you are driving via a ferry crossing from either northern Europe or the UK, then load the boot up with crates of cheap larger and bottles of Vodka. Travel to Norway is no problem, the country has a good road and rail network which connects well with international airports as well as domestic airports. Accommodation is pretty good with the best and most affordable being cabins which cater for groups. Hotels will burn a stupidly big hole in the pocket so unless you have a gold card avoid them.

Overall Norway is OK and the local riders are cool, everyone speaks good English so you'll be able to find out easily where the best happenings are, on and off the slopes. Norwegian riders are very much influenced by American trends in terms of styles of riding - 99% soft boots, and in terms of fashion and attitude, laid back easy going party animals. Who rip in the pipe.

NORWEIGAN DRIVE GUIDE

Break down - tel - Norges Automobil +47-22 34 1400

Vehicles drive on the Right

Speed On:	Motorway	Dualcarage	Single	Urba
	80-9080-90	80-90	50km/h	
Towing:	80 80	80	50km/h	

Seat belts - Compolsory for front and back if fitted

Tolls - Payable on somr new roads

Alchol level = 0.05%

Driving age limit - 18 Or 20 depending on vehicle

Document to carry: International Driving permit ,

Vehicle Reg,Green Card,Country Identifaction,

Number Plates, Hire Docs

Fuel -Sold in Litres

Firt Aid Kit - Recomended

Warning Triangle - Compolsory

Snowchains - Recomended

FACT FILE

Status	Constitunal Monich
Capital	Oslo
Area	324,219 sq km
Population	4.3 million
Language	Norweigan
Currency	Kroner
Neighbouring Countries	Findland, Russia, Sweden
Winter snowboard periods	November to May
Summer snowboarding	May to August
Highest Mountain	Galdhopiggen 2472 m
Country Snowboard styles	Freeride/Freestyle 99%
	Alpine/Caring 1%
	Soft boots 99%
	Hard boots 1%
Drugs	Canabis is illegal
Death penalty	No capital punishment
Military Service	Nationals have to joint the army
Alcohol drinking age	Age 18 for beer and 20 for spirits.
Age of consent for sex	Male 16-Female 16

GEILO

Geilo is a winter sports area that not only is up to the mark, but also has a lot going for it. If all you're looking for is a simple no nonsense place that offers some good terrain to ride then this place should do the trick. Geilo is a popular Norwegian resort as well as being the biggest in the country. About 3 1/2 hours from Norway's capital Oslo, Geilo is situated in the Hallingdal Valley the largest mountain plateau in Europe. On your arrival in the village you are met with a good spread of services and happening things. The well spread out town, which is also easy to get about, lies close to the slopes making for easy attack of the runs first thing in the morning. The slopes rise up on two sides of the valley with terrain that is well looked after leaving lots of corduroy tracks to mess up in the early hours. Geilo's slopes will suite intermediate and novice riders mostly, there's nothing here to set the old heart racing for advance or even competent riders, although there are a few black graded runs but don't get too excited, they won't take long to conquer. The two separate areas which are not connected, rise up to give a maximum lift height of 1173 meters. If you want to ride both places you'll have to take a snow taxi which you will have to pay for extra to your lift pass. The Vestila area which is actually the smaller of the two, has the longer runs, with a mixture of easy blues, reds and a couple of blacks to carve up with some trees to check out as well. Furthermore the 5 lifts get you around with ease, even shy beginners will be happy. On the main and bigger area you'll find the terrain is much the same. Though there are a couple of challenging runs to suit freeriders, beginners are given a much bigger choice of slopes to tackle starting out at the base areas with good flats higher up and easy runs back into the village. Freestylers wanting air will find the hits in the 100m long halfpipe the place from the quarter pipes, spines and rails found in the two fun parks. Night riding on four flood lit slopes is possible before hitting the bars.

Around the town Geilo is not the cheapest place, with a choice of fancy hotels to less expensive cabins and apartments which are the best options. There are a number of good options to eat out and with Geilo's 6 discos and selection of bars, you will be able to big out and get messy but it will require a hammering with a credit card or a hole in the wall bank machine. Check out Hos Johs'n.

Winter snowboard periods between Nov and May.

No summer snowboarding

Top Station	1173m
Base	800m
Vertical Drop	275m
Longest run	2 Km
Ride area	25km
Snowmaking	12km

Terrain ability suits:

● Beginner	22%
● Intermediate	56%
● Advanced	22%

Terrain Ride styles suits:

Freeride	55%
Freestyle	30%
Alpine/Carve	15%

Half pipe and 2 fun parks

1996/97 Lift pass guide

Days	Junior	Adult
1/2	120-	160-
1	145-	195-
5	460-	605-
Adult season pass 2450-		

Lifts open 9.30am to 4.30pm
Nigh riding daily

Chair lifts	4
Drag lifts	14

Lift policy is rear foot free on drag lifts and snowboard leashes are required.

Photo: Tourist Office Geilo

Snowboard Instruction
1 hour lesson 250-
2 hour lesson 450-
Kids as young as 3 catered for.

Snowboard and boot hire
1 day hire for standard board 250-
2 day hire for standard board 400-
5 day hire for standard board 850-

Snowboard repair & service
Full base tune service 200-

Snowboard Shop/s
Vestlia Ski Center
Tel +47-320 88340
Per Bye
Tel + 47-320 90 650

Eat at
Vidda Restaurant
Bifferiet

Night Time hangouts
Hos Johsin, a beer cost 40-
Recepten, a beer cost 40-
Laven, a beer cost 40-

Photo: Mark Webster

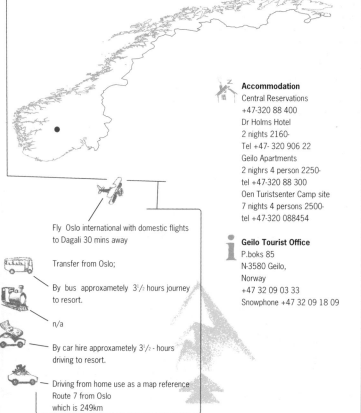

Accommodation
Central Reservations
+47-320 88 400
Dr Holms Hotel
2 nights 2160-
Tel +47- 320 906 22
Geilo Apartments
2 nighrs 4 person 2250-
tel +47-320 88 300
Oen Turistsenter Camp site
7 nights 4 persons 2500-
tel +47-320 088454

Geilo Tourist Office
P.boks 85
N-3580 Geilo,
Norway
+47 32 09 03 33
Snowphone +47 32 09 18 09

Fly Oslo international with domestic flights
to Dagali 30 mins away

Transfer from Oslo;

By bus approxametely 3$\frac{1}{2}$ hours journey
to resort.

n/a

By car hire approxametely 3$\frac{1}{2}$ - hours
driving to resort.

Driving from home use as a map reference
Route 7 from Oslo
which is 249km

HEMSEDAL

Whether you're a frequent visitor to Norway or a first timer to any mountain resort range, what you will notice about Hemsedal is it's the nearest they come in Norway to resembling the resorts of the Alps. Hemsedal's height, location and use of snow cannon's help to insure a good snow record and long season starting from November and going on to May. You get a lot here, although on a lower level to it's foreign cousins, Hemsedal still offers steeps, deeps, big bowls and loads of good piste riding on a well spread out mountain range. This is a resort that has been attracting riders of all ages for years, especially freestylers. The slopes lie about 3 kilometres from the main town and are reached by a free shuttle bus. The terrain will appeal to all standards, with 40 kilometres of well prepared piste for freeriders to carve up as well as being ideal for beginners. The runs are serviced by a good lift system which unlike some neighbouring resorts is not all drag lifts, making life for novices that bit easier. The few hard booters who dare grace the slopes will find the runs known as the Hemsedalsloypa and Kuleloya's the place to lay out some carves, these may not be the longest two runs in the world but they are also not for first timers. The Sahaugloypa is also a decent run on which to get some speed together. In many of Norways resorts the runs are usually very short, so it comes as a welcome relief to find a run that last for more that two seconds. The Turistloypa run is the longest descent around the area and although it's not at all testing even for novice riders still in nappies, it's still worth a blast if only to avoid being on a lift again. Riders looking for some hits and trees should take the Holdeskarheisen and Roniheisen chairs to reach some cool terrain including a tight gully to pull air from. The area offers plenty of easy flats for beginners at the base as well as higher up with easy options to ride home.

Hemsedal off the slopes is pretty cool and has a good snowboard scene. The cheapest options for accommodation are the camping cabins which you can load with heaps of riders. The Rjukandefoss is a cool place to stay at but if you want something close to town then check out the Totten Ferie apartments. The main snowboard hang out is the Hemsedal Cafe where booze, which is expensive, flows nicely.

Winter snowboard periods between Nov and May.

No summer snowboarding

Top Station	1450m
Base	650m
Vertical Drop	800m
Longest run	6 Km
Ride area	40km
Snowcannons	145

Terrain ability suites:

● Beginner	53%
● Intermediate	27%
● Advanced	20%

Terrain Ride styles suits:

Freeride	60%
Freestyle	25%
Alpine/Carve	15%

Half pipe and fun parks

1996/97 Lift pass guide

Days	Junior	Adult
½	130-	170-
1	155-	210-
5	580-	750-
Night ride pass		
	65-	90-

Pass of 2 days or more covers night riding

Lifts open 9 am to 4.30pm
Nigh riding 3 nights a week

Chair lifts	4
Drag lifts	11

Lift policy is rear foot free on drag lifts and snowboard leashes are required

Photo: Tourist Office Hemsedal

Snowboard Instruction
5 day lesson 390-

Snowboard and boot hire
1 day hire for standard board 250-
2 day hire for standard board 400-
6 day hire for standard board 500-

Snowboard repair & service
Full base tune service 200-

Snowboard Shop/s
Hemsedal Sport
Tel +47-32 06 03 50
Totten Sport
Tel + 47-32 06 05 77

Snowmobile rides

Ice Climbing

Snow Holing

Hangliding and Paragliding

Eat at:
Hemsedal Cafe

Night Time hangouts
Hemsedal Cafe
Elgen Bar
Garasjen

Accommodation
Central Reservations
+47-32 06 07 00
Hemsedal Cafe
tel +47- 32 06 06 15
Rjukandefoss
tel +47-32 06 21 74
Totten Ferie Apartments
tel +47-32 06 21 00

Hemsedal Tourist Office
PO Box 3
N-3560 Hemsedal
+47 32 06 01 56
Snowphone +47 32 06 01 56

Fly Oslo International with
domestic flights to Dagali
1¹/₂ hours

Transfer from Oslo;

By bus approxametely 3¹/₂
hours journey to resort.

By train to Goi then transfer
by bus to the resort

By car hire approxametely
3¹/₂ hours driving to resort.

Driving from home use as a map
reference Goi. Oslo is 220km

VASSFJELLET

Vassfjellet is not a tourist resort that is perched way up high on a mountain, boasting millions of kilometres of piste and dozens of hotels. No this place is a locals place and serves the masses from neighbouring towns and the city of Trondheim. When you live in a city you go snowboarding in the easiest and cheapest way so a trip up to Vassfjellet

is just what Trondheimís riders do in large numbers. If your on a road trip and fancy some different then check this place out its pretty cool and very snowboard friendly, with a large number of students riders from Trondheinís University. They are given student concession on lift passesí so if your doing the college or Uni number be sure to carry your students card. The evenly matched freeride, freestyle and carving terrain offers every level of rider something to take on. This is by most standards a very small resort with just 10kms of piste, (4kms flood lit for night riding), which wont take the average rider to many hours to conquer.

Though its not going to hold the attention of advanced riders for to long if your looking for major big powder bowls or dozens of big cliff jumps, the longest run to keep the mind occupied is 3.5 kms which is respectable and offers the opportunity to speed past the on looking skiers. The best way to search out any powder or any good hits is to call in at the local snowboard school, there's no ride guides here, but the guys at the club will help you out. There are however plenty of trees to cut through and a couple of big hits to be found but were not talking massive. Freeriders roaming around will find some banked walls and a gullies to check out while freestylers will find that the 2 half pipes and fun park is the best place to get air, both pipes are really good and grommets will soon be emulating their freestyle heros of both walls in the pipe or of the selection of rails and hits in the park.

First time riders will find this place more than enough to start out with, the local school looks after tuition and will take kids down to 4 years old. You can hire snowboard equipment at the slopes however for a bigger choice check out Sport Extreme in Trondheim, where they stock the lot. At the end of the day every one heads off back to Trondheim by a regular bus service, where theres a huge selection of places to sleep at or eat and drink in. Theres also a skate board shop and half pipe to ride.

Winter snowboard periods between Nov and May.

No summer snowboarding

Top Station	670m
Base	200m
Vertical Drop	470m
Longest run	3.5Km
Ride area	10km
Snowcannons	7

Terrain ability suits:

Beginner	35%
Intermediate	50%
Advanced	15%

Terrain Ride styles suits:

Freeride	60%
Freestyle	35%
Alpine/Carve	5%

2 Half pipe and a fun parks in the Boarder Cross Arena.

Snowboard shop to check out Sport Extreme in Trondheim. Tel +47 73 90 54 00

1 days snowboard lession 300-
1 day board and boot hire 250-
Full base service 100-

1996/97 Week day lift pass

Days	Junior	Adult	Students
1 /2	80-	100-	80-
1	100-	120-	100
2	200-	240-	200-
7	560-	690-	560-

Lifts open
10 am to 10pm weekdays
10 am to 5 pm weekends

Drag lifts	3
Button lifts	1
Rope tows	1

Bike lift (the only one in the world used in the summer)
No ride rules.

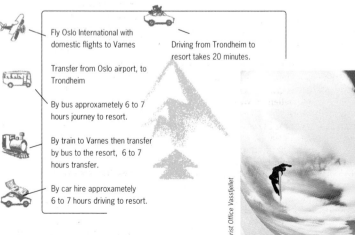

Fly Oslo International with domestic flights to Varnes

Driving from Trondheim to resort takes 20 minutes.

Transfer from Oslo airport, to Trondheim

By bus approxametely 6 to 7 hours journey to resort.

By train to Varnes then transfer by bus to the resort, 6 to 7 hours transfer.

By car hire approxametely 6 to 7 hours driving to resort.

Tourist Office Vassfjellet

OPPAL

Oppal; is one of Norway's main resorts situated 125km south of Trondheim. One of Norway's biggest areas Oppal will appeal (as with much of this country) to easy going piste loving freeriders. Although the off piste here is actually quite good. The 80km of piste are for beginners mainly, there's nothing for advanced riders to get excited about, and even intermediates will soon tire of this place. The somewhat uneven terrain will give ground grommets something to spin over but won't please hard boot carvers to much. The longest run of 5.5 km is the best place to lay out some arcs while freestylers will find the park and pipe the place to get air from. Beginners will find the Stolen area the easiest place for the early moves. Off the slopes there's not a great deal going on. There are a few good places to kip but night time is a bit naff and more importantly booze is bloody expensive.

Winter snowboard periods between Nov and April.
No summer snowboarding

Top Station	1300m
Base	545m
Longest run	5.5Km
Ride area	65km

Terrain ability suits:

● Beginner	52%
● Intermediate	30%
● Advanced	18%

Terrain Ride styles suits:
Freeride	45%
Freestyle	30%
Alpine/Carve	25%

Pipe and Park

Full resort Details
tel +47 72 42 17 60

VALDRES

Valdres: is a small unassuming typical Norwegian resort with a good reputation amongst Norway's snowboarder population. The tree lined runs will suit intermediate freeriders and air heads. Carvers looking for lots of wide open flats will be disappointed, as well advanced riders looking for major hits or gullies with big walls. However there is some extreme stuff to keep freeriders happy and the open and tight trees are pretty cool. Grommets will find enough logs to slide down. The fun park and pipe are also good and offers the best chance of pulling some good air. First timers should have no problem here, the flats at the base area are full-on for collecting the first bruises. The local snowboard school will help you out with your early moves.

Lodging is the usual Norwegian offering with a number of decent chalets or apartments to choose from. Night time, turn up the walkman!

Winter snowboard periods between Nov and April.
No summer snowboarding

Top Station	1040m
Base	1000m
Longest run	2Km
Ride area	11km
Snowcannons	5

Terrain ability suits:

● Beginner	30%
● Intermediate	50%
● Advanced	20%

Terrain Ride styles suits
Freeride	65%
Freestyle	25%
Alpine/Carve	10%

Pipe and Park

4 lifts no ride rules

VOSS

This is a very popular Norwegian resort. The 40kms of piste is well marked out and groomed to suit carvers and plain freeriders. The limited off piste here is not bad and you will be able to go deep, above and below the tree lines. The wood also allows for some good shredding with loads of logs to grind. Carvers will find Voss a good challenge, with some good piste to lay some big lines especially on the Raugstad run. Freestylers don't get caught trying out the ski jump, you're not allowed, check out the trees instead where you will find hits. Voss is ideal for novices particularly on the Hangur area.

The town offers good accommodation, plenty of eating joints, 6 pubs and 4 cheesy discos. The place is not bad just heavy on the pocket.

Winter snowboard periods between Nov and May.
No summer snowboarding

Top Station	945m
Base	55m
Vertical Drop	650m
Longest run	1500Km
Ride area	40km

Terrain ability suits:

● Beginner	66%
● Intermediate	7%
● Advanced	27%

Terrain Ride styles suits:
Freeride	55%
Freestyle	20%
Alpine/Carve	25%

Full resort Details tel +47 56 51 00 51

RIDER'S OWN NOTES ON NORWAY

SPAIN

If you thought that Spain was just about castanets, bull fighting and hot tacky seaside resorts inhabited by Britain and Europe's finest villainy then think again. Its also about snowboarding, not intense but certainly worth more than a mention. Although Spain's disgusting reputation for animal rights (bull fighting is simply sick) and it's eighties explosion of package holiday haunts is one thing, its two main mountain ranges with almost thirty resorts offering ample for some full on snowboarding are another. The two mountain areas in question are the Pyrenees in the north of Spain along the French border and in the south the area known as Sierra

Nevada near Granada. Top international freestyler Sergio Bartrina hails from here too. The thing to remember about Spain is that even though some of the resorts have been around for some time they are not up to much and some are stupidly small. Spain hasn't always had the greatest snow record and with many not being the most up to date resorts there's very little artificial snowmaking to help out when the real stuff is lacking. Resort facilities are not the greatest either with little or no snowboard facilities, sad options for places to doss and poor snowboard hire options. However this is generalising because the big areas like Sierra Nevada are an easy match for the rest of Europe, indeed it will put a lot of northern places to shame. The Spanish tend to be a bit like there Mediterranean Italian cousins, they love to pose and in doing so end up looking stupid in sad ski wear. Snowboarding is fairly well received though out its resorts, the majority of which are situated in the north and can prove tricky to reach with a bit of an unsure travel service. Your best bet is to hire a car at airports and drive, this way you can leave quickly if you hate a particular place and can move on to the next area. One last point, Spanish snowboarding may not work out as cheap as you think, so don't just think of it as just a cheap alternative to France or Austria though it is certainly cheaper than Switzerland.

Spanish Snowboard Association
Gran Via 29,8∞ Oficina 4
28013 Madrid- Spain
+34.1. 5222 803

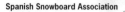

Status	Constitutional Monarchy
Capital	Madrid
Area	504;880 sq km
Population	38,959,000
Density	77 people per sq km
Language	Spanish, (Catalan and Basque)
Currency	Peseta
Neighbouring Countries	France, Portugal
Winter snowboard periods	December to April
Summer snowboarding	Zero
Highest Mountain	Mulhacen 3478 m
Country Snowboard styles	Freeride/Freestyle 35%
Alpine/Carving	65%
	Soft boots 40%
	Hard boots 60%
Drugs	Cannabis and dope are illegal
Death penalty	No capital punishment
Military Service	Nationals joint the army by choice
Alcohol drinking age	Age 18.
Age of consent for sex	Male 16, Female 16
Prostitution	Illegal

SIERRA NEVADA

It seems amazing, wrong even, that you can quite easily snowboard in the morning then pop down to the beach just over an hour away for a huge seafood scoff and a swim. But at the Sierra Nevada centre of Pradollano this is exactly the case. Situated at the southern tip of Spain it's possible from the high point Veleta to see the Atlas mountains of Morocco across the Med. That's Africa! Once you're ready to go snowboarding the main gondola deposits you in 'Borreguiles' directly onto fantastic beginners teaching piste, go up higher and you go to the next level where it's steeper, the angles being great for freecarving – just that perfect angle to really lay 'em out in perfect control. Just below the peak of Veleta at 3398m traverse to the 'Olimpica' and where this crosses the 'Diagonal' kick hard to your left and travel off piste on an itinerary known as 'Tajos de la Virgen'. The view above you is truly stunning. A bowl edged with dramatic cliffs and ice blue snow. Along this run are rolling jumps verging into vertical kickers. Kick back again towards the piste 'Cartujo' and make use of the piste edge with it's many varied banked sides. Take the 'Dilar' chair up towards the Radio Telescope then walk along the ridge and view below you the huge expanse of off piste which you have just travelled over on the chair. Take any line, the slope is a good safe angle with an easy traverse back to the 'Solana' piste and the Dilar chair. Night skiing is done on the 'Rio' slope. The days for this you would have to check with the ticket office but we think that it is one of the best lit night runs ever. Getting around the village which is extremely steep is pretty tough on foot so note this for your early morning club sessions. There is a bus service but this stops at 12.00. Alternatively there's a chair lift that links the various levels to the centre of the village. For this you will need a valid lift pass. Remember to go to Granada. With the new road built for the "Campionatos de Esqui 96" it's a complete doddle to motor down for a look around. It takes between 20 and 30 minutes. You can catch a bus which costs 600 pesetas (£3.50). Sun protection is a necessity. Forget it and fry dude. Being so far south and at 2100m + you will need it.

If you like night life then you will have plenty to go at here, but it's a little different to the rest of Europe. Nothing happens until 9.30pm when people start to go out for dinner, this will typically last 3 hours, so bars and clubs don't get going until at least midnight. Then it rocks. It will be no trouble to stay out until 7/8 in the morning and you won't get bored. The shop to visit is Surfin' run by Miguel Bonal - "El Capitan". You cannot fail to love his little logo - El Surfito. They are a good core shop with a great bunch of riders and instructors. Its been going since 1988.

Winter snowboard periods between Dec and April.

No summer snowboarding

Top Station	3398m
Resort height	2100m
Vertical Drop	1348m
Longest run	7.5km
Ride area	61km of piste
Snowmaking 22km of piste cover	

Terrain ability suits:

● Beginner	55%
● Intermediate	32%
● Advanced	14%

Terrain Ride styles suits:

Freeride	35%
Freestyle	5%
Alpine/Carve	65%

Snowboard hire

Days	Board
1	3000
2	5500
3	7500
4	8500
5	9500

El Edwardo del Spring

Lift Pass price guide
Spanish Pesetas

	High season		Low season	
	Adult	Child	Adult	Child
1/2 day				
	2350		2100	
1 day				
	3150	2050	2725	1850
5 days				
	13900	9259	12100	7950
6 days				
	16000	10500	13950	8950
Night pass 700				

Lifts open 8.30am to 4pm week

Cable Cars	2
Chair lifts	8
Drag lifts	9

Sierra Nevada Tourist Office

Rider: Joe in the Laguna area.
Photo: Dward

Rider: Dave Furneau overlooking
the town. Photo: Dward

i **Sierra Nevada Tourist Office**
Monachil, Granada
Spain
(+34-(9) 58 24 91 11
Reservations(+34-(9) 58 24 91 11
Snowphone(+34-(9) 58 24 91 11

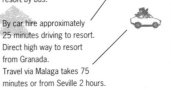

Fly to Granada International
Airport

Transfer from the airport;

By bus approximately 35 minutes journey to resort.

By train to Granada transfer to
resort by bus.

By car hire approximately
25 minutes driving to resort.
Direct high way to resort
from Granada.
Travel via Malaga takes 75
minutes or from Seville 2 hours.

QUICK RIDE AROUND TWENTY
OTHER SPANISH SNOWBOARD RESORTS

	Top station	Base	Ride Area (km)				

Boi-Taull — 2475 — 2030 — 17 — ●Beg 59% — ●Int 29% — ●Adv 12% — Lifts 8
Wide open flats, best for novices, suits carvers, bore freestylers and advanced riders.
No accommodation . To Barcelona or Zaragoza. Resort info +34-9-3 414 66 60

La Molina — 2537 — 1400 — 27 — ●Beg 52% — ●Int 37% — ●Adv 11% — Lifts 20
Trees, gullies and runs to suit freeriders and freestylers of all levels.
Some accommodation. To Barcelona or Zaragoza. Resort info +34-9-72 89 21 76

Masella — 2535 — 1600 — 42 — ●Beg 45% — ●Int 41% — ●Adv 14% — Lifts 10
OK freeriding, lots of trees, suit all levels with some hits for freestylers.
Some accommodation. To Barcelona or Zaragoza. Resort info +34-9-72 89 01 06

Port Aine — 2440 — 1650 — 18 — ●Beg 44% — ●Int 50% — ●Adv 6% — Lifts 6
Wide flats good for carvers, a few open trees for freeriders, good for beginners.
No accommodation. To Barcelona or Zaragoza. Resort info +34-9-73 62 03 25

Port del Comte — 2400 — 1700 — 31 — ●Beg 39% — ●Int 45% — ●Adv 16% — Lifts 15
Trees, trees and more trees, suit intermediate freeriders, some short advanced runs
Some accommodation. To Barcelona or Zaragoza. Resort info +34-9-73 48 09 50

Rasos Peguera — 2050 — 1850 — 14 — ●Beg 43% — ●Int 57% — ●Adv 0% — Lifts 5
A couple of boring flat piste to suit novices and intermediate carvers, freestylers forget it.
No accommodation. To Barcelona or Zaragoza. Resort info +34-9 3 821 03 79

Super Espot — 2555 — 1500 — 20 — ●Beg 50% — ●Int 35% — ●Adv 15% — Lifts 7
OK for freestylers and freeriders not looking for much, short runs through trees
Some accommodation. To Barçelona or Zaragoza. Resort info 34-9-73 63 50 13

Nuria — 2268 — 1964 — 9 — ●Beg 44% — ●Int 44% — ●Adv 12% — Lifts 4
Boring with nothing of note, the few short runs will suit intermediate carvers.
Some accommodation. To Barcelona or Zaragoza. Resort info +34-9-72 73 07 13

Vallter 2000 — 2600 — 1900 — 12 — ●Beg 50% — ●Int 33% — ●Adv 17% — Lifts 7
Boring open flats, OK for novices, a tiny bit of off piste for intermediate freeriders.
No accommodation. To Barcelona or Zaragoza. Resort info +34-9-72 74 00 22

Astun — 2324 — 1650 — 28 — ●Beg 39% — ●Int 50% — ●Adv 11% — Lifts 14
Wide open spaces for carving intermediates. OK for new school ground grommets
Some accommodation. To Barcelona or Zaragoza. Resort info +34-9-74 37 30 34

Candanchu — 2400 — 1560 — 22 — ●Beg 32% — ●Int 50% — ●Adv 18% — Lifts 24
Wide open spaces for carving intermediates. OK for new school ground grommets
Some accommodation. To Barcelona or Zaragoza. Resort info +34-9-74 37 31 94

Cerler — 2364 — 1500 — 21 — ●Beg 24% — ●Int 62% — ●Adv 14% — Lifts 13
Good for intermediate freeriders, some hits and trees for freestylers to play in.
Some accommodation. To Barcelona or Zaragoza. Resort info +34-9-74 55 10 12

Panticosa — 1900 — 1200 — 14 — ●Beg 43% — ●Int 55% — ●Adv 7% — Lifts 7
Short runs for intermediate and novice carvers. Easy to reach beginner areas.
Some accommodation. To Barcelona or Zaragoza. Resort info +34-9-74 48 81 25

Alto Campo — 2175 — 1650 — 11 — ●Beg 36% — ●Int 64% — ●Adv 0% — Lifts 10
Mostly red runs of boring hard boot carving featureless terrain.
Some accommodation. To Zaragoza. Resort info +34-9-42 75 40 01

San Isidro — 2155 — 1500 — 20 — ●Beg 35% — ●Int 50% — ●Adv 15% — Lifts 13
Good chances for beginners and novice riders to progress. Crap for others.
Some accommodation. To Zaragoza. Resort info +34-9-42 75 40 01

Valgrande Pajares — 2155 — 1500 — 20 — ●Beg 35% — ●Int 50% — ●Adv 15% — Lifts 13
Short open flats suit beginners learning to carve. Crap for all others.
Some accommodation. To Zaragoza. Resort info +34-9-85 49 61 23

Valdesqui — 2280 — 1880 — 11 — ●Beg 82% — ●Int 18% — ●Adv 0% — Lifts 10
Best for total beginners only, crap for others.
No accommodation. To Madrid. Resort info +34-9-1 515 59 39

Valdelinares — 2024 — 1880 — 7 — ●Beg 71% — ●Int 29% — ●Adv 0% — Lifts 5
Riding for those who are brain dead because there's nothing to think about.
No accommodation. To Madrid. Resort info +34-9-74 60 16 71

La Pinilla — 2273 — 1500 — 16 — ●Beg 44% — ●Int 50% — ●Adv 6% — Lifts 12
Good chances for beginners and novice riders to progress. Some off piste for freeriders
Some accommodation. To Zaragoza. Resort info +34-9-11 55 03 04

Valdezcaray — 2024 — 1880 — 7 — ●Beg 71% — ●Int 29% — ●Adv 0% — Lifts 5
Not in the least bit testing, nor in the least bit interesting.
No accommodation. To Zaragoza. Resort info (34-9-41 35 42 75

FORMIGAL

Located in the Pyrenees, a stone's throw from the French border is the resort of Formigal, a Spanish purpose built affair which is OK for most riders in particular intermediates wanting some easy freeriding. The well looked after pistes are pretty wide and open allowing carvers the chance to show off as they crank over some hard edges. The slopes are largely crowd free especially week days which means you can roam about and explore the terrain without to many daft Spanish skiers (friendly but a bit loco) getting in the way. One thing this place is not and that is a freestyle paradise, though like any resort in the world it also depends on what you're in to, for instance new school ground grommets wanting to just fakie down flat pistes with the odd spin will love it. They can fanny around on loads of easy runs, however big air dudes won't and can't! Beginner areas will really help with quick progression (not that there's a great deal to progress too), instruction is available at the local ski school.

Village is basic with few accommodation options. Eating and boozing is definitely not hardcore but it's also not to pricy with a couple of cafe's, bars and disco to check out.

Winter snowboard periods between Dec and April. No summer snowboarding

Top Station	2376 m
Resort height	1476m
Vertical Drop	900m
Longest run	7km
Ride area	50 km of piste
Snowmaking	

Terrain ability suits:

● Beginner	41%
● Intermediate	48%
● Advanced	11%

Number of lifts 18

Formigal Tourist Office
Sallent De Gallego
(+34-9-74 58 81 25
Reservations(+34-9-74 58 81 25
Snowphone(+34-9-74 58 81 25

International airport, Zaragoza
Transfer time 3 ½ to 4 hours

BAQUEIRA BERET

Baqueira Beret is one of Spains main resorts, and one of its most poncy, attracting a fair number of the Spanish Ski elite. Fortunately this purpose built haunt is not to bad to ride which is a point not missed by the International Snowboard Federation who have held both slalom and half pipe events here. The terrain is spread out over 4 connecting areas all of which are easy to reach and will largely appeal to leisurely freeriders with a number of reds to try with the odd hint of a steep and trickle of trees to shred. Overall the area is going to give hard boot carvers the most interest with some decent width red runs for experienced carvers and a good number of easy blues for the less talented edge merchants. Like much of Spain there's no major amounts of natural freestyle terrain but still hits to get air and a few drop off's to try. Beginners are well catered for on the easy to reach blue's which are served by chair lifts making it possible to get around all the areas at some stage. Tuition at the ski school is ok, and hire of boards is available but don't go looking for a big fleet of demos to rent.

Accommodation is close to the slopes consisting of a number of pricey hotels to affordable apartments and chalets. Eating and entertainment is simply boring and not snowboard style, still there is a supermarket for packet food and carry outs.

Winter snowboard periods between Dec and April. No summer snowboarding

Top Station	2510m
Resort height	1500m
Vertical Drop	900m
Longest run	3.6km
Ride area	75 km of piste

Terrain ability suits:

● Beginner	45%
● Intermediate	46%
● Advanced	9%

Half pipe

Number of lifts 22

Baqueira Beret Tourist Office
Viella (Lerida) Spain
+34-9-73 64 50 25

International airport, Zaragoza
Transfer time 3 to 4 hours

SWEDEN

Sweden the nation of blues eyes, blonde hair, Fiords, Abba and some of the best freestylers around. Male pros like Johan Olofsson, Ingemar Backman, Staahlkloo Pontus (??eh!) and females Jennie Waara and Jenny Jonsson, all of whom can seriously rip. Sweden emulates it's neighbouring cousin Norway in almost every aspect; cold climate, short winter days and expensive beer. Like Norway and Finland, Sweden has a lot of listed resorts - approximately 150, however 70 or so cater for just cross country skiing rather than going down hills. As this can be a cold country with many areas suffering high winds and sometimes very unpredictable snow conditions, and couple this with the fact that the resorts are often small may be why so many Swedes head down to France and Austria leaving their own resorts crowd free. What's not cold about Sweden are the locals and their acceptance of snowboards on the slopes. There's a strong Swedish snowboard culture that is very much freestyle and freeride oriented, taking a lot of influence from the US and adapting things to suit. Resorts have long been encouraging and supporting snowboarding, with pipes and parks as well as offering a high level of snowboard instruction. The resorts which suit intermediate riders most also allow for some hard-core stuff and will certainly appeal to beginners. Hard boot carving is possible but its not major. Soft boots ripping up the well looked after slopes are more the norm and better suited.

Resorts facilities and services are basic but acceptable and cater well for groups. Sweden has had the reputation of being very expensive and although prices have dropped considerable over the last few years, things are still expensive especially beer in bars and clubs. Still, getting around the country is not the worst although you may have to do some travelling to reach some of the far flung resorts. Air, bus and rail services are damn good. Over all Sweden may not be the most adventurous country in which to ride, nor the most extreme but it's still worth a road trip especially in June when you can still ride some places on good snow in tees and shorts; what's more the Swedes are cool and full on party animals

Swedish Ski Ass/Snowboard,
SSA
Idrottens Hus
12387 Farsta
Sweden
+46 8605 6300

Rider: Magnus Noren. Photo: Vincent Skoglund

Status	Constitutional Monarchy
Capital	Stockholm
Area	449,964 sq km
Population	8.5 million
Language	Swedish
Currency	Krona
Neighbouring Countries	Finland - Russia - Norway
Winter snowboard periods	November to June
Summer snowboarding	June to August
Highest Mountain	Mt Kebnekaise 2117 m
Country Snowboard styles	Freeride/Freestyle - 99%
	Alpine/Caring - 1%
	Soft boots - 99%
	Hard boots - 1%
Drugs	Cannabis is illegal
Death penalty	No capital punishment
Military Service	Males have to do national service at 18
Alcohol drinking age	Age 18 in restaurants,
	20 in liquor stores
Age of consent for sex	Male 15 - Female 16

Name	Dis	Ranking
Females		
Jennie Warra	HP	4
Jenny Jonsson	HP	10
Marie Birki	GS	27
Males		
Ingemar Backman	HP	8
Pontus Staahlkloo	HP	25
Andres Hagman	HP	26
Jacob Soederqvist	HP	26
Johan Olofsson	HP	36
Oskar Norberg	HP	48
Stefan Sundqvist	HP	51
Rickard Rickardsson	SL	30

Dis = Discipline
HP = Half Pipe
GS = Giant Slalom
SL = Slalom

ARE

Unlike many Swedish resorts, this isn't a poxy little hill – it's a good size mountain that will give all rider styles and levels a fairly good time. Are is a sprawling place that offers some decent off piste riding that can be tackled by going heli boarding. Carvers will find a few black runs to check out, especially the Slalombacken race run. Freeriders will find the best powder and drops off's on the Areskutan areas. For freestylers there is a good pipe to ride while novices will find the easy flats no problem to take on.

Staying in Are is no big deal, there's a mixture of accommodation options which isn't always cheap. To eat check out Broken Dreams for a burger and the Country Club for a lively beer. The Garage snowboard shop is the main place to get the best low down on Are.

Winter snowboard periods between Nov and May.
No summer snowboarding

Top Station	1300m
Base	372m
Longest run	6.5Km
Ride area	90km

Terrain ability suits:

● Beginner	54%
● Intermediate	36%
● Advanced	10%

Terrain Ride styles suits:

Freeride	50%
Freestyle	30%
Alpine/Carve	20%

44 lifts no ride rules

Full details Tel +46 (0)647 17700
Nearest airport Ostersund 110km.

FUNASDALEN

A full on OK place no matter what you're into. Located just a stones throw from the Norwegian boarder, Fundasdalen has attracted the attention of the I.S.F who now hold regular pro events here which should indicated its snowboard worth. Powder and good freeriding are in fairly good supply, catering more for intermediate freeriders rather than the hard core extreme cliff jumper. Freestylers have plenty of small hits to go for as well as the offerings from the pipe. Beginners will get on here with ample of easy flats to keel over on, however be warned the drag lifts could pose a few hic-cups.

Bedding down in Funasdalen is simple with self catering the norm. You can even stay in caravans close to the slopes. Night time is simply Swedish.

Winter snowboard periods between Nov and May.
No summer snowboarding

Top Station	1000m
Base	750m

Terrain ability suits:

● Beginner	40%
● Intermediate	50%
● Advanced	10%

Terrain Ride styles suits:

Freeride	50%
Freestyle	35%
Alpine/Carve	15%

20 lifts no ride rules

Full details Tel +46 (0)647
Nearest airport - Roros in Norway.
Fly to Stockholm transfer 10 hours

RIKSGRANSEN

Look north to Lapland and just in the far reaches you will find Riksgransen nestled on the skirts of the Arctic circle. The main thing to note about this resort is that it's not a normal winter area. The season doesn't get going until the end of February. The late season however provides for a long one that lasts well into June making this a good place to try out for tee shirt riding in early summer. No one will want to spend a two week trip riding here, it gets boring early on especially if you are of the grade that can ride. However the comparatively featureless terrain is well suited to freeriding with some off piste that has steeps and hits to take on. Off the slopes what you get is very basic, the main place to kip is the Riksgransen Hotel. You can also pig out with a choice of restaurants with burgers on the menu. Remember to bring extra batteries for your Walkman because there's no happening life style or night life here. This is a road trip haunt for a group of riders in a van. However you can fly via Stockholm to domestic airport Kiruna 3 hours away or take the train which stops just meters from the village.

SWITZERLAND

Forget the huge costs of everything, forget the small red knives, V-shaped chocolate, dodgy bank accounts and cuckoo clocks, and OK Switzerland is hardly in the Worlds top ten of 'Movers & Shakers' list. But be sure of one thing and that is Switzerland is a snowboarders country and it has the terrain to prove it. This small, land-locked country covering about 41,288sq km with a recorded 315 resorts is unbelievably rich and has some of the most impressive snowboard resorts in the world. The Swiss have gained their riches by shrewdness, getting in on the act early, so it's no wonder their resorts have been welcoming snowboarders for some time and providing them with a huge variety of services. It's never been a big deal for areas to build pipes and fun parks - some of the tiniest resort have had them since way back. When it comes to money Switzerland is costly - budget boarders be warned and gold credit card holders be prepared to notch up as much mileage with your card as your snowboard!. Nothing is cheap. This is not an easy country where by you can scam your way around, though thankfully a lot of resorts have bunk houses and youth hostel that help to keep cost down. Beer in bars - silly, lift pass - silly, heli boarding - silly, silly, silly, hire and instruction - silly, food not only in restaurants but supermarkets - silly. Yet you can get by and have a major time because the terrain and the variation of it is great. Steeps, powder, wide long carving pistes, pipes, parks, boarder cross circuits, open and tight trees (it is in many places discouraged from riding through trees on the grounds of environmental concerns) and beginner friendly slopes. It's all here. What you find in Switzerland is a decent mixture of the old and new. Many resort are made up of rickety old chalets that look the part, while others are sprawling modern affairs. Verbier is a huge and very impressive place, spoilt only by the fact that its damn expensive and that it attracts Royalty and idiots on Big Foot skis. While at the other end of the scale little old Braunwald with its half pipe is cool and sad git free.

The Swiss style reflects close neighbour Austria, with a fusion of French carving to a high level, though the all in one sad ski suits let the side down. It's fair to say now that hard boots are as common as soft boots, especially in the more expensive resorts. However there is a very healthy freestyle/freeride scene with a strong skateboard influence. The Swiss seem to be able to produce as many top Freestylers as Alpine riders and each year the ISF rankings reflect this. One of the notable points about Swiss snowboarding is its emphasis on instruction, a superb effort with very high levels of tuition. Along with the well established Swiss Snowboard School they take the subject serious and all levels and styles are well catered for probably better than any where else in the world.

Getting to Switzerland is no problem with all the main airports having good connection options to resorts buy bus, car hire or train, many having good rail services that wind their way up to some of the smallest places.

Life style in Switzerland is cool reflecting street American with an accent! The locals know how to party, even if their music leaves a lot to be desired, the booze is good (pricy), food bland unless you're after cardboard burgers from you know who, or pizza which is better here than in Italy. Skaters will find ramps and a skatescene in a lot of main towns or cities.

Status	Federal Democracy
Capital	Bern
Area	41,288sq km
Population	7 million
Language	French/German/Italian/Romansh
Currency	Swiss Franc
Neighbouring Countries	Austria, France, Germany, Italy, Liechtenstein
Winter snowboard periods	November to May
Summer snowboarding	May to August
Highest point	4634m Monte Rosa
Country Snowboard styles	Freeride/Freestyle: 60%, Alpine/Carving: 40%
	Soft boots 60%
	Hard boots 40%
Drugs	Cannabis is illegal
Death penalty	No capital punishment
Military Service	Male nationals have to joint the army at 19
Alcohol drinking age	Age 16.
Age of consent for sex	Male 16, Female 16

FACT FILE

Rider: Danny Wheeler. Photo: Sang Tan

Zurich
Zug
Luzern
Bern
Interlaken
SWITZERLAND
Chur
Davos
Savoginin
St. Moritz
Laussane
Zweisimmen
Chateau-doex
Les Mosses
Leysin Anzere Montana
Geneva
Morgins   Aigle Sion   Crans
Champery   Verbier   Saas Fee
Martigny-ville   Zermatt

SWISS DRIVE GUIDE

Break down - Tel - Automobile Club +41-(031) 22 47 22

Vehicles drive on the Right

Speed On:	Motorway	Dualcarage	Single	Urban
	120	100	80	50km/h
Towing				
	80	80	80	60km/h

Seat belts - Compulsory for front and back if fitted
Tolls - Payable on some roads
Alcohol level = 0.08%
Driving age limit - 18
Documents to carry: International Driving permit, Vehicle Erg,
Green Card, Country Identification, Number Plates, Hire docs.
Fuel - Sold in Litres
First Aid Kit - Recommended
Warning Triangle - Compulsory
Snowchains - Recommended

181

DAVOS

Davos is not just a major snowboard resort, it's also a massive town that offers just about all you need to have a cool time. This very happening place offers you the lot; deep powder, loads of trees, big natural hits, halfpipes, funparks, boarder cross circuit and night riding on over 315km of terrain. Davos is located in an area that makes it ideal to check out many other resorts, however the stuff here is enough to keep any rider busy for a long time. Split between two main areas the one to check most for snowboarders is the runs on the Jakobshorn which you can reach with ease via a couple of cable car rides. From the top station, which is well above the tree lines, advanced or intermediate freeriders will find a number of testing blacks which mellow out into reds as they lead straight back down to the Ischalp mid section. From here you could carry on down through the trees to the base or if you want an easy final decent then there's an easy blue that snakes its way home, ideal for beginners. Carvers looking for some long open runs to crank some big turns on won't be disappointed, the 10k red run into the village of Serneus is full on and you should be carving big style at the end of this one. The off piste opportunities here are mega and best checked out with the services of a guide. The run down to Teufi from Jakobshorn is pretty cool, but you will have to bus back to Davos. Beginners wanting to get to grips with things should go see the guys at the 'Top Secret snowboard school', the instructors really know how to turn you from a side standing numpty into a powder hound. At the top station of Jackobhorn novices are treated to wide open easy flats which are serviced by drag lifts or a short cable car ride. Alternatively there are plenty of very easy runs lower down on the Parsenn slopes.

In the town of Davos you really do get snowboard life style, the only real problem is that it doesn't come too cheap. However that said Davos has what is said to be the worlds first snowboard hotel which is a cool place that offers a number of ride and stay packages at affordable prices, there's also a bar and the nights can be very lively. Alternatively you could park the camper van in the waste area of the train station but remember this is a high resort which means cold nights. There's also a youth hostel. Around the town you can find plenty of places to eat. 'Snack Bar 1' is the place for a burger and pool while the Schutzen is a good bar to check out with live music.

Winter snowboard periods between Dec and April.

No summer snowboarding

Top Station	2850m
Base	1560m
Vertical Drop	200m
Longest run	12Km
Ride area	315km
Snowmaking	minor

Terrain ability suits:

● Beginner	30%
● Intermediate	40%
● Advanced	30%

Terrain Ride styles suits:

Freeride	60%
Freestyle	30%
Alpine/Carve	10%

Half pipe, **fun parks** and **boarder cross** areas on the Jakobshorn area.

Photo: Davos Tourist Office

1996/97 lift pass guide
½ day tickets from Sfr 23 - 39
1 day tickets from Sfr 27 - 52
2 day tickets from Sfr 50 - 100
5 day tickets from Sfr 105 - 200

Lifts open 8am to 4.45pm and 8am to 5.15pm from Feb

55 lifts
Lift policy is snowboard leashes are compulsory but there are no rear foot rules.

Photo: Davos Tourist Office

Snowboard Instruction
$^1/_2$ day lesson from Sfr 130 to 145
1 day lesson from Sfr 230 to 250
5 day lesson from Sfr 215 to 240

Snowboard and boot hire
1 day hire for standard board Sfr 53
2 day hire for standard board Sfr 83
5 day hire for standard board Sfr 161

Snowboard repair & service
Full base tune service Sfr40

Snowboard Shop
Top Secret Snowboard Centre
Tel +41 081 413 73 74

Hangliding & Paragliding

Climbing and Climbing wall

Eat at
Snack Bar 1
Pizzeria Padrion

Night Time hangouts
Bolgenschanze Hotel
Snober Stubli
Schutzen
Club Billard

Photo: Davos Tourist Office

SWITZERLAND – DAVOS

Accommodation
Central Reservations
+41-0 81 415 21 21
Bolgenschanze Hotel
from 600- a week per person.
*Packages with lift pass
Tel +41-0 81 414 90 20

Davos Tourist office
Promenade 67
CH-7270 Davos
Switzerland
Tel +41- 0 81 415 21 21
Web http://www.davos.ch
Email davos@davos.ch

Fly to Zurich international

Transfer from airport;

By bus approximately
$2^1/_2$ hours journey to resort.

Trains from Zurich arrive in
the centre of Davos.

By car hire approximately
2 hours driving to resort.

Driving use as a map
reference via Zurich
autoroute N3 exit Ladguart
28 = Davos is 148km
from Zurich.

LEYSIN

Leysin is located in the French parts of Switzerland. Lesser known for skiing, the resort goes out of its way to make it a snowboard friendly place. Since 1992 Leysin has been playing host to the I.S.F World Pro Tours (normally scheduled in January). In a good winter Leysin offers you everything that makes a riders heart beat with pace. This is a resort that will keep adventure seeking advanced riders happy while also appealing to first timers with a number of easy slopes reached without having to use a drag lift straight away. Freeriders have plenty of great terrain to discover with tree runs down to the village or extreme terrain with bowls and cliffs which you can reach by dropping into just on your right side at the arrival on the 'Berneuse'. You should also check out the official off piste runs that give you the feeling of riding back country. For example try the route behind 'Tour D'Ai' starting at the top of 'Chaux de Mont'. Euro carvers will be able to lay out some big turns on the wide flats of the Berneuse and the Chaux de Mont. For a longer run that won't test you too much give the blue run that bases out in the village a go. Freestylers will be able to spin huge airs in the remaining bits of the ISF pro tour pipe, which is normally maintained, however don't be shy and ask for a shovel at the nearby lift hut. As well as the pipe the fun park, located between Berneuse and 'Mayen', has quarter pipes and gaps to ride. Mind you it's not usually built until the end of February. Beginners can get going at the nursery slopes which have easy to use rope tows before venturing up by cable car to slopes on the Berneuse, however the drag lift at the Chaux de Mont is tricky and will pull off first timers. Note, beginners should not go to the top of this lift.

Around Leysin life's is very easy going with a lot of Americans hanging around due to the 2 American colleges based here. There's no great skate scene although a skate park is being planned for the coming season. The local ski/snowboard shops are nothing special nor are they cheap, but you will at least be able to rent some good equipment including demo boards. For a cheap bed the best option is the really cool bunk house called 'The Vagabond' which has a cool bar. Alternatively Chalet Ermina is a really nice. For a beer at night there are a number of good options which are all late and lively. Plenty of parties happening here.

Winter snowboard periods between Dec and April.

No summer snowboarding

Top Station	2200m
Base	1300m
Vertical Drop	2199m
Longest run	5Km
Ride area	60km
Snowcannons	10

Terrain ability suits:

Beginner	40%
Intermediate	30%
Advanced	30%

Terrain Ride styles suits:

Freeride	50%
Freestyle	20%
Alpine/Carve	30%

Half pipe fun parks and boarder cross areas between Berneuse and Mayen.

Page rider Thomas Reider - a cool Swiss freestyler.

1996/97 lift pass guide
Swiss francs

	Child	Adult
¹/₂ day	14	24
1 day	21	34
2 days	40	66
5 days	88	147
7 days	115	191
Season	365	520

Lifts open 8.30am to 5pm	
Gondolas	2
Chairlifts	7
Drag lifts	10
No ride rules.	

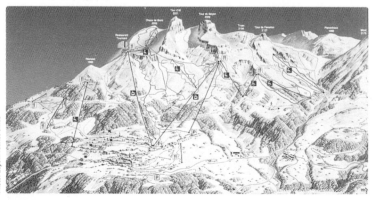

Snowboard Instruction
½ day lesson Sfr 26
6 half day lessons Sfr 115
School caters for 7 years old

Snowboard and boot hire
1 day hire for standard board Sfr 57
2 day hire for standard board Sfr 100
5 day hire for standard board Sfr 182

Snowboard repair & service
Full base tune service Sfr 30

Snowboard Shops
Hefti Sports
(ski snowboard shop)
Tel +41 0 25 34 2621

Heli Boarding (V-expensive)
Tel +41 0 25 34 14 01

Paragliding, a 15 minute flight Sfr 100
Tel +41 0 77 382 602

Climbing and climbing wall

Skateboarding
Ramps and hits in Aigle 15km away.

Eat at
La Lorraine for Pizza
Feydeys Restaurant for fondues

Night Time hangouts
Club Vagabond - booze and OK music.
Top Pub with juke box and a pool table
Club 94 playing euro pop.

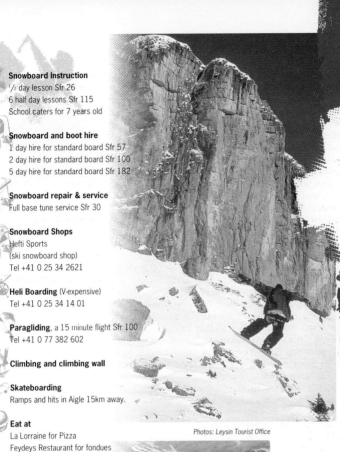

Photos: Leysin Tourist Office

Photo: Bunk House Vagabond

Accommodation
Central Reservations
+41-0 25 34 22 44

Club Vagabond
from Sfr 25 a bunk.
Tel +41 0 25 34 13 21

Restaurant Feydey
rooms from Sfr 36 a night
Tel +41 0 25 34 11 47

Leysin Tourist office
PO Box 100
CH - 1854 Leysin
Switzerland
Tel +41- 0 25 34 22 44
web - http://www.leysin.ch
e mail:o.t.leysin@ping.ch

Trains from Geneva in the Leysin via
Aigle takes 2 ½ hours

By car hire approximately 1½ hours
driving to resort.

Fly to Geneva international

Transfer from airport;

Driving from home use as a map
reference from Geneva autoroute
N1-direction Lausanne-Montreux-
Aigle Leysin.

By bus approximately 2 ½ hours
journey to resort.

VERBIER

A massive resort where boarding is still fairly small – less than 5% of slope-users, but don't fret, the attitude here is pretty cool and snowboarders are welcomed. Verbier has the reputation of being a classy expensive haunt and Brit skiers are well in evidence on their sad Big Foot skis doing the stupid hat number. However the snow record is good and even in a poorish season, it's still possible to ride to the resort in April. Although the large amount of terrain gives all levels of riders something to get their teeth into, Verbier is essentially a freeriders resort, with easily accessible powder, trees, hard-pack, cliffs, hits and extremes some conquered by a hike first. The European Extreme Boarding comp went off in Verbier in March 96 which should give you a guide to some of the awesome terrain on offer. The Mont Gele cable car serves no piste, just a series of off-piste runs and couloirs of varying extremity; tuck your balls or equivalent away before you get up here. The less squeamish should check out the areas round the back of 'Lac des Vaux' – the Col des Mines, 7 Vallon d'Arbi routes steer you towards wide open powder fields with the words 'session me' written all over them. Hard booters will enjoy several different runs but the best is undoubtedly the long wide red piste that goes from the top of 'Attelas II' all the way back to the Medran lifts. There's also some cool stuff at 'Savoleyres' and 'Ruinettes'. Freestylers have a park and pipe to jib around in Siviez, but to be honest the natural stuff around La Chaux and Lac des Vaux lifts are the places to check out. The main beginner areas are actually banned to snowboarders. This means that first timers are mostly faced with steeper slopes. The best options are the runs at Savoleyres where you are certain to be doing a few 180 arse spins. Some lifts here can be a bit tricky so keep to the slow chair lifts. A tip is lift pass checking is slack so think on, but don't get caught.

Off the slopes this is Royals, city slickers & lottery winners only. Verbier costs huge wadges of cash no matter what it is. There no such thing as a scene and most of the dudes here have never heard of a skateboard. Bedding down is costly and if you get caught scamming on some-ones floor you could face a 200 S.Franc fine. Over all this is not a place to head for on a tight budget unless you have a few degrees in scamming. To get the best info check out 'No Bounds' or 'Extreme' snowboard shops.

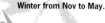

Winter from Nov to May.

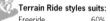

Summer snowboarding on the Mont Fort Glacier

Top Station	3330m
Base	1500m
Vertical Drop	1830m
Longest run	7Km
Ride area	400km
Snowmaking	20km

Terrain ability suits:

Beginner	32%
Intermediate	42%
Advanced	26%

Terrain Ride styles suits:

Freeride	60%
Freestyle	20%
Alpine/Carve	20%

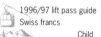

Half pipe fun parks at Coles des Gentaines

Photo: Verbier Tourist Office

1996/97 lift pass guide
Swiss francs

	Child	Adult
¹/₂ day	22	37
1 day	29	49
2 days	57	95
5 days	129	215
7 days	189	281
Season	604	1007

Lifts open 8.45am to 4.15pm

Cable cars	5
Gondolas	11
Chairlifts	25
Drag lifts	29

No ride rules.

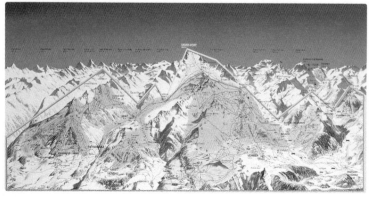

Page rider Nick Dales a nice chap from England

Snowboard Instruction
¹/₂ day group lesson Sfr 35
5 day group lesson Sfr 110
1 day private lesson Sfr 310

Summer camps contact
Mountain High +41 21 320 2288

Snowboard and boot hire
1 day hire for standard board Sfr 57
2 day hire for standard board Sfr 100
5 day hire for standard board Sfr 182

Snowboard repair & service
Full base tune service Sfr 30

Snowboard Shops
No Bounds Tel +41 0 26 31 55 56
for Sales-Hire-Instruction-Repair
(Snowboard shop)
Xtreme Tel +41 0 26 31 7810
for Sales-Hire-Instruction-Repair
(Snowboard shop)

Heli Boarding 7 flights Sfr 375 each

Climbing and Ice climbing lesson Sfr 35

Photo: Verbier Tourist Office

Eat by buying food at the supermarkets
(restaurants are 'V' expensive).

Night Time hangouts
Le Pub where a beer cost Sfr 3.50
The Montfort Pub for various music
Big Ben Pub for booze and pool

Accommodation
Central Reservations
+41-0 26 31 62 22

1 week studios 2 person Sfr
650
2 week studios 4 person Sfr
2530

Verbier Tourist office
CH 1936
Verbier
Switzerland
Tel +41- 0 26 31 62 22
http://www.verbier

Fly to Geneva international

Transfer from airport;

By bus approximately 2 hours
journey to resort.

Trains via Martingy to Le Chable
station then bus into the resort.

By car hire approximately 1¹/₂ hours
driving to resort.

Driving from home use as a map
reference from Geneva autoroute
N1-direction Lausanne N9-Montreux-
exit Martigny 21 = Verbier

SWITZERLAND – VERBIER

ANZERE

This is one of Switzerland's custom built resorts that stems back to the sixties. Built at an altitude of 1500m this has helped this relatively small resort to have a reliable and good snow record on slopes that get a lot of sun, allowing for plenty of tanning. Anzere is a fun, happy-go-lucky place that will appeal to the no drama snowboarder. A lot of families hang out here as does the gentle piste loving geriatric ski brigade. However snowboarders can mingle with ease with both and riders are not ignored or snubbed. The 40km of runs are simple and all styles will find something to keep them happy appealing most to novices and riders just getting things sorted out. Anzere would be worth a visit for a few days if you're on a road trip, but a two weeker will prove to be a bit of a bore for advanced riders. Hard boots and euro carvers are much in evidence here with the terrain lending itself well to some good edge-to-edge riding. Carvers who are competent will find the black that runs under the Pas-de-Maimbre gondola worth a visit, it should be said that this run could be a red however it's OK and will allow for a few quick turns. Freeriders in softs will also fair well on this run as well as areas found off the Les Rousses and Le Bate chair lifts. The trees at the lower parts although not extensive do offer some pine shredding, (the Swiss don't particular like the woods cut up so be aware you may encounter a few sharp tongues from the locals). One thing Anzere is not is an extreme freestylers resort. Freestyle ground hogs can spin off a number of natural hits, and there's ample area for practising your switch stance especially on the runs frequented by the oldies who are leisurely sliding around on their two wooden planks. Beginners should achieve the most on the well matched easy slopes, which can be tackled by taking the Pralan-Tsalan chair lift and then by using the drags (hold on tight nappy wearers).

Anzere is a well laid out village with a good choice of head-rest mainly tailored to the Credit card riders, although budget snowboarders will find affordable beds in a selection of apartments and chalets. Village Camps offer decent priced lodgings while The Avenir does the best pizza. Night time it's best to check out in La Grange, and the Rendezvouz. A cool place to hang out and get the best low down on Anzere is at Central Sports where you can rent gear and have you board tweaked to perfection.

Winter snowboard periods between Nov and April.
No summer snowboarding

Top Station	2420m
Base	1500m
Vertical Drop	862m
Longest run	6Km
Ride area	40km

Terrain ability suits:

● Beginner	40%
● Intermediate	50%
● Advanced	10%

Terrain Ride styles suits:

Freeride	45%
Freestyle	10%
Alpine/Carve	45%

Halfpipe, Fun park and Boarder Cross

1996/97 Week day lift pass

Days	Adult	Child
1	36	22
2	67	42
4	124	73
7	194	112

Lifts open 8.30am to 4.30pm
12 lifts
No ride rules

Snowboard hire
Central Sports
Tel +41 (0) 27 38 16 76
Crazy Corner
Tel +41 (0) 27 398 40 00

1 day hire Sfr 53, 5 days Sfr 161.
3 hour lesson Sfr 40

Accommodation
Village Camps
Tel +41 (0) 22 776 20 60

Anzere Tourist office
CH- 1972 Anzere
Switzerland
Tel +41 (0) 399 20 00
http://www.anzere.ch

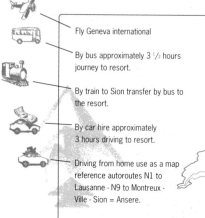

Fly Geneva international

By bus approximately 3 ½ hours journey to resort.

By train to Sion transfer by bus to the resort.

By car hire approximately 3 hours driving to resort.

Driving from home use as a map reference autoroutes N1 to Lausanne - N9 to Montreux - Ville - Sion = Ansere.

CRANS MONTANA

One of Switzerland's top snowboard resorts, Crans Montana is pretty outstanding and a total full on place with loads going on. Crans is one area and Montana the other which both fuse together to provide 160km of all level, all rider style terrain. Snowboarders have been cutting up theses slopes for years which has lead to a resort with some of the best snowboard instruction and facilities anywhere in Europe. For all the area has to offer, advanced riders are not always tested, with the terrain largely covering intermediate or novice levels. The hardest listed run is the black that runs down from Toula chair which is best tackled in softs as the unevenness in parts are better ridden in something where you can easy absorb the bumps at speed. However there is still plenty of long reds to check out, the red run that drops away from the Plaine Morte down to the village of Les Barzettes is perfect for carvers to lay out some big lines and with a length of 7.5km you have plenty of time to get it right. Freeriders in search of off piste and fresh powder need to hook up with a guide and set off to areas around the Plaine Morte Glacier where you can make your way to nearby Anzere. The bit through the tunnels makes this well worth the effort. The area known as the Faverges is cool and for riders with some savvy there are some decent steeps to tackle - watch out for the thigh burning traverse on the way back. For those who can afford it you can do some cool heli boarding to some major terrain. Freestylers are well sorted here with a good pipe on Pas du Loup which can be reached by the Montana-Arnouvaz gondola. The fun park at Aminona is loaded with rails spines and gaps, new schoolers will love it, and for those who want to find out how to ride a pipe correctly and learn how to get big airs there's a number of schools that will help out. Beginners are treated to a variety of no nonsense blues which may require some navigation in order to get around with out having to tackle drag lifts all the time.

Lodging is plentiful here, pricey perhaps but good options, with apartment blocks and chalets possible within easy reach of the lifts. Snowboard life style is good, with a number of cool hangouts and excellent snowboard shops to check out. There's also a local snowboard club 'Vauge Blanche' where you can find out all need to know about the place.

Winter snowboard periods between Nov and April.
No summer snowboarding

Top Station	3000m
Base	1484m
Vertical Drop	1500m
Longest run	7.5Km
Ride area	160km
Snowmaking	6km

Terrain ability suits:

● Beginner	38%
● Intermediate	50%
● Advanced	12%

Terrain Ride styles suits:

Freeride	40%
Freestyle	25%
Alpine/Carve	35%

2 fun parks with half pipe and hits located on Pas de Loup and at Aminona

Snowboard shops
Avalanche Pro Shop.
Tel +41 (0) 27 402 424.
Pacific Surf Shop.

Snowboard instruction
via Surf Evasion / Montana Ski School
Swiss Snowboard School
Avalanche Pro Shop.

5 days snowboard lesson
from Sfr 190
1 day board and boot hire Sfr 53

Full base service from Sfr 30

42 lifts, no rear foot binding rules but leashes are required.

Heli boarding
contact Surf Evasion

Crans-Montana Tourist Office
PO Box 372- CH-3962
Switzerland
Tel +41 (0) 27 41 30 41
http://www.crans-montana.ch/

SWITZERLAND – ANZERE, CRANS MONTANA

— Fly Geneva international

— By bus approximately 2 1/2 hours journey to resort.

— By train to Sierre transfer by bus to the resort 20km.

— By car hire approximately 2 hours driving to resort.

— Driving from home use as a map reference autoroutes N1/ N9 via main towns Montreux and Martigny and Sion.

SAAS FEE

If you having a bit of a dilemma about where to go in Switzerland then here end it, because Saas Fee is one of the jewels in the crown. This is simply Switzerland at its best, a major Dogs B's place which you can cut up all year round thanks to the Glacier. A true snowboard resort with everything – steeps, deeps, banks and walls, big hits and ample wide open banzai runs where you can get some serious speed. Plus of course, trees and easy terrain for first timers along with two half pipes all year round and a third during the winter as well as a fun park for freestylers. Saas Fee is the home to Killer Loops test centre and the place where a lot of manufactures hold camps and board testing programmes during the summer months. K2 hang out here for race training. This is a place where all levels can start out and progress on over 135km of well looked after pisted terrain serviced by high tech lifts as well as loads of off piste. Advanced riders are provided with ample chances to prove themselves. The runs under the Mittelallalin restaurant at the top are major, carvers or freeriders can test your way down a series of black/red runs before easing out to some easy stuff as you base out at the bottom. The runs off the Hinterallalin drag lift will sort out the wimps with some really cool freeriding to be had and some steeps to go for. For freestylers with balls or the equivalent check out the hits on the Mittaghorn where you will find a natural pipe. The park located of the Mittelallalin is loaded with gaps, Q pipes, spines and hits to get cool air from. The pipe are open all year round enabling air heads to practice till they drop. Learners are not left out, Saas Fee has plenty of novice runs to cut your first tracks on with those at the base serviced by easy to use drag lifts and those midway and at the top reached by cable car and Funicular.

The town is cool with options to kip close to the slopes in hotels or Chalets. Life style is good and the main hangouts for hangover material are in the Blackbull bar, the Happy bar and the Go-Inn. The main shops which are really laid back and very helpful are Popcorn Snowboard point and Powder tools.

Winter from Nov to May
Summer snowboarding best between May & Aug

Top Station	3600m
Base	1800m
Vertical Drop	1776m
Longest run	14Km
Ride area	135km
Snowcannons	7

Terrain ability suits:

● Beginner	50%
● Intermediate	25%
● Advanced	25%

Terrain Ride styles suits:

Freeride	45%
Freestyle	25%
Alpine/Carve	30%

3 Half pipes and a fun park with Q-Pipes & Rope tow Boarder cross has 2 tunnels

1996/97 Week day lift pass

Days	Junior	Adult
½	26	46
1	32	56
2	60	102
7	165	290

Lifts open 8.30 to 16.00 daily
34 lifts
Ride rear foot free

Snowboard shops
Popcorn Snowboard Point
Tel +41 (0) 27 958 19 14
Powder Tools
Tel +41 (0) 89 220 77 92
1 day board and boot hire Sfr 250
Full base service Sfr 100

Snowboard Instruction
Paradise Snowboard School
Tel +41 (0) 28 57 46 18
1 days snowboard lesson Sfr 300

Saas Fee Tourist Office
CH-3906 Saas Fee
Switzerland
Tel +41 (0) 28 57 14 57
Reservations +41 (0) 28 59 11 20
Snowphone +41 (0) 28 57 12 72
web-http://www.saas-fee.ch

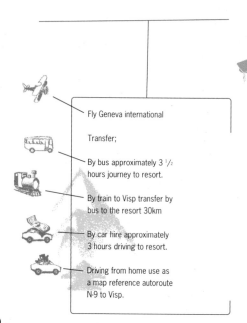

Fly Geneva international

Transfer;

By bus approximately 3 ½ hours journey to resort.

By train to Visp transfer by bus to the resort 30km

By car hire approximately 3 hours driving to resort.

Driving from home use as a map reference autoroute N-9 to Visp.

SAVOGNIN

Just two hours from Zurich lies this relatively unknown resort that is fast becoming a magnet for snowboarders out for a good time with out all the hustle and bustle of the bigger resorts. Fortunately the ski press don't mention Savognin which leaves this crowd free little gem free for snowboarders to cut at will. The natives are friendly and happy to have snowboarders on their slopes. Local riders are cool and have their own club where you can find out about the best hits and runs or where to get messy in the evenings. The 80 km of piste are well worth checking out and will certainly give intermediate and beginners something to think about. Advanced riders are going to be disappointed if it's testing stuff your after because there is none really. You can have bit of excitement on the black run known as the pro Spinatsch that runs from the Tigignas chair lift which is also the location of the fun park, but it doesn't take too long to conquer if you know what you're doing on your edges. Although freestylers and freeriders can boogy around with ease this is basically a hard boot carvers resort. The well groomed runs allow for some cool arcing, in full view of the lifts allowing the Oxbow wearers to show off their latest designer jumpers and sad flowery yellow pants. A good run that will suit all level carvers whether your in softs or hards is the Cresta Ota which runs down from the Piz Cartas summit. Freestylers will find the best air to be had in the fun park or in the pipe (apart from a few cliff jumps to go) which is tooled up with fun boxes, gaps, spines, rails and Q pipes. For some natural hits check out the stuff on the area called Tiem which will suit new schoolers very much. Beginners are looked after with a number of easy blues and the option of being able to slide back to base at the end of the day on easy runs, however novices are going to have to make do with drag lifts to get around though there are some chair lifts.

Off the slopes is nothing major. There are some good places to kip, eat or drink at, the main snowboard hang-outs are Housebar, Hotel Danilo that has pool and a Disco or the Zerbratent Paulin where a beer cost Sfr 4

Local rider Peder Plaz is head of the Codgias Sursettras snowboard club he can help you out with all you need to know about Savognin. Call the tourist office for details.

Winter snowboard periods between Dec and Apr.
No summer snowboarding

Top Station	2713m
Base	1200m
Vertical Drop	1513m
Longest run	7Km
Ride area	80km
Snowcannons	40

Terrain ability suits:

● Beginner	35%
● Intermediate	63%
● Advanced	2%

Terrain Ride styles suits:

Freeride	22%
Freestyle	13%
Alpine/Carve	65%

Half pipe and fun park.

Snowboard shop:
Snowboard-In
Tel +41 (0) 684 12 52
1 day board & boot hire Sfr 53
Full base service Sfr 35

Snowboard Instruction
1 ½ days group lesson Sfr 95
2 ½ days group lesson Sfr 140
5 days group lesson Sfr 180

1996/97 Week day lift pass

Days	Junior	Adult
½	21	33
1	26	44
2	48	85
7	135	228

Lifts open 8.30 to 4pm
17 lifts
Rear foot free and leashes required.

Savognin Tourist Office
CH-7460- Savognin
Switzerland
Tel +41 (0) 684 22 22

By bus approximately 2 hours journey to resort.

By train 3 hours 50 minutes

By car hire approximately 2 hours driving to resort.

Fly Zurich international with domestic flights to Samedan 1¼ hours

Transfer from Zurich;

Driving from home use as a map reference towns, Tiefencastel, Julier

ENGELBERG

Slap bang in the middle of Switzerland is the town of Engelberg un-tarnished from hoards of holiday ski crowds. This is a resort that has one of the longest verts in Switzerland and snow on the Glacier allowing boarding into June. The 82km of piste area is split into two, rising either side of the village with the most snowboarding happenings on the Titlis slopes which can be reached by funicular, gondola and cable cars. Once up at the top you will find the runs lend themselves best to intermediate carvers with the Odd bit of difficult stuff mixed in. Just before you get to the Rotair Fun Park there's an interesting black to check out. Off piste is good and will appeal to advanced freeriders, the Laub is a steep wall running down from the Titlis but be warned, don't mess with this one - you will come off worst. Freestylers can play in the park decked out with obstacles, there's also some good natural stuff to go for. Learners will be OK here, there are some easy runs on the mid section of the Tiltis which drop back to the base and around Trubsee.

Any resort that is a neighbour to Klosters which attracts Britain's Royal two plankers in their designers sad git stuff is bound to be pricy and yes, Engelberg is. However you can find places to kip and the El Burro Loco Mexican serves affordable food. Night time happens in the Angel Pub and in El Burro Loco Mexican where a beer sets you back Sfr 4. There's also a snooker and pool hall to idle the night away.

Winter snowboard periods between Nov and April. Summer snowboarding to June

Top Station	3020m
Resort height	1050
Vertical Drop	2000m
Longest run	12km
Ride area	82km
Snowcannons	6

Terrain ability suits:

● Beginner	22%
● Intermediate	48%
● Advanced	30%

Fun Park and Halfpipe

26 lifts No ride rules
Lifts, 8.30 to 16.30 daily
1 day Adult pass, Sfr 47; 5x =Sfr 187
1 day Child pass, Sfr 28; 5x = Sfr 102

Snowboard Instruction
Swiss Snowboard School
+41 (0) 637 40 50
1 day lesson Sfr 88; 5 days Sfr 378.

Engelberg Tourist Office
Klosters 3 CH-6390, Engelberg
Switzerland.
+41 (0) 637 37 37

Nearest international airport Zurich
Transfer time 1 ½ hours

LENZERHEIDE-VALBELLA

Here is a place that is not too familiar with most, but this classy resort has some 150 km of piste to destroy, 2 half pipes to catch major air from and 2 fun parks in which you are offered all sorts of toys that grommets can play with for days. Lenzerheide and Valbella are in fact two separate areas nestled around the Heidsee lake but link up on the slopes that extend from both sides of the valley, offering heaps and heaps of easy terrain that beginners will love. On the Danis slopes which has the greater of the runs, novices with a bit of go in them, can start from the top of 4 points and gently ride all the way back down collecting a few ice burns as you fall. Riders looking for hard core freeriders in search of extremes or deep wood forget it. This it not your resort. However carvers wanting to come to terms with the art can do so with great ease on a selection of red and blue runs. If you take the cable car up to the Rothorn you can give it some on the Totalpi which is cool, it also offers some decent freeriding down to Motta which has about the only black rated runs. Freestylers will find fun park and pipe located at Scharmon and on the Danis side down from the Statzertali chair lift.

Both towns offer loads of places to doss with group accommodation the cheapest. For nosh check out Da Elio for a pizza and for a beer Ninos Pub is OK (a beer cost Sfr 4). Joy-Club is the main Disco where you can get a game of pool but a small beer will set you back about Sfr 6.

Winter snowboard periods between Dec and April. No summer snowboarding

Top Station	2865m
Resort height	1500m
Vertical Drop	1450m
Longest run	11km
Ride area	150km
Snowcannons	6

Terrain ability suits:

● Beginner	46%
● Intermediate	40%
● Advanced	14%

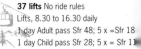

2 Fun Parks and 2 Halfpipes

37 lifts No ride rules
Lifts, 8.30 to 16.30 daily
1 day Adult pass Sfr 48; 5 x =Sfr 18
1 day Child pass Sfr 28; 5 x = Sfr 1

Snowboard Instruction
Primus Snowboard School
+41 (0) 81 384 67 17
1 day lesson Sfr 75, 5 days Sfr 360

Lenzerheide Tourist Office
7078 Lenzerheide
Switzerland.
+41 (0) 384 3434

Nearest international airport Zurich
Transfer time 2 hours

TOGGENBURG

Toggenburg is a region that offers a lot of snowboard terrain with the best to be found leading from the hamlet of Wildhaus. The area is somewhat basic and should appeal to true riders touring around in a van who are looking for a stop over for a few days. To be honest you are not going to want to hang out here for more than a week or so (unless you pull a local!). Never the less it still has something to offer favouring novices and intermediates best. Advanced riders can take on a couple of runs especially when it has just dumped, check out the stuff down from the Hinterrug, it offers some excellent freeriding but you have to hit it on the right day. The tree stuff here isn't going to freak you out, it mainly consists of some open tree riding but like much of Switzerland its not welcomed on environmental grounds, (they should cut the stuff down and use the wood for roach papers then there would be no hassles). Freestylers do get the chance to fly with gullies and banked walls to launch out from as well as some extremes and big drop off's to check out, and if that wasn't enough there are two halfpipes and two fun parks to satisfy all those doing it in mega baggy strides.

Lodging and night time is very laid back, with farm houses the best offering. For life style check out Pferdestall or Willi's Music bar, not happening but certainly OK.

Winter snowboard periods between Dec and April.
Summer snowboarding to June

Top Station	2262m
Resort height	894m
Vertical Drop	1300m
Longest run	5km
Ride area	82km
Snowcannons	3

Terrain ability suits:

● Beginner	30%
● Intermediate	50%
● Advanced	20%

2 Fun Parks and 2 Halfpipes

20 lifts
Rear foot free rules
Lifts, 8.00 to 16.30 daily
1 day Adult pass Sfr 42; 5 x = Sfr 164
1 day Child pass Sfr 29; 5 x = Sfr 114

Snowboard Instruction
Toggenburg Ski /board School
+41 (0) 74 5 17 22
1 day lesson Sfr 60; 5 days Sfr 140.

 Area Tourist Office
9658 Alt, St. Johann. Wildhaus, Switzerland.
+41 (0) 71 999 18 88

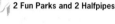 Nearest international airport Zurich
Transfer time 1 hours.

ZERMATT

This is probably one of the most famous resorts in Europe, though it could be questioned why. Maybe it's to do with its very elitist status. What the heck, it can be ridden in the summer when all the fur clad numpties have gone home on the Theodul Glacier. This actually an impressive place with extensive heliboarding on offer as well as some major terrain to be conquered by all levels and ride styles. For all the money this place seems to attract it can't be said to be well spent when you see how the 73 lifts are connected. Riders who have made the grade then the runs of the Stockhorn are the ones to check out, both carvers and freeriders should be able to match the blacks. However if it is full on freeriding off piste you want without splashing out large wadges on Heliboarding then check out the Garten area. Beginners are not spoilt and it could prove to be a bit tricky if you don't keep an eye out or study a piste map. Freestylers are however spoilt with good natural hits and a pipe and park to gain big air from.

Zermatt which goes over board with sad Brit apre skiers is a stupidly pricy place so staying, eating and partying is not cheap. You will need your major scam head on if you're on a tight budget.

Winter between Dec and April.
Summer snowboarding on the Theodul – Klein glacier

Top Station	3820m
Resort height	1620m
Vertical Drop	2203m
Longest run	15km
Ride area	245km
Snowcannons	6

Terrain ability suits:

● Beginner	33%
● Intermediate	45%
● Advanced	22%

1 Fun Park and 1 Halfpipe
on the Klein Matterhorn

73 lifts – No ride rules
Lifts, 8.00am to 5pm daily
1 day Adult pass Sfr 60; 5 x = Sfr 250
1 day Child pass Sfr 30; 5 x = Sfr 125

Snowboard Instruction
Stoked Snowboard School
1 day lesson Sfr 80, 3 days Sfr 220

 Zermatt Tourist Office
3920 Zermatt
Switzerland.
+41 (0) 27 967 01 81

 Nearest international airport Zurich
Transfer time 2 hours.

QUICK RIDE AROUND TWELVE OTHER SWISS SNOWBOARD RESORTS

Resort	Mountain Information and Travel.

	Summit	Resort	Ridable Piste	Lifts
Adelboden	2350m	1350m	166km	51 lifts

Simple laid back place which is excellent for beginners and OK for intermediate air heads with good natural terrain. Good carving to be had. Heaps of accommodation to choose from. Life style good at the Alpenrosli. Full details Tel +41 (0) 33 73 80 80.

	Summit	Resort	Ridable Piste	Lifts
Andermatt	2963m	1444m	56km	13 lifts

Deep powder for freeriders, steeps, big hits and park for freestylers, but total beginners beware, this is not nappy land. Cool snowboard shop to visit. Accommodation in Chalets. Life style very quite – crank up the Walkman.
Full details Tel +41 (0) 44 674 54

	Summit	Resort	Ridable Piste	Lifts
Braunwald	1900m	1300m	25km	7 lifts

Happy little resort where freestylers can play in the pipe and novices can practice 180 arse spins on easy slopes. Good place for ground grommets. Accommodation at the youth hostel. Life style OK and with a Skate scene
Full details Tel +41 (0) 55 643 11 08.

	Summit	Resort	Ridable Piste	Lifts
Engadine	3303m	1673m	350km	60 lifts

Big area suiting freeriders looking for powder and freestylers for big air in the park and half pipe. Euros in hards will like this place with good flats. Lots of accommodation options including a youth hostel. Life style Good
Full details Tel +41 (0) 82 6 65 73

	Summit	Resort	Ridable Piste	Lifts
Grachen	2920m	1615m	40km	12 lifts

Quite little resort that links with St. Niklaus to offer some cool no dramas freeriding as well as providing freestylers with 2 pipes. Beginner friendly to. Small place with good lodging. Life style not as pricy as its neighbours.
Full details Tel +41 (0) 28 56 27 27

	Summit	Resort	Ridable Piste	Lifts
Gstaad	3000m	1000m	250km	69 lifts

Rich pickings to be had on and off the slopes in a big area suiting every one, with 3 fun parks for flyers and twisters to do their thing in. For a bed check out the youth hostel. Life style full on, even a Tex- Mex.
Full details Tel +41(0) 30 83 200

	Summit	Resort	Ridable Piste	Lifts
Laax	3018m	1020m	220km	32 lifts

Alpine powder heaven for advanced freeriders. 2 half pipes and a park for big air. Cool for beginners and full on for carvers with loads of long runs. Lodging in apartments is a good option. Life style very Swiss and not that bad. Full details Tel +41 (0) 81 921 43 43

	Summit	Resort	Ridable Piste	Lifts
Les Diablerets	3000m	1155m	200km	74 lifts

Carvers check this one out. Freestylers and freeriders give the boarder cross a go. Beginner total friendly slopes which can't be said for the lifts. Kip at apartments or B&B's. Life style – walkman, and supermarkets for booze. Full details Tel +41 (0) 25 53 13 58

	Summit	Resort	Ridable Piste	Lifts
Meiringen	2433m	1230m	60km	15 lifts

Quite, crowd free freeriders resort with nothing too testing but plenty of good terrain. Euro carvers also get some good flats to cut up. Beginner friendly slopes. Bed down at the youth hostel. Life style, check out the Lyons Pub. Full details Tel +41 (0) 36 71 39 22

	Summit	Resort	Ridable Piste	Lifts
Pontresina	3000m	1800m	350km	64 lifts

Easy access to a number of areas appealing to most, especially novices. Area has 3 pipes and a fun park. Riding on the Glacier is possible into July. Accommodation limited, good Lifestyle but crank up the walkman.
Full details Tel +41 (0) 81 842 64 88

	Summit	Resort	Ridable Piste	Lifts
Scuol	2783m	1244m	80km	15 lifts

Euro carvers place with wide flats. Good for freestylers with a big pipe and a park. Cool snowboard school for beginners to find out the basics. Accommodation limited but good Lifestyle.
Full details Tel +41 (0) 81 864 93 39

	Summit	Resort	Ridable Piste	Lifts
Villars	2217m	1253m	200km	74 lifts

Laid back area not testing. Will suit carvers who want the long wide stuff. Some cliffs for freestylers and a half pipe. Very beginner friendly slopes. Good lodging services. Lifestyle good, check out Garage for a beer.
Full details Tel +41 (0) 25 35 32 32

RIDER'S OWN NOTES
ON SWITZERLAND

EASTERN EUROPE
Bulgaria - Czech Republic - Poland - Russia

Eastern Europe believe it or not offers amazing snowboarding opportunities on major mountains. However the biggest problem is who's shooting who, because one minute you have a top resort the next it's a battle ground. Still if you do decide to try out the east then remember that on the whole travel can be a bit of a nightmare. Some places have bugger all

Dombaj. Photo: Haus Hansbauer

services, resorts are in the main some what undeveloped, and rules and regulations slack to say the least. But the big big plus about any part of Eastern Europe is the cost - cheap cheap cheap; and the experiences. It's worth ducking and diving from the lead sparrows when you can buy booze at such silly low prices. So what if the slopes are not of the same high tech stuff as in western Europe. Who cares if the runs are not pisted to perfection. Freeriders will love the unevenness. Freestylers may not find half pipes or fun parks with table tops all over the place but things are changing and there is ample natural freestyle terrain to be had. Carvers too will be pleasantly surprised in some parts with enough opportunity to lay out big carves. Beginners are provided with user friendly slopes which is not so true of lifts, so be prepared for the odd bit of drag lift tackle. Snowboard instruction is not up to much yet and you will only really be able to get basic tuition, but again this is changing.

Overall resort services are very basic with basic and cheerful accommodation and simple restaurants and bars. It doesn't matter what bars are like when alcohol is so cheap. Snowboard hire is not too hot but you can get soft bindings and the odd demo board. There's also a lot of dodgy and dubious fake boards mass made in certain countries.

Local people are very friendly and eager to see that you have a good time. A good way of visiting any of the countries and resorts is to hire or take your own RELIABLE car or van. It's well worth checking with travel operators before leaving to find out the latest problems and the best options for travel and places to kip.

Rider: Mike Hunt at Zakopane, Poland. Photo: Sang Tan

BULGARIA

BOROVETS

Best known of the Bulgarian Resorts, with a wide range of facilities and life style activities (including sumo wrestling). Borovets has one of the largest and highest ridable areas in Eastern Europe having hosted several world cup events.

The terrain here is mainly suited to intermediate carvers, with nothing too challenging for experienced riders. The 35km of piste are split into three areas offering open runs, lines through trees and some beginner friendly stuff at the base.

The French designed lift system is OK and snowboarding is welcomed with both hire and instruction available. The modern hotels offer a high value area in the famous Bulgarian wine belt, but beware of food shortages. Night time is OK and goes on until the early hours of the morning.

Winter snowboard periods between Nov and May.
No summer snowboarding

Top Station	2543m
Base	1317m
Vertical Drop	1193m
Longest run	6.5Km
Ride area	37km

Terrain ability suits:

● Beginner	32%
● Intermediate	64%
● Advanced	4%

13 lifts no ride rules.

Nearest international airport: Plovdiv 101km away.

Full resort details
Balkantoursit Borovets
2010 Borovets, Bulgaria
Tel +359 2 835210

Photo: Borovets

PAMPOROVO:

Pleasant purpose-built centre in pine forests. There may be something in the air here as many of the locals live to be 100+, or it may be just because this claims to be Europe's sunniest resort, averaging 270 sunshine days annually onto easy slopes that will please novices, entertain intermediates carvers but bore the heck out of advanced Freestylers.

Limited accommodation but what you do get is OK. The evenings are carried on in a number of bars and 2 discos if you want to strut your stuff with cheap plonk in you. Local food should be tried in the Tschewermeto restaurant. Prices are very low compared to Alpine resorts.

Season starts Dec, ends April. Top Station 1926m Base 1620 Vertical Drop 480m
Longest run 4Km Ride area 22km 13 lifts ●Beg 73% ●Int 18% ●Adv 9%
Travel via international airport: Plovdiv 80 km from the resort.
Full details: Tourist office Pamporovo AG. Bulgaria. Tel +359 3021 438.

VITOSHA:

Close to the Bulgarian capital, Sofia, a gondola takes riders from the city limits to Aleko (1810 metres). In good snow conditions an off-piste descent of 1295 vertical metres is possible. Alternative ascent via two chairlifts from Dragalevtsi or via the 23km mountain road from Sofia. Reliable snow (average base depth 3 metres) and plenty of sunshine in the summit bowl. Trees for freeriders to check out. No pipe for freestylers but flats for euro carvers and easy stuff from the top to the base for beginners.

The village offers a number cheap hotels. Night time check out Hotel Prostor or head down to Sofia.

Season starts Dec, ends April. Top Station 2115m Base 1810 Vertical Drop 600m
Longest run 6.5Km Ride area 37km 11 lifts ●Beg 10% ●Int 37% ●Adv 10%
Travel via international airport Sofia 32 km from the resort.
Full details Balkantoursit, Boulevard Vitosha 1 Bulgaria. Tel +359 2 43331

CZECH REPUBLIC

SPINDLERUV MLYN:

The Czech republic's largest and best known resort, Spindleruv is a scattered community centred around the old village of St. Peters, which has heaps of history and old buildings dating back as far as the 1800's. There are several ridable areas and snow cover is usually good to late April. Best runs can be found on Medvedin and around Svaty Petr. The later is probably the most modern area in Czech with a detachable quad. Extensive snowmaking and night riding. Moreover an interchangeable lift ticket is offered. A chairlift ascends Snezka (1602 m), Czechs highest mountain but no runs lead down to the valley.

Season starts Dec, ends April.   Top Station 1310m   Base 718   Vertical Drop 495m

Longest run 3.5Km   Ride area 25km   21 lifts   ●Beg 45%   ●Int 40%   ●Adv 15%

Travel via international airport Prague 165 km from the resort.

Full details Tourist office Spindleruv Mlyn, Bedrichov 19. Tel +42 438 93656.

ZELEZN RUDA:

One of the largest ski centres in the Czech Republic centred on this 16th century mining settlement. The Spicak snow area with its 9 lifts is most popular with advanced snowboarders, linked by a shuttle bus to the other slopes (but lift ticket is only valid on Spicak). Pancir is served by a long chair and offers very easy trails. Prices are low but slightly higher than in the rest of Czech due to lots of German visitors. Great slopes on nearby (Bavarian) Arber mountain.

Season starts Dec, ends March.   Top Station 1200m   Base 754   Vertical Drop 364m

Longest run 2.2Km   Ride area 15km   26 lifts   ●Beg 60%   ●Int 35%   ●Adv 5%

Travel via international airport Prague 180 km from the resort.

Full details Tourist office Lyzarsky areal Belveder 34004. Tel +42 186 97132.

LOUCNA – KLINOVEC:

Snowboard friendly resort – Season starts Dec, ends April.

Top station 1240m   Bottom lift 860m   Resort height 830m   Vertical drop 380m

Longest run 2km   Ride area 11km   ●Beg 60%   ●Int 30%   ●Adv 10%

Lifts 12, 1 single chair 11 drag lifts, uphill capacity 5800 persons an hour

Fly to Prague 140 km from resort. Full details Tel +42 396 96262

JANSKE LAZNE:

Snowboard friendly resort - Season starts Dec, ends April

Top station 1275m   Bottom lift 640m   Resort height 620m   Vertical drop 380m

Longest run 2km   Ride area 11km   ●Beg 58%   ●Int 34%   ●Adv 8%

Lifts 11, 1 Gondola , 10 drag lifts, uphill capacity 7000 persons an hour

Fly to Prague 160 km from resort .Full details Tel +42 439 94661

PEC POD SNEZKOU:

Snowboard friendly resort - Season starts Dec, ends April

Top station 1602m   Bottom lift 705m   Resort height 769m   Vertical drop 355m

Longest run 2km   Ride area 12km   ●Beg 60%   ●Int 35%   ●Adv 5%

Lifts 23, 2 chairs lifts, 21 drag lifts, uphill capacity 11,500 persons an hour

Fly to Prague 175 km from resort. Full details Tel +42 439 962 475

ROKYTNICE NAD JIZEROU:

Snowboard friendly resort - Season starts Dec, ends March

Top station 1300m   Bottom lift 630m   Resort height 543m   Vertical drop 670m

Ride area 13km   ●Beg 67%   ●Int 25%   ●Adv 8%

Lifts 15 drag lifts, uphill capacity 6500 persons an hour

Fly to Prague 150 km from resort. Full details Tel +42 439 92694

POLAND

Polish snowboard Population	12000
Polish snowboard association set up	1992
Number of associations members	210
Membership cost to join	2 USD

Association is independent of any skiing group and fully supports the International Snowboard Federation over the Olympics and NOT the Federation of Skiers.
Riders from other countries are welcome to joint the Polish snowboard Association and ride together across the universe.

Poland has 70 snowboard clubs spread across the country, the first known independent snowboard shop was Star Sport which opened in 1993 located at Piotr Starowicz, ul. Partyzantow 63, Bielsko-Biake.

Poland favours 60% freeride, 30% freestyle and 10% Alpine carve
Polish riders are 80 % soft boot riders and 20% hard booters.
During 1995/96 approximately 5000 snowboards were sold in Poland, split as 3000 freeride, 1500 freestyle and 500 Alpine carve.

Polish snowboard mags or publication with snowboard articles.
'Narty and', Address: ul.Sw. Tomasza 30/9a Krakow
'Slizg', Address: Warsaw
'Gory', Address: ul. Librowszczyana 3 Krakow.

Poland has at least 1 snowboard manufacture.
Polands most Popular riders are, Malgorazate Rosiak and Jagna Marczulajtis.
Polands most popular snowboard personality is Dariusz Rosiak.

To find out more about Poland contact the Polish Snowboard Association, they are damn fine people, major helpful and cool riders.
Polski Zwiazek Snowboardu
ul. Wyzwolenia 59/60, 43-300 Bielsko-Biala Poland.

ZAKOPANE

Originally a 17th Century forestry settlement, Zakopane has been a centre for Polish intellectuals for the past century. This picture post card town (with a few ugly Communist era blocks) is also Poland's best known resort. The nearest ridable area (3km) is Kasprowy Wierch where there is high Alpine boarding in two treeless bowls. Other nearby areas are Gubalowka and Nosal. 14 of the lifts quoted locally are drag lifts dotted around the town. Whereas lifts are not state of the art, life style and nightlife is ahead of many alpine competitors. Cheap booze is the key dudes especially the Jagermeister.

Top 1960m Bottom 830m Vertical drop 929m
Longest run 8.5km Ride area 27km ●Beg 13% ●Int 43% ●Adv 44%
Lifts 6 uphill capacity 3500 persons an hour
Fly to Warsaw 300km from resort. Full details: Zakopane Travel Agency Tel + 48 165 15947

Rider: Russ Ward. Photo: Sang Tan

RUSSIA

DOMBAJ

This was a Mecca for German heli-snowboarders until the Russian government refused to give visas for this region one year ago. Actually the Chechnya war took place several hundred kilometres away and Dombaj could become an alternative to the Rockies again as soon as fighting finishes. Situated 90km west of Elbrus, Dombaj is surrounded by 4000 m peaks of which Bjela Jakaja (nickname: Caucasian Matterhorn) is the most impressive.

Five hotels with a total bed base of 900, some chalets and the base of the gondola create the peaceful village. Modern Kassbohrer snowcats are a contrast to the old fashioned lifts. But groomers are not always on duty. Be aware to face ungroomed terrain even on all designated trails. Meeting point for snowboarders is the UFO a futuristic, small hotel in the middle of the ride area at 2250 m. Although Dombaj officially belongs to Europe, culture is much influenced by the Orient.

Season starts Nov, ends June.
Top Station 3050m Base 1600 Vertical Drop 1450m
Longest run 5km Ride area 17 runs
●Beg 35% ●Int 30% ●Adv 35% 11 lifts
Travel via international airport Mineralinyje Vody.
Full details Tourist office Dombaj Stavropol Territory.
Tel +7 86522 78168
For details on Heli-boarding call Andreas Rhul in Germany on +49 2837 515.

ITKOL

The two cable cars of Itkol start right at the foot of Mt. Elbrus. The 5633 m volcano in the Caucuses was the highest summit in Europe until geographers decided that it is actually in Asia. The lifts take snowboarders from 1800m to an altitude of 3900m. Riding is exceptionally cheap (as is heli boarding option) but lifts often broken down so a Cat tow to the mountaineering base camp, a big metal covered structure at 4200m usually offered as alternative. Black Sea can be seen at the horizon. The chairlift between 3900m and 4000m seldom operates but summer snowboarding is an option. The run from the base camp to the valley offers a 2400 m vertical. If you are in good shape, hire a mountain guide and ascend Elbrus for an ultimate 3833m vertical experience. Needless to say that Elbrus offers impressive off-piste options.

Closest airport is Mineral
Further details try the following addresses: Cet Neva High Venture Travel,
Antonenko Street 5, 190000 St. Petersburg, Russia, Tel. +7-812-1106509, Fax 1106097, or Intourist Itkol, Kabardin - Balkar ASSR, RF - Itkol.

CHEGET

Antiquated lift infrastructure and a very frontier feel to one of Russia's top winter sports centres. Ticket prices for the three chair and two drag lifts are ludicrously low for hard currency holders, who can also afford to queue jump. Located at the same latitude as Vail and offering almost the same vertical (914 m), Cheget (1500 m) was inaugurated in 1964. The mountain is full on, a jagged, steep-flanked peak, shoulder-to-shoulder with other giant crags. Despite Centuries of settlement in the valley, the mountains are still untouched wilderness. Not marvellous but just barely acceptable is the scant amount of developed terrain, basically ungroomed. There is no rental equipment available at Cheget. If you plan on going bring your own. 1 mountain restaurant.

Closest airport is Mineral
Further details try the following addresses: Cet Neva High Venture Travel,
Antonenko Street 5, 190000 St. Petersburg, Russia, Tel. +7-812-1106509, Fax 1106097, or Intourist Itkol, Kabardin - Balkar ASSR, RF-Itkol.

Dombaj

JAPAN

Forget politics, to hell with diplomacy and stuff the money talking hype, because this is not a great country to shell out and go snowboarding in, unless you're a well sponsored rider with mega bucks who will put up with anything in order to earn a crust and get a front cover shot.

For a country that is quick to jump on the band wagon of trendy new things with the opportunity of making a few Yen, it's somewhat odd to find that Japan has more resorts that ban snowboarding than anywhere else in the world, yet there are thousands of loyal Japanese snowboarders who are cool riders with a good attitude. Manufacturers went into overdrive in Japan and are now paying for it because they've over estimated the market and produced too many boards. The country is now awash with unsold produce because to many money grabbing corporates put out the wrong vibes.

Japan is an expensive place and snowboarding doesn't come cheap. If you're living in Australia or New Zealand then it may be worth a quick hop over to see what's on offer but if your coming from Europe or America it's going to be a long expensive journey to make when you have better on your door step. There are an estimated 700 resorts spread out over the 4 main islands. Resorts are generally low level affairs that broadly offer basic short runs and none too adventurous terrain where novices and early intermediates will fair best. Freeriders will find the odd steeps, some big bowls and trees to shred while freestylers are provided with perfectly groomed half pipes. Beginners will manage but don't get excited with the thought of progressing on to major hard-core terrain. Resort marketing literature will boast about how many lifts they have, however instead of this being an advantage it has the opposite effect, because it attracts far more punters than the slopes can cater for and in-turn leaves the slopes way overcrowded.

If you do decide to give Japan a go check with a travel operator on what package deals are available and get them to confirm that riding is allowed at the place you're heading for. Travel is no big deal and resorts can be reached by car or bus and in many cases you can get close by train with short transfers by bus. Lodging and services at resorts differ but are good and of high standard, however the Japanese don't like hard core snowboarders partying big style or trashing the place so be warned.

MOUNT MADARAO

Snowboard at Madarao Kohgen & Tangram. Two resorts on Mt. Madarao, combined offer one of the biggest areas in Japan, with trees for freeriders to shred. Life style: loads of bars plenty of accommodation though expensive.

Fly to Matsumoto in Nagano.
Top: 1350m Bottom: 800m
●Beg 30% ●Int 40% ●Adv 30%
Ride area 300 acres with 25 lifts.
Info Madaras +81 269 64 3214
Info Tangram +81 262 58 3511

RUSUTU

Snowboarding allowed but not all over. Located on the Hokkaido mountain. Big family favourate place with 3 mountains to ride. Flats for speed seeking carvers.

Fly to Chitose in Sapporo.
Top: 995m Bottom: 400m.
●Beg 35% ●Int 35% ●Adv 30%
Ride area 420 acres with 20 lifts.
Resort info +81 136 46 3331.

KIJIMADAIRA

Very snowboarding frendly one of the most in Japan riding allowed all over. Ok freeriding to be had on featureless terrain. Longest run for carvers to slice up is 3km.

Train to Liyama then bus - 30mins.
Top: 1300m Bottom: 500m.
●Beg 40% ●Int 40% ●Adv 20%
Ride area 15km with 15 lifts.
Resort info +81 269 82 3434.

JOETSU KOKUSAI

Snowboarding allowed at this big, by Japanese standards, area which stages pro events. Boring for advanced riders, Ok for early intermediate slow freeriders

Train to Echigo Yuzawa - 20 mins.
Top: 950m Bottom: 215m.
●Beg 40% ●Int 50% ●Adv 10%
Ride area 25km with 35 lifts.
Resort info +81 257 82 1030.

HACHIMANTAI

Cool little snowboard hang out that has night riding and stages pro events. Perfect for beginners with a long run for carvers and freeriders to mess up.

Train to Morioka then bus 1½ hrs
Top: 1000m Bottom: 540m. 8 lifts.
●Beg 50% ●Int 40% ●Adv 10%
Resort info +81 195 78 2577.

International Snowboard Association Asia
MC Bldg 2F, 4-36-4 Yoyogi
Shibuya-ku. Tokyo 151, Japan.
tel +81 3 33377 0285

Japan Snowboard Association
Mac Shibuya Bldg 4F, 15-10
Nanpeidai Shibuya-ku.Tokyo 150
tel +81 3 5458 2661

JAPAN

SOUTHERN HEMISPHERE

The southern hemisphere is that part of the globe that lies below the equator. Universal snowboard guide gives a very brief description in this issue of USG, however a full -in-depth ride guide to the stuff down under will feature in our next issue and our special summer supplement.

Rider: Bjorn Leines in Chile. Photo: Scott Needham

AUSTRALIA

Australia's winter sports grounds where you can snowboard are located on the eastern mountain ranges on the state boarders of New South Wales and Victoria. Australia's high ground has its very own distinctive flavour and characteristic's. They may not compare in stature to the far higher European Alps but still have varied terrain with snow gums and mountain ash. Australia's season normally kicks in around June, and ends at the end of September or mid October.

NEW SOUTH WALES resorts are located in the Kosciusko
National Park which has the highest summit in the country.

Charlotte Pass; 500km from Sydney is the highest village in New South Wales. Small resort that will suite everyone with 5 lifts to get you around.
Stay at the Kosciusko Chalet. Info Tel: +61 561 700.

Perisher Blue; 520 km from Sydney is one of the biggest resorts in Australia with terrain spanning out over 4 mountain peaks all accessed with one lift ticket. There is a fun park and pipe. Night riding on Tuesdays.
Accommodation and life style at Jindabyne or Perisher. Info Tel: +61 56 2457

Mount Selwyn; 500km from Sydney is the small family resort ideal for beginners. The terrain has 11km of piste serviced by 12 lifts.
Stay at Adaminaby, Tumut or Coona. Info Tel: +61 549 488.

Thredbo Alpine Village; 550km from Sydney, is one of Australia's top resorts with 65 marked runs with a fun park and pipe serviced by 11 lifts.
Youth Hostel accommodation bars and shops. Info Tel: +61 59 4100.

VICTORIA; Victoria's resorts are in the North-Eastern part of the
state. Lower than the resorts in New South Wales they still get the same degree of snow.

Mount Baw Baw; 163km from Melbourne and one of the nearest, has terrain for novices and intermediates on snow gum and alpine ash terrain.
The village has Beds, bars and food joints. Info Tel: +61 3 764 9939.

Mount Buffalo's; 320km from Melbourne is the place where Australia's first lift was put in. This is a beginners resort with 7 easy to use lifts.
Resort services at the Tatra Inn complex. Info Tel: +61157 551 500.

Mount Butler; 240km from Melbourne has a modern lift system of 26 lifts to carry you over its 80km of piste that offer good levels with something to take on.
Beds, bars and food joints available in the village. Info Tel: +61 3 650 9798

Falls Creek; 380km from Melbourne this is a Euro style place with 80 runs, backed up with snow-making facilities for all grades and styles.
Beds, bars and food joints available in the village. Info Tel: +61 57 57 2718.

Mount Hottam; 373km from Melbourne, this is said to be the place for powder and some testing riding, with off piste and lodging on the slopes. Beds, bars and food joints available in the village.
Info Tel: +61 57 59 3632.

TASMANIA; In the south tip of the country are the resorts of
Tasmania, snow cover however is not so good as the other areas.

Ben Lomond; 60km from Launceston has the best of what is on offer in the state. With terrain to please advanced riders and novices with 8 lifts.
Accommodation at the town of Blessington. Info Tel: +61 2 33 8011.

Further Australian contacts.
Snowave Snowboarding Adventure Holidays.
9c Clarke St, Po Box 556, Crows Nest NSW 2064. Tel: +61 2 901 3008

Australian Snowboard Association.
22 Beattle St, Balmain NSW 2041. Australia Tel: +61 2 818 5047

NEW ZEALAND

Amuri: Snowboarder friendly, elevation at 2118m up to 2456m. Natural half pipe. 10-15 runs, 2 lifts. Full info + 64 (03) 315 7125

Broken River: Getta Grip snowboard weekends boarder cross and big air events. Night riding, 4 tows. Full info + 64 (03) 384 9018

Coronet Peak: 428m of vert with bowls. Terrain suits Beg 15%, Int 45%, Adv 40%. Heliboarding but no park or pipe. Area has 6 lifts. Nearest accommodation and services 18km. Full info +64 (03) 442 7653

Cardrona: All level terrain with big bowls. Half pipe and fun park with 4 lifts covering the area. Terrain suits Beg 20%, Int 55%, Adv 25%. Nearest accommodation and services 33km. Full info +64 (03) 443 7411

Craigieburn Valley: Awesome terrain available on field, and a short hike off the top of Top Tow, along ridge to Middle Basin and beyond, 500m drop into Big Bend. Natural lips and halfpipe. 3 tows with assistance for beginners. Full info + 64 (03) 3666 6644.

Fox Peak: Elevation to 2254m 4 lifts. Full info + 64 (03) 688 1870.

Manganui: Come prepared for a 20 minute walk and one of the gruntiest nutcracker lifts. 2 natural half pipes 4 lifts. Full info + 64 (06) 765 7669.

Mt. Hutt: 655m of vert with terrain to suit Beg 25%, Int 50%, Adv 25%. Nearest accommodation and services 25km. Full info +64 (03) 302 8811

Mt. Cheesman: Elevation to 2250m 2 lifts. Full info + 64 (03) 379 5315.

Mt. Lyford: Snowboarders welcome with base elevation at 1500m up to 1740m. Ride area 7 kms runs to suit Beg 30%, Int 35%, Adv 35%, over a rolling basin serviced by 6 lifts. Pipe, Park and Heli boarding. Accommodation and services 4km away. Full info + 64 (03) 315 6178.

Mt. Olympus: Elevation to 2250m 3 lifts. Full info + 64 (03) 329 1823.

Mt. Robert: Elevation up to 1673m. 4 tows. Full info + 64 (03) 548 8336.

Ohau: Elevation to 2153m 2 lifts. Full info + 64 (03) 438 9885.

Porter Heights: Snowboarders welcome with base elevation at 1280m up to 1980m with terrain to suit Beg 20%, Int 50%, Adv 30%. 3 tows. Fun park. Cliff jumps, Good off piste to be had. Heli Boarding by arrangement. Accommodation and services 40km. Full info + 64 (03) 379 7087.

Rainbow Valley: A half pipe and small terrain park were introduced last year. This season there's is a groomer blade for the half pipe. Area has 20 runs serviced by 4 lifts. Heli Boarding. Accommodation and services 20km away. Full info + 64 (03) 765 5493

Turoa: Good off piste but no trees. Suite Beg 20%, Int 60%, Adv 20%. Nearest accommodation and services 18km. Full info +64 (06) 3858 465

Temple Basin: Discover Bill's Basin - endless powder. 84 runs serviced by 4 lifts. Natural quarter pipe for regular riders. Lots of events. Full info + 64 (03) 377 7788

Treble Cone: Top snowboard friendly New Zealand resort, to suit Beg 15%, Int 45%, Adv 40%. Heaps of off piste but no trees. Fun park with logs and slides. Half pipe, gullies and banked walls for freestylers. Base at 1250m up to top lift at 1750m. Ride area serviced by 5 lifts. Accommodation and services 28km away. Full info + 64 (07) 892 3738

Tukino: Snowboarders friendly with elevation up to 2056m. 3 lifts.

Turoa Ski Resort: Turoa welcomes snowboarders with base elevation at 1625m up to 2300m. Half pipe and fun park with 12 lifts. Full info + 64 (07) 892 373

Whakapapa: Terrain consists of some of the best natural gullies in New Zealand serviced by 24 lifts. Resort has a half pipe and fun park and regularly stage snowboard events. Accommodation and services 26km away. Full info + 64 (07) 892 3738

Steve Eakin

ARGENTINA

LAS LENAS

Generally regarded as the best snow resort area in South America today. It was dropped on to the wilderness of the High Andes in 1983 and wasted no time in establishing its international credentials by staging a world cup event in 1985 and 1986. It's reputation as the most expensive place to go in Argentina seems to be borne out by the continual patronage of wealthy Brazilians, the Argentinean upper classes and well heeled North Americans through the lobby of the five-star Hotel Piscis. Valle de Las Lenas means "the firewood valley" - ironic, as there's not a tree to be seen in the lunar landscape. There really is absolutely nothing to see, a strange experience for even the most travelled snowboarder. The nearest town is 69km away, there's just a desert like barrenness. The focus is therefore on the impressive area, which combines French lifts and German snowcats with the snow, sunshine and service of a Colorado resort. The south American contribution is the spectacular Andean backdrop. The cluster of hotels looks like a Martian colony but the lifts access a ski area of top Alpine proportions. The Marte lift accesses more expert terrain than any other lift on planet Earth. No boarder could ever try every option available - there's exposure on all sides, dozens of ridges, daunting gullies, bowls and chutes - all with the added bonus of uninterrupted vertical madness. Less vertically-challenged snowboarders will prefer to ride the short Iris poma at the top of Marte. It accesses the summit and huge bowls for endless turns. The Jupiter and Apollo runs lead down in a big, six kilometre long curve.

The only thing that might cut you short on this manicured snow course is the wind, as Las Lenas suffers from it bad, along with avalanche danger.

Season starts June, ends Nov.
Top Station 3430m   Base 2256   Vertical Drop 1230m
Longest run 7Km   Ride area 59km   14 lifts
●Beg 48%   ●Int 32%   ●Adv 20%

Travel via international airport Mendoza 444 km from the resort.
Full details Las Lenas Tourist office Arenales 707. Tel + 54. 1 3132121

BARILOCHE/GRAN CATEDRAL

Overlooking some cool scenery around Lake Nahuel Huapi, Gran Catedral is South Americas biggest single snowboard mountain. Snow at the base cannot be guaranteed due to low elevation. But Argentina's first and only cable car lifts boarders to Punta Rifugio (1850 m) where wide open snowfilled bowls stretch out seemingly endlessly. Climate is mild and sunny, lots of sundecks. New management promised a lot of improvements including new quads.

Season starts June, ends Oct.
Top Station 2160m   Base 1050   Vertical Drop 1130m
Longest run 6Km   Ride area 72km   28 lifts
●Beg 54%   ●Int 33%   ●Adv 13%

Travel via international airport Buenos Aires 1615 km from the resort.
Full details Tourist office Gran Catedral, Paraguay 783. Tel +54. 1 3122420.

Argentinean Snowboard Association,
Zabala St, 2679 P8-1426 Buenos Aires-KF
Tel +54 1 796 1951

CHILE

VALLE NEVADO

At the bottom of the 5,430 metre high El Plomo mountain, three resorts have merged to become the biggest rideable area in the Southern Hemisphere - super modern Valle Nevado, noble La Parva and traditional El Colorado. Valle Nevado sits like an eagle's nest on a ridge of Cerro Negro. The terrain is high above the treeline, giving boundary-less off-piste options in the numerous bowls, corries and valleys. Since Chileans are fond of dancing, many runs are named after dances - Tango, Twist and naturally the Lambada. These dances tend to be rather slow however and there is a lack of really demanding sites, but after snowfalls the powder is excellent. By taking a helicopter to El Plomo's summit you can extend the vertical to 3900 metres. The incredible length of the ascent is the main enjoyment of the descent however, the snow conditions are hard and the glaciated walls extremely steep above 4000 metres. Today the resort's only real failing in attracting those North Americans, is that virtually none of the staff speak English. The food served in the seven restaurants is excellent however and guests at the resort can ride in neighbouring La Parva on the same lift ticket, and in El Colorado for a $15 supplement.

Season starts June, ends Oct.
Top 3650m   Base 3025m   Vert 615m
Longest 5km   Ride area 35km   9 lifts
●Beg 47%   ●Int 44%   ●Adv 9%

Travel via international airport Santiago 60 km.
Full details Valle Nevado Tourist Office. Tel + 56. 2 206 0027

TERMAS DE CHILLIAN

Termas de Chillian (1680m) nestles in the woods beneath the volcano Chillian Nuevo. The earth has not yet quite cooled here. Hot springs bubble up between the rocks, steam rises into the air, bringing with it a smell of sulphur. Back in 1945 some visiting French ski instructors enthused: "The best and most fascinating runs in the world are found in the springs and snows of Chillan". Huge amounts of snow fall on to the volcano. Tree lined runs descend towards the resort and there can be great boarding through the woods themselves in the lower section of the rideable area, known as the Bosque del Nevado.

Above there the Don Otto lift (South America's longest chair at 2,500 metres) reaches the start of boarders heaven at 2,490 metres. Wide powder-filled bowls, bump-filled couloirs, steep sidewalls and chutes open up beneath you. The greatest treasure is the huge Pirigallo Bowl on the east side of the top station. Here the expert snowboarder can descend through a primitive landscape of steaming pools and flowing mud for a true "fire and ice" encounter. A two hour hike to one of the two summits opens up more terrain (there is also a helicopter service in the Spring at a cost of $70US). The glaciated face of the Nevado summit (3212 metres) is the more pedestrian of the two, whilst the Volcan (2950m) is much more challenging. The Shangri La run should also not be missed, descending over 2000 metres to the original site, a distance of some 14km. For those staying on the marked piste, the most exciting is the 5.5km long Pista Tres Marias.

Life style is relaxed and informal, centred as it is on the steaming hot open air pool of the Hotel Pirigallo with a glass of Chile's 'national drink', the Pisco Sour, made of grape schnapps and lemon juice.

Season starts May, ends Oct.
Top Station 2570m   Base 1680   Vertical Drop 890m
Longest run 6Km   Ride area 40km   8 lifts
●Beg 65%   ●Int 25%   ●Adv 10%

Travel via international airport Santiago
480 km from the resort. Full details
Centro de Ski Termas de Chillan, Av.
Providencia 2237 Santiago.
Tel +56. 2 251 5776.

Chilenish Snowboard Association
Objec Tiflun Ltda. Vitacura 5534 Vitacura,
Santiago, Chile. Tel +56 2 218 2879

A QUICK RIDE AROUND THE REST OF THE GLOBE

The following is a compilation to countries where you may be able to snowboard, either on real snow, or artificial slopes. You should contact a country's snowboard association to obtain exactly where you can, or can not go. It would also be a good idea to call a national tourist office to find out travel and visa services. The information given includes countries that have had resorts which now may well no longer exist, as well as countries that have an increased number resorts and those under construction including indoor and dry slope areas.

AFRICA AND MIDDLE EAST

Algeria
Reportedly has 2 resorts the highest point is Mt Tahat 2918m.
The country's population is 25 million. Travel around is very dodgy.

Iran
Reportedly has 3 resorts the highest point is Qolleh-Ye 5604m.
The country's population is 54.6 million. Travel around is dangerous.

Israel
Reportedly has 1 resort the highest point Mt Atzmon 1208m.
The country's population is 4.6 million. Travel around is possible.

Jordan
Reportedly has 1 resort the highest point Jaal Ramm 1754m.
The country's population is 4. million. Travel around is not easy.

Lebanon
Reportedly has 6 resorts the highest point Qurnat As-Sawda 3088m.
The country's population is 2.7 million. Travel around is tricky.
There are more than 2000 snowboarders in Lebanon. Snowboarding started here in 1991. The country has a least six resorts to ride however more are developing as the country evolves. The Lebanese Snowboard Association which began 1993 was founded by Antoine Abou-Samara and Habib Abou-Samara. Today the LSA which is recognised by the Lebanese Government and the ISF, has 250 members and regularly stages pro events.
Lebanese riders on the international scene;
Antoine Abou-Samara, Mazen Sidani, Rania Khalaf, Samer Mansour.
Lebanese Snowboard Association, PO box 90-328 Jdeideh El Maten, Lebanon. Tel +961 3 733 695

Morocco
Reportedly has 1 resort the highest point is Mt. Toubkal 4165m.
The country's population is 25 million. Travel around is not great.

South Africa
Reportedly has 3 resorts the biggest being Tiffindell. The highest point is Mt. Aux Sources 4165m.
The country's population is 25 million. Travel around is not great.
Resorts include artificial slopes

SOUTH AMERICA

Bolivia
Reportedly has 1 resort. The highest point is Mt. Tocoputi 2918m.
The country's population is 7.3 million. Travel around is not convenient.

Brazil
Reportedly has 1 resort. The highest point is Mt. Pico de Banderia 2890m
The country's population is 150.3 million. Travel around is not convent.

Ecuador
Reportedly has 1 resort. The highest point is Mt. Chimboraz 6272m.
The country's population is 10.5 million. Travel around is not convent.

Peru
Reportedly has 1 resort. The highest point Mt. Huascaran 6768m.
The country's population is 21.5 million. Travel around is not convent.

ASIA

Armenia
Reportedly has 2 resorts. The highest point is Pik Konnunizma 7494m
The country's population is 3.4 million. Travel around is not dodgy.

China
Reportedly has 5 resorts. The highest point is Mt Everest 8848m
The country's population is 1.2 billion. Travel around is restricted.

Georgia
Reportedly has 2 resorts. The highest point is Pik Konnunizma 7494m
The country's population is 5.5 million. Travel around is dangerous.
Georgian Snowboard Association, Club Marco Polo, Gudauri Georgia.

Kirghizatan
Reportedly has 1 resort.
The country's population is 16.8 million. Travel around is very dodgy.

India
Reportedly has 5 resort. The highest point is Nanda Devi 7817m.
The country's population is 300 million. Travel around is slow.

Pakistan
Reportedly has 1 resort. The highest point is K2 8611m.
The country's population is 122.6 million. Travel around is OK but slow.

Nepal
Reportedly has 1 resort. The highest point Mt. Everest 8843m.
The country's population is 19 million. Travel around is OK but slow.

South Korea
Reportedly has 19* resorts. The highest point Halla-San 1950m.
The country's population is 42.8 million. Travel around is OK.
*includes artificial dry slopes

Taiwan
Reportedly has 1 resort. The highest point Yu Shan 3997m.
The country's population is 20.8 million. Travel around is OK.

Turkey
Reportedly has 8 resorts. The highest point Mt. Ararat 5185m.
The country's population is 55.8 million. Travel around is OK but slow.

EUROPE

Belgium

Reportedly has 12* resorts the highest point is Botrange 694m
The country's population is 9.8 million. Travel around is good.
* artificial dry slopes
Belgium Snowboard Association - Valerian Pirate 8, Impasse de l'Avenir, 4020 Liege, Belgium. Tel +32 41 429 904

Bosnia

Reportedly has 15 resorts the highest point is Triglab 2864m.
The country's population is 4.4 million. Travel around is dangerous.

Croatia

Reportedly has 2 resorts the highest point is Jtland 1730 m.
The country's population is 4.7 million. Travel around is not easy.

Denmark

Reportedly has 12* resorts. Travel around is good.
* includes artificial dry slopes
Danish Snowboard Association - Vejlebrovej 91, 2635 Ishoje. Denmark. Tel +45 316 42311

Holland

Reportedly has *51 resorts the highest point is Vaalserberg 321m.
The country's population is 14.9 million. Travel around is good.
* artificial dry slopes
Holland's snowboard association was founded in 1988 by Hank Snel. The association is linked to the countries ski association. To date there are 500 members. Holland has a strong dry slope culture. There is no real snow mountain resorts.
Holland's 1996 snowboard champions are:
Frank Germann, male rider age 25 riding Burton.
Maureen Terhorst, female rider age 21 riding Burton.
Paul Schoenmakers male junior rider age 15 riding Freesurf
Miriam Vijfvinkel junior female rider age 18 riding Kemper.
*Snowboard Holland (SH) Po Box 82100, 2508 EC Den Haag, Netherlands. Tel +31 70 352 5821

Hungary

Reportedly has 19 resorts the highest point is Mt. Kekes 1015m.
The country's population is 10.5 million. Travel around is not convenient
* Hungarian Snowboard Association, Podmaniczky u.13, 1065
Budapest, Hungary. Tel + 36 1 1121 429.

Iceland

Reportedly has 12 resorts the highest point is Oraefajokull 2119m.
The country's population is 3.7 million. Travel around is OK .

Liechtenstein

Reportedly has 5 resorts the highest point is Grauspitze 2599m.
The country's population is 28,000. Travel around is good.

Lithuania

Reportedly has 5 resorts.
The country's population is 3.7 million. Travel around is not convenient

EUROPE

Macedonia
Reportedly has 3 resorts. The highest point is Solunska 2540m
The country's population is 2 million. Travel around is convenient.

Romania
Reportedly has 9 resorts. The highest point is Negoiu 2543m
The country's population is 23. 2 million. Travel around is not easy.

Serbia
Reportedly has 25 resorts the highest point is Gerlachovsky 2655m
The country's population is 9.7 million. Travel around is dangerous.

Slovak Republic
Reportedly has 100 resorts the highest point is Gerlachovsky 2655m
The country's population is 5.6 million. Travel around is slow.

Rider: Anthony Youngin O'hau, NZ. Photo: Scott Needham

PORTUGAL

Has 1 resort. The highest point is Estrela 1991m.
The countries population is 10.2 million. Travel around is good.

Portugal has only one resort called 'Serra da Estrela' where you can ride on snow. The area is very low altitude and conditions are not always that favourable. Most riders only check the place out at weekends. If the locals want to ride longer than a weekend they tend to visit Sierra Nevada in Spain and Val D'Isere or Isola 2000 in France.

Snowboard Population	2000
Portuguese snowboard association set up	1996
Number of associations members	85

Association is independent of any skiing group and fully supports the International Snowboard Federation over the Olympics and NOT the Federation of Skiers.
Riders from other countries are welcome to join the Portuguese snowboard Association and ride together across the universe.
The country has 4 snowboard clubs.
Portugal's style favour: Freeride 30%, Freestyle 60% , Alpine/Carve 10% with 60% hard boots and 40% soft boots.

Portuguese snowboard mags or publications with snowboard articles:
'Surf Portugal', Apartado 137, 2765, Estoril, Portugal.
'Portugal Rad', Rua Santo, Estevao Lt 196/98, Casal Da Silveira, 2675 Odivelas, Portugal.
'Surf Magazine', Apartado 7525, 2720 Alfragide Portugal.

To find out more about Portugal contact the Portuguese Snowboard Association they are really cool people, helpful and making things happen in their country.
Portuguese Snowboard Federation, Rua Nova De Sao Mamede 29-1200, Lisboa, Portugal.
Tel +35101 385 2722.

Rider: Artur at Sierra Da Estrela. Photo: Nuchi

Rider: Joado Filipe. Photo: Pedro Silva

RIDER'S OWN CHECK OUT

Name _____

Address _____

_____

_____

_____

Telephone/s _____

Private _____ Business _____

Fax _____ Mobile _____

Riders in case of emergency details _____

Contact _____ Relationship _____

Address _____

_____

_____

_____

Contacts Telephone/s _____

Private _____ Business _____

Fax _____ Mobile _____

Riders blood group _____ Blood donor (Yes no) ___

Organ Donor(Yes no) _____ Doctors Tel _____

Important numbers to remember _____

Name _____ Location _____

Tel _____ fax _____

Name _____ Location _____

Tel _____ fax _____

Name _____ Location _____

Tel _____ fax _____

Local snowboard shop

Name _____ Location _____

Tel _____ fax _____

Local snowboard Club/Association/Hangout

Name _____ Location _____

Tel _____ fax _____

For reason of identification security and insurance _____

Rider's Passport number _____

Rider's snowboard serial number _____

Snowboard length _____ Style _____ Colour _____

WORLD RIDE
TIME DIFFERENCES

Photo : Rob Woodall / Wade McKoy at Jackson WY, USA.

World Ride time differences

Place	Country	Time	off GMT
Adelaide	South Australia	21:30	+9^1/$_2$
Amsterdam	Netherlands	13:00	+1
Athens	Greece	14:00	+2
Auckland	New Zealand	24:00	+12
Berlin	Germany	13:00	+1
Bombay	India	17:30	+5^1/$_2$
Brussels	Belgium	13:00	+1
Bucharest	Romania	14:00	+2
Budapest	Hungary	13:00	+1
Buenos Aires	Argentina	9:00	-3
Cape Town	South Africa	14:00	+2
Chicago	USA	6:00	-6
Copenhagen	Denmark	13:00	+1
Geneva	Switzerland	13:00	+1
Helsinki	Finland	14:00	+2
Istanbul	Turkey	15:00	+3
Jerusalem	Israel	14:00	+2
Lisbon	Portugal	12:00	GMT
London	Great Britain	12:00	GMT
Madrid	Spain	13:00	+1
Melbourne	Australia	22:00	+1
Montreal	Canada	7:00	-5
Moscow	Russia	15:00	+3
New York	USA	7:00	-5
Oslo	Norway	13:00	+1
Ottawa	Canada	7:00	-5
Paris	France	13:00	+1
Peking	China	20:00	+8
Perth	West Australia	20:00	+8
Prague	Czech Republic	13:00	+1
Quebec	Canada	7:00	-5
Rio de Janeiro	Brazil	9:00	-3
Rome	Italy	13:00	+1
San Francisco	USA	4:00	-8
St Petersburg	Russia	15:00	+3
Stockholm	Sweden	13:00	+1
Sydney	Australia	22:00	+10
Tokyo	Japan	21:00	+9
Vancouver	Canada	4:00	-8

International Codes
(dialled from the UK)

Andorra	00 376
Australia	00 61
Austria	00 43
Bahrain	00 973
Belgium	00 32
Brazil	00 55
Canada	00 1
China	00 86
Czech Republic	00 42
Denmark	00 45
Egypt	00 20
Finland	00 358
France	00 33
Germany	00 49
Greece	00 30
Hong Kong	00 852
Hungary	00 36
India	00 91
Ireland	00 353
Israel	00 972
Italy	00 39
Japan	00 81
Luxembourg	00 853
Mexico	00 52
Norway	00 47
Pakistan	00 92
Poland	00 48
Portugal	00 351
Russia	00 7
Spain	00 34
Sweden	00 46
Switzerland	00 41
Turkey	00 90
USA	00 1

UK international code 00 44

_____

_____

_____

_____

_____

_____

_____

_____

_____

_____

_____

_____

_____

_____

_____

_____

_____

_____

CONVERSIONS FOR WEIGHTS AND MEASURES

Convert	X by	Convert	X by
Inches to Centimetres	2.54	Litres to Gallons	0.22
Centimetres to Inches	0.3937	Gallons to Litres	4.546
Feet to Meters	0.3048	Litres to Pints	1.761
Meters to Feet	3.281	Pints to Litres	0.568
Yards to Meters	0.9144	Ounces to Grams	28.35
Meters to Yards	1.094	Grams to Ounces	0.0352
Miles to Kilometres	1.609	Kilograms to Pounds	2.205
Kilometres to Miles	0.6214	Pounds to Kilograms	0.4536
Sq. Inch to Sq. C/meters	6.452	Kilogram to Stones	0.158
Sq. C/meters to Sq. Inch	0.155	Stones to Kilograms	6.35
Sq. Meters to Sq. Feet	10.76	Tons to metric Tonnes	1.016
Sq. Feet to Sq. Meters	0.0929	Metric Tonnes to Tons	0.984
Sq. Yard to Sq. Meters	0.8361		
Sq. Meters to Sq. Yards	1.196		
Sq. Miles to Sq. Kilometres	2.59		
Sq. Kilometres to Sq. Miles	0.3861	Speed	
Acres to Hectares	0.4047	Mph 30 50 60 70 80 90 100	
Hectares to Acres	2.471	KPH 48 80 96 112 128 144 160	

_____

_____

_____

_____

_____

_____

_____

_____

_____

_____

_____

_____

_____

_____

_____

_____

_____

_____

_____

CONVERSIONS FOR WEIGHTS AND MEASURES

Temperature Scale

	32	40	50	60	70	75	85	95	105	140	175	211	°F
	0	5	10	15	20	25	30	35	40	60	80	100	°C

Temperature Conversions

°C (Celsius) = 5/9 (°F-32)   °F (Fahrenheit) = 9/5 (°C+32)

EARTH FACTS

Largest desert is the Sahara at 8400 000 sq. Kilometres.
The hottest place is Al'Azizyah in Libya at 58°c.
The coldest place is Vostock in Antarctica at -89°c
The wettest place is Tutunendo in Columbia with 11770mm of rain.
The driest place is the Calma Atacama Desert in Chile.
The circumference around the equator is 40,075 km with the distance to the centre of the earth approximately 6370km. The earth's surface is approximately 510,065,600 sq. km of which 71% is water. The earth travels at 29.8 km per second and is 385,000km from the moon.

Nowhere is without bounds and can not be conquered on a snowboard. ??????!!!!!!!!!!

FLYING AROUND THE GLOBE. DISTANCES IN KM

	Amsterdam	Cairo	Chicago	Delhi	Hong Kong	London	Los Angles	Montreal	Moscow	Paris	Perth	Rome	Sydney	Tokyo
Cairo	2042													
Chicago	4109	6135												
Delhi	3985	2753	8119											
Hong Kong	5926	5098	7827	2345										
London	217	2187	3956	4169	5979									
Los Angles	5559	7589	1746	8781	7231	5442								
Montreal	3422	5431	737	7421	8564	3252	2482							
Moscow	1338	1790	5500	2698	4839	1550	6992	4393						
Paris	261	1995	4140	4089	5987	220	5663	3434	1540					
Perth	9118	7766	11281	5013	3752	9246	9535	12402	8355	12587				
Rome	809	1329	4828	3679	5773	898	6340	5431	1478	688	8309			
Sydney	10390	9196	9324	6495	4586	10565	7498	9980	9425	10150	2037	10149		
Tokyo	6006	6362	6286	3656	1807	6218	5451	6913	4668	6208	4925	6146	4640	
Washington	3854	5859	590	7841	8385	3672	2294	493	4884	3843	11829	4495	9792	6763

Rin tin chin, Adrian Corrigal

MOUNTAIN HIGH

8848m	Mt. Everest	Himalayas
8611m	K2	Himalayas
8586m	Kangchenjunga	Himalayas
8500m	Lhotse	Himalayas
8470m	Kangchenjunga S Peak	Himalayas
8470	Makalu 1	Himalayas
8420m	Kangchenjunga W Peak	Himalayas
8380m	Lothse E Peak	Himalayas
8170m	Dhaulagiri	Himalayas
8150m	Cho Oyu	Himalayas
7723m	Muztag	Himalayas
7710m	Kongur	Himalayas
7590m	Minya Konka	Himalayas
7495m	Pik Kommunizma	Himalayas
6960m	Aconcagua	Andes
6908m	Ojos Del Saldo	Andes
6768m	Huascaran	Andes
6542m	Sajama	Andes
6485m	Illampu	Andes
6190m	Mt Mckinley	Rockies
6050m	Mt Logan	Rockies
5895m	Kilimanjaro	Africa
5700m	Citaltepetl	Mexico
5670m	Damavand	Elburz
5642m	Elbrus	Caucasus
5620m	Ras Dashan	Caucasus
5199m	Kirinyaga	Africa
5110m	Ruwenzori	Africa
5140m	Vinson Massif	Antarctica
5029m	Jaya	New Guinea
4808m	Mt Blanc	French Alpes
4418m	Mt Whitney	Rockies
4201m	Maunakea	Hawaii
3795m	Erebus	Antarctica
3764m	Mt Cook	New Zealand
3764m	Fuji-san	Japan
3718m	Teide	Pyrenees
3404m	Aneto	Pyrenees
2230m	Mt Kosciusko	Australia
1344m	Ben Nevis	Scotland

*The largest mountain range is the Andes.

DRIVING AROUND EUROPE. DISTANCES IN KM

Martin Robinson at Saas Fee. Photo, Sang Tan

	Athens	Barcelona	Brussels	Calais	Geneva	Hamburg	Lisbon	Lyons	Madrid	Marseilles	Milan	Munich	Paris	Rome
Barcelona	3313													
Brussels	2963	1318												
Calais	3175	1326	204											
Geneva	2610	803	677	747										
Hamburg	2977	2018	597	714	1118									
Lisbon	4532	1304	2084	2052	1936	2671								
Lyons	2753	645	690	739	158	1159	1778							
Madrid	3949	636	1558	1550	1439	2198	668	1281						
Marseilles	2865	521	1011	1059	425	1479	1762	320	1157					
Milan	2282	1014	925	1077	328	1238	2250	328	1724	618				
Munich	2179	1362	747	977	591	2565	805	724	2010	1109	331			
Paris	3000	1033	285	280	513	877	1799	471	1273	792	856	821		
Rome	817	1460	1511	1662	995	1751	2700	1048	2097	1011	586	946	1476	
Vienna	1991	1802	1175	1381	1019	1155	2935	1157	2409	1363	898	428	1249	1209

UNIVERSAL SNOWBOARD GUIDE

Tee Shirts, Sweats and Caps

The Trip Sweat Top
with embroided logo
£24.99
Sizes - S/M/L/XL
Colour: Burgundy Parade

No Dramas Short sleve
Tee with embroided logo
£18.00
Sizes - S/M/L/XL
Colours: Moss-Clover-
Storm-Black-White

USG Embroided Caps
£16.00

wee lad, Bruce

UNIVERSAL SNOWBOARD GUIDE

Baseball Journey Jackets

Embroided front, back and down the right arm

Sizes   Small
Medium
Large
X Large

Colour   Red

£99
Exclusive with
limited availability

To order fill out the order
form over the page

Posers:
Graham
Gordon
Ian

Hang out at Barcelona Airport

UNIVERSAL SNOWBOARD GUIDE PRODUCTS

Journey Jackets   **£99.00**
Sizing
Small - Medium - Large - Extra Large
One Colour - Red

Short Sleeve tees   **£18.00**
Colours
Moss-Storm-Clover-Black-White
Sizes - S - M - L - XL

Sweat Shirts   **£24.99**
Colour = Parade
Sizes - S - M - L - XL

Caps   **£16.00**

UK Post and Packing: Add £3 per Journey Jacket
Overseas: add £6.50

Tees, Sweats and Caps add £1.50 per item
Overseas orders add £2.00

Cut out the order form and send with your Cheque, Postal
order or International money order in GBP £'s, made payable
to Ice Publishing.

Post to:

Ice Publishing
45 Corrour Rd
Dalfaber
Aviemore
Inverness-Shire
PH22 1SS

PRODUCT
ORDER FORM

Item	Size S / M L / XL	Qty	Colour	Price
Journey Jacket				
Short sleeve Tee				
Sweat shirt				
Caps				
			Sub Total	
			Post & Packing	
			Total Enclosed	

Name
Address
Post Code
Telephone

Steve (Numpty) Crampton

Universal Snowboard Guide extra copies

Please send me ___ copies @£14.99. P+P £1.50

Total amount enclosed   £ _____

Name _____

Address _____

_____

_____

_____

Post Code _____

Telephone _____

Send cheque or postal order made payable to "Ice Publishing"
to: Ice Publishing, 45 Corrour Rd, Dalfaber,
Aviemore, Inverness-shire. PH22 1SS.

Universal Snowboard Guide extra copies

Please send me ___ copies @£14.99. P+P £1.50

Total amount enclosed   £ _____

Name _____

Address _____

_____

_____

_____

Post Code _____

Telephone _____

Send cheque or postal order made payable to "Ice Publishing"
to: Ice Publishing, 45 Corrour Rd, Dalfaber,
Aviemore, Inverness-shire. PH22 1SS.

Universal Snowboard Guide extra copies

Please send me ___ copies @£14.99. P+P £1.50

Total amount enclosed   £ _____

Name _____

Address _____

_____

_____

_____

Post Code _____

Telephone _____

Send cheque or postal order made payable to "Ice Publishing"
to: Ice Publishing, 45 Corrour Rd, Dalfaber,
Aviemore, Inverness-shire. PH22 1SS.

Ice Publishing. 45 Corrour Rd., Dalfaber,
Aviemore, Inverness-Shire, PH22 1SS.
Tel / Fax: 01479 810362

Universal Snowboard Guide extra copy coupon.

✂

Ice Publishing. 45 Corrour Rd., Dalfaber,
Aviemore, Inverness-Shire, PH22 1SS.
Tel / Fax: 01479 810362

Universal Snowboard Guide extra copy coupon.

✂

Ice Publishing. 45 Corrour Rd., Dalfaber,
Aviemore, Inverness-Shire, PH22 1SS.
Tel / Fax: 01479 810362

Universal Snowboard Guide extra copy coupon.

✂

Reserve a copy of Universal Snowboard Guide book 2 1997/98 with this voucher and receive:

- More snowboard friendly resorts.
- Loads more info

Universal Snowboard Guide 2 1997/98.

Please reserve me a copy of USG 2

Name _____

Address _____

_____

_____

Post Code _____

Telephone _____

Universal Snowboard Guide 2 1997/98.

Please reserve me a copy of USG 2

Name _____

Address _____

_____

_____

Post Code _____

Telephone _____

Universal Snowboard Guide 2 1997/98

Voucher

Universal Snowboard Guide 2 1997/98

Voucher

If you would like to feature as a USG page rider then let us know where you're going and when so that we can send you details.

Let us know what you think of USG 1 and what you would like to see featured in USG 2.

If you have any special resort information then send it what ever it is.

Let us know about your clubs, associations, main shops and hangouts.

If things are going down in your town or city then let us know and we will broadcast it big style.

Cheers Riders.

Universal
Snowboard
Guide

Snowboard

Skating

Climb and raft

summer action

available spring 1997

Snowboard camps
Summer test programmes
Mountain bike trails
White water rafting
Climbing
Hanging out summer style
Skate board scene

**For advertising contact
Ice Publishing on
01479 810 362**

I fancy a beer now.